International Taxation in an Integrated World

International Taxation in an Integrated World

Jacob A. Frenkel, Assaf Razin, and Efraim Sadka

The MIT Press
Cambridge, Massachusetts
London, England

336.2
F87i

This book was set in Palatino by Asco Trade Typesetting Ltd., Hong Kong and printed and bound in the United States of America.

Library of Congress Cataloging-in-Publication Data

Frenkel, Jacob A.
   International taxation in an integrated world / Jacob A. Frenkel,
Assaf Razin, and Efraim Sadka.
      p.   cm.
   Includes bibliographical references and index.
   ISBN 0-262-06143-0
   1. Taxation.   2. Fiscal policy.   3. International economic relations.   4. International economic integration.   I. Razin, Assaf.   II. Sadka, Efraim.   III. Title.
HJ2305.F74   1991
336.2—dc20   91-3396
                                                                          CIP

To our parents:
Lea and Kalman-Hillel Frenkel
Dora and the late Mordechai Razin
Lucy and Moshe Sadka

Contents

Preface

This book is a first attempt to integrate elements from two distinct disciplines in economics: public economics and international economics. The impetus comes from the ongoing process of economic integration and policy coordination in the world economy, especially among the industrial countries. The trend toward a borderless economy is particularly evident in the 1992 process of economic integration of the European Community. The increased economic integration brings into focus new issues of public policy. Notable examples are international tax competition, international tax harmonization, and the location and destination of production, consumption, savings, and investments in the world economy. In a sense this book can be viewed as a complement to Frenkel and Razin, *Fiscal Policies and the World Economy*, which applies the intertemporal approach to international fiscal policies. Recent developments in the theory of public economics have also incorporated the intertemporal approach, thereby laying the ground for the integration of the two disciplines into the unified treatment presented here.

The book is written for a wide professional audience: graduate and advanced undergraduate students in economics departments, business schools and research organizations, academic scholars, and business and public sector professionals.

Part I, which provides a review of stylized facts, sets up key main issues of international taxation and the implications for the international movements of goods and capital. To offer a self-contained treatment of the subject matter, we devote part II to the review of the modern approach to international macroeconomics and international taxation. Part III analyzes the international transmission of various tax and budget policies. The implications of the analysis are illustrated by means of dynamic simulations of the consequences of international tax harmonization. These simulations highlight the significance of incorporating international considerations in the design of tax policies. Part IV provides a rigorous treatment of optimal open economy tax policy. This analysis aids in determining the optimal level and composition of taxes in national economies that are at once sovereign politically and interdependent economically within the integrated world economy. Concluding remarks, extensions, and references are provided in part V.

Some of the material in the book draws on our previous work: chapter 1 draws on Jacob A. Frenkel, Assaf Razin, and Steve Symansky, "International Spillovers of Taxation," in Assaf Razin and Joel Slemrod (eds.), *Taxation in the Global Economy*, University of Chicago Press, 1990; chapter 3 draws on Jacob A. Frenkel and Assaf Razin, *Fiscal Policies and the World Economies*, MIT Press, 1987; chapter 4 draws on Alan Auerbach, Jacob A. Frenkel, and Assaf Razin, "Notes on International Taxation," mimeo, February 1989; chapter 6 draws on Jacob A. Frenkel and Assaf Razin, "Real Exchange Rates, Interest Rates and Fiscal Policies," *Economic Studies Quarterly* 37, June 1986; chapter 7 draws on Jacob A. Frenkel and Assaf Razin, "Budget Deficits Under Alternative Tax Systems: International Effects," *IMF Staff Papers* 35, no. 2, June 1988; chapter 8 draws on Jacob A. Frenkel, Assaf Razin, and Steven Symansky, "Simulations of Global Effects of VAT Harmonization," in Siebert Horst (ed.), *Reforming Capital Income Taxation*, Tübingen, Mohr: Institute für Weltwirtschaft on der Universität Kiel, 1990; chapter 9 draws on Assaf Razin and Efraim Sadka, "Integration of the International Capital Markets: The Size of Government and Tax Coordination," in Assaf Razin and Joel Slemrod (eds.), *Taxation in the Global Economy*, University of Chicago Press, 1990; chapter 10 draws on Assaf Razin and Efraim Sadka, "Efficient Investment in the Presence of Capital Flight," *Journal of International Economics*, 1991; and chapter 11 draws on Assaf Razin and Efraim Sadka, "International Tax Competition and Gains from Tax Harmonization," *Economics Letters*, 1990–91.

Parts of this research was conducted while Assaf Razin and Efraim Sadka were visiting scholars at the International Monetary Fund. In the course of our research we have benefited from comments and suggestions by Joshua Aizenman, Julian S. Alworth, Alan Auerbach, Eitan Berglas, Lans Bovenberg, David Bradford, William Branson, Willem Buiter, Guillermo Calvo, Sijbren Cnossen, Avinash Dixit, Michael Dooley, Rudiger Dornbusch, Martin Feldstein, Robert Flood, Alberto Giovannini, Roger Gordon, Arnold Harberger, Elhanan Helpman, James Hines, Glenn Hubard, Takatoshi Ito, Mervyn King, Charles McLure, Jack Mintz, Hans-Werner Sinn, Joel Slemrod, Vito Tanzi and John Whalley.

We have also benefited from presentations and discussions in various seminars held at the International Monetary Fund, the National Bureau of Economic Research, the Centre for Economic Policy Research, the Korean Development Institute, the Institute for World Economy at Kiel University, Tel Aviv University, New York University, the Bank of Israel, the University of Chicago, and the World Bank. We thank the participants in these seminars for their comments and suggestions. We also wish to thank Terry Vaughn, the economics editor of The MIT Press, for his patience and support.

We wish to dedicate this book to our parents, Lea and Kalman-Hillel Frenkel, Dora and the late Mordechai Razin, and Lucy and Moshe Sadka.

I

Facts and Concepts

1

Stylized Facts on Tax Systems

The removal of economic borders among independent tax jurisdictions—local, state, national, or otherwise—has immense implications for both the structure and the overall burden of the tax system in each of these jurisdictions. When capital, labor, goods, and services can move freely from one tax jurisdiction to another, the tax base becomes global, and its distribution among the various tax jurisdictions becomes endogeneous to all the various tax systems.

For instance, whether a U.K. consumer purchases a tradable good from domestic production or imports it from France or Germany depends on the value-added taxes (VAT) that France or Germany levy, if any, on their exports to the United Kingdom and on the value-added tax levied by the United Kingdom on domestic production and on imports. Thus, the amount of tax revenue that the U.K. government collects from the purchases of U.K. consumers depends on the French and German tax systems as much as on its own system.

Similarly, whether a U.K. resident invests his savings domestically or channels it to France or Germany depends on the taxes levied in France and Germany on the capital income of U.K. residents originating in France and Germany, respectively, and on the tax levied by the U.K. government on its residents on their foreign-source capital income. Hence, the amount of tax revenue collected by the U.K. government from the savings of U.K. residents depends on the French and German tax systems as much as on the U.K. tax system.

A common rule of tax theory and policy (based on considerations of economic efficiency) is to focus taxes on factors of production and goods in relatively inelastic supply and to abstain from taxing, or to tax only lightly, factors of production in relatively elastic supply. The removal of international economic borders renders the domestic supply of tradable goods and internationally mobile factors of production more elastic, thereby forcing national governments to lower taxes on mobile factors of production (especially capital) and tradable goods, or otherwise make indirect border tax adjustments (such as applying the residence principle for income taxation or the destination principle for value-added taxation—for details see chapter 2). Naturally then, less mobile factors (for example, land and labor) and nontradable commodities (especially services) become major sources of tax revenues.

A federal system (such as the United States) is a model example of economic integration among states. Capital, labor, and (tradable) goods move freely across state borders, and no direct border taxes are allowed by law. In such a federal system, the ability of individual states to tax income and goods is severely constrained. Thus taxes on mobile factors of production—capital and labor in this case—account for less than one-quarter of total state and local tax revenues in the United States (see table 1.1). Almost one-third of all tax revenues comes from property taxes, which are largely taxes on immobile factors. Similarly, the possibility of cross-border shopping, mail- and phone-order shopping, and the like, tends to narrow the rate differentials of sales taxes among states.

1.1   Tax Structures in Industrialized Countries

The most important features measuring the incentive effects of tax systems—on investment, savings, labor supply, etc.—are the *marginal rates* of tax. As a conceptual matter, the marginal rate of tax is a relatively clear

Table 1.1
Sources of tax revenue—state-local fiscal systems (fiscal 1982)

Type of tax	Amount (in millions)	Percentage
Property	$ 89,253	31.4%
Sales & excise	89,305	31.4%
Motor fuel	10,942	3.8%
Individual income	55,129	19.4%
Corporation income	14,258	5.0%
Motor vehicle and operator's license	6,732	2.3%
Other	18,967	6.7%
Total	$284,586	100.0%

Source: James M. Buchanan and Marilyn R. Flowers, *The Public Finances: An Introductory Textbook*, Irwin, 1987, p. 324.

term. In practice, however, owing to the complexity of the tax code involving progressivity of taxes, exemptions, tax credits, tax evasion, delays and advances in payments of taxes, and the like, the empirical counterparts to the conceptual marginal tax rates are less clear. For this reason we base our illustrations in this section on measures of *average rates* of tax. These average tax rates are also relevant for analyzing tax incidence and as measures of tax revenues and tax burdens.

We present stylized facts concerning average tax rates in the seven major industrial countries (the Group of Seven): Canada, the United States, Japan, France, Germany, Italy, and the United Kingdom.[1] Owing to intercountry differences in the tax code, in the factors underlying tax collections, and in the relative share of state and local governments in total tax revenue, the international comparison of tax rates is quite complex. Keeping these empirical difficulties in mind, we highlight some key features of intercountry differences in direct and indirect tax rates.[2]

Figure 1.1, featuring total tax rates for the Group of Seven countries, highlights the international diversity of this measure of the tax burden. Whereas in Japan and the United States the total tax rate was less than 30 percent in 1986, rates in the rest of the OECD were substantially higher, reaching close to 45 percent in France.

The other noteworthy feature apparent in figure 1.1 is the different degrees of variability over time in this measure of tax rates. For example, whereas for some countries (e.g., Italy, France, and Japan) this measure of tax rates exhibits a positive trend in the period 1973–1986, for other countries there is no such pronounced trend. Since the mid-1980s, following the lead of the United Kingdom and the United States, other industrialized countries have launched a process of gradual tax reforms. As these reforms are generally governed by the principle of *revenue neutrality*, the overall burden of taxation is not scheduled to change.

The total tax rate provides some information regarding the overall tax burden. However, key decisions concerning investment, saving, and labor supply depend also on the detailed composition of taxes. We turn next, therefore, to examine more detailed information on the tax structure. Figure 1.2 exhibits the consumption-tax rate. As is evident, the highest consumption-tax rate prevails in France (about 15 percent), whereas the lowest rates prevail in Japan and the United States (about 3 percent). The figure also reveals the upward trend (during the 1980s) prevailing in Canada, Italy, and the United Kingdom, whose rates have risen to about 10 percent (the rate prevailing in Germany). In this context, the sharp increase in the U.K. tax rate associated with the decision in 1979 to nearly double

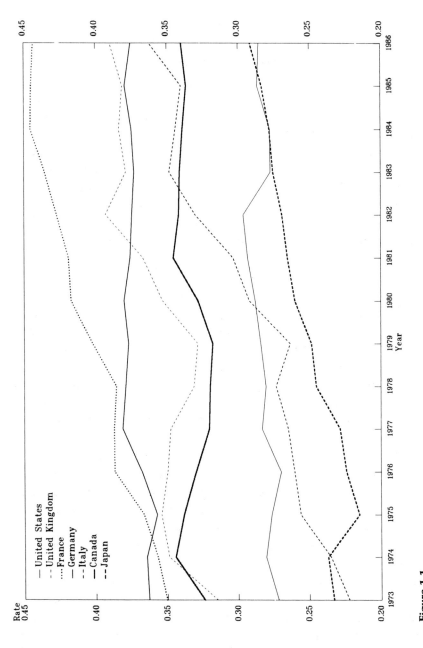

Figure 1.1
Total tax rates

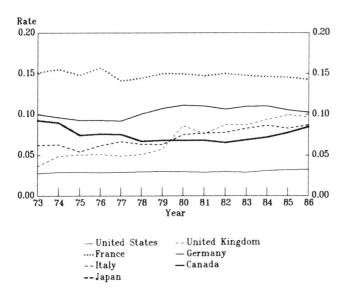

Figure 1.2
Consumption tax rates

the value-added tax rate is especially noteworthy. The intra-European differences among consumption-tax rates are of special relevance in view of the VAT harmonization proposals associated with the plans for the single market in Europe of 1992 (for details, see chapters 2 and 8).

Figures 1.3–1.5 exhibit various measures of income tax rates. The individual income tax rates shown in figure 1.3 reveal the international diversity, with rates ranging from about 10 percent in France to about 22 percent in Canada. Also noteworthy is the upward trend in the Italian individual income tax rate.

The income tax rates shown in figure 1.4 include both individual and corporate taxes. Based on this measure, the highest tax rates prevail in Canada and the United Kingdom. The magnitude of the U.K. tax rate reflects the relatively high corporate income tax. The lowest tax rate (about 10 percent) prevails in France. The significant decline of this measure in 1982 in the United States reflects the sharp fall in the (effective) corporate income tax rates associated with the Tax Act of 1981. The Tax Reform Act of 1986 reduced the statutory income tax rates on individuals and corporations but abolished several investment incentives, benefits to capital income (e.g., low tax rates on capital gains), etc. As a result, the average income tax rate declined only moderately.

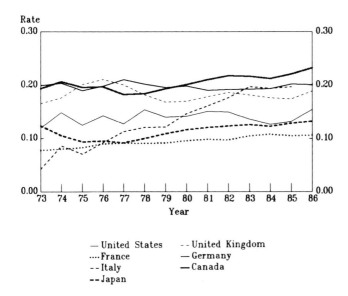

Figure 1.3
Personal income tax rates

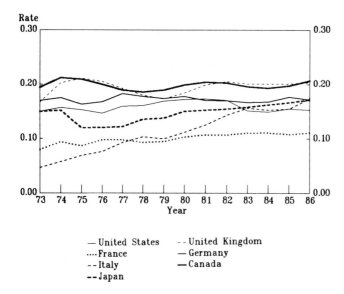

Figure 1.4
Income tax rates

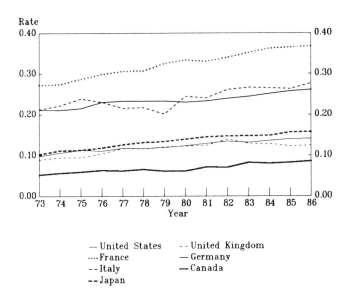

Figure 1.5
Social Security and payroll tax rates

The role of social security and payroll tax rates and the international diversity thereof is represented in figure 1.5. We first note the upward trends prevailing in all major industrial countries. A second noteworthy feature is the roles played by these tax rates relative to the income tax rates in Canada and France. Whereas France has the highest social security and payroll tax rate (exceeding one-third), Canada has the lowest rate (below 10 percent). This ranking of Canada and France is the opposite of the one shown in figure 1.4 pertaining to the individual income tax rate.

Table 1.2 presents summary data on the various tax rates in the Group of Seven countries. The international diversity of these rates within Europe is noteworthy in view of the tax harmonization plans for Europe of 1992. Of special relevance for international tax harmonization is the situation within the European Community (EC). On the eve of the integration of 1992, major differences in the composition and level of taxes still exist in the EC, as figure 1.6 demonstrates. The highest burden, as measured by the gross domestic product (GDP) share of all taxes, prevails in the Benelux countries, France, Ireland, and Italy. The rate in the United Kingdom is close to the average prevailing in the EC. The Federal Republic of Germany (FRG) and Spain enjoy the lowest burdens. The consumption tax burden (VAT and other excises) is highest in Denmark, Greece, Ireland, and Portugal. It is lowest in the FRG, Italy, and Spain.

Table 1.2
Average tax rates in the major industrial countries (general government), 1986

	Total tax rate	Consumption tax rate	Individual income tax rate	Income tax rate	Social Security and payroll tax rate
Canada	34.0	8.5	23.2	20.6	8.6
United States	28.5	3.3	15.5	15.3	14.1
Japan	29.2	...	13.2	17.2	15.7
France	44.4	14.3	10.6	11.1	36.8
Germany	37.5	10.3	20.0	17.2	26.1
Italy	36.2	8.7	...	17.4	27.7
United Kingdom	39.0	9.7	18.9	20.3	12.4

Source: Computed from OECD (1987a) and OECD (1987b).
Note: Our measure of the consumption-tax rate is computed as the ratio of general taxes on goods and services (including value-added taxes, sales taxes, and other general taxes on goods and services) to private final consumption. For income taxes we use various measures distinguished between individuals and corporations as well as between social security and the more conventional definition of income taxes. Accordingly, the personal income tax rate is computed as taxes on incomes, profits, and capital gains of individuals divided by compensation of employees (a broader internationally comparable tax base is unavailable). The income tax rate is computed as the taxes on income, profits, and capital gains (including individual and corporate taxes) divided by the compensation of employees plus property and entrepreneurial income. The social security and payroll tax rate is computed as social security contributions and payroll taxes of the work force divided by compensation of employees. Finally, the total tax rate is computed as taxes on income, profits, and capital gains plus social security contributions plus payroll taxes plus property plus taxes on goods and services, all divided by GNP and GDP. To maintain a consistent use of the OECD data, we have used GNP for the United States, Japan, and Germany and GDP for Canada, France, Italy, and the United Kingdom.

1.2   International Integration of Capital Markets

The gains from trade are obviously not limited to international trade in goods and services. The potential gains from international flows of capital are equally important. Indeed, the industrialized world has gradually witnessed a large increase in the volume of international capital movements in the form of borrowing and lending, bond transactions, direct foreign investments, and the like, of which the full integration of the capital markets of Europe in 1992 is an outstanding example.

In economies that are open to international flows of capital, net capital exports are accounted for by the difference between national saving and investment. Of course, *net* capital exports do not fully measure flows of

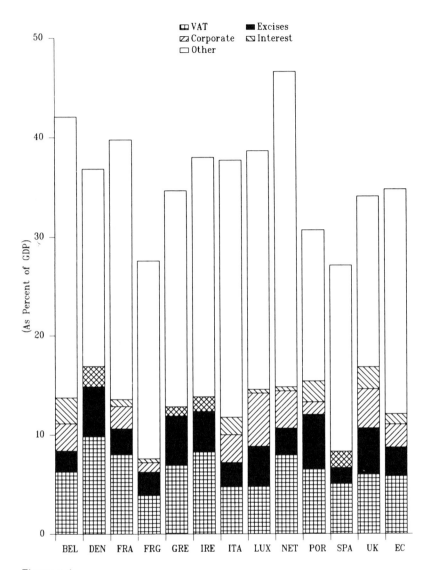

Figure 1.6
Shares of taxes in GDP: European Community 1989
Source: Lans A. Bovenberg and George F. Kopits, "Harmonization of Taxes on Capital
Income and Commodities in the European Community," IMF, 1990.

Table 1.3
Gross international capital movements of the seven major industrial countries, 1970–1989

	(percentages of GNP/GDP)			
Country	1970–1974	1975–1979	1980–1984	1985–1989
Canada	5.9	5.9	7.9	5.6
France	7.0	9.0	8.6	11.2
Germany (FRG)	6.0	9.2	9.9	14.2
Italy	9.4	4.9	5.2	3.7
Japan	3.3	2.4	5.4	19.5
United Kingdom	6.4	11.4	26.6	32.6
United States	2.5	3.4	4.8	5.8

Source: International Monetary Fund.

capital into and out of the country. Typically, removal of barriers to international capital movements is followed by a two-way increase in *gross* capital flows, which is not necessarily reflected in the net export of capital.

Table 1.3 shows the developments in the measure of *gross* international capital movements of the seven major industrial countries during the 1970s and 1980s. The volume of international capital movements is measured in this table by the *sum* of capital exports and capital imports. To normalize the units of measurement and facilitate intercountry comparisons, the volumes of capital movements are expressed as percentages of GNP (or GDP). The information shown in table 1.3 reveals the dramatic increase in capital movements from the early 1970s through the late 1980s. In this regard the United Kingdom and Japan stand out. In both, gross capital flows (as percentages of GNP) rose about fivefold during the two decades (from 6.4 to 32.6 in the United Kingdom, and from 3.3 to 19.5 in Japan). In the United States and Germany, the share of gross capital flows in GDP more than doubled during the period. These changes reflect the very rapid integration of world capital markets. In fact, in recent years the degree of integration of capital markets (as measured by gross capital movements) has grown more rapidly than the degree of integration of goods markets (as measured by the gross volume of trade in goods and services).

The intergration of capital markets in the world economy (coupled with a reduction in border tax adjustments) narrows the differences among interest rates across countries, when quoted in the same currency. To illustrate this point (especially for the second half of the 1980s), figures 1.7 and 1.8 portray the difference between domestic and offshore interest rates in two major industrial countries, France and the United States.

The integration of international capital markets is also reflected in the narrowing of the differences among *real* interest rates in various countries.

To illustrate this point, we define the (realized) real interest rate in any country as the nominal interest rate in that country adjusted by its inflation rate, measured by (realized) changes in the consumer price index. Because the latter includes the prices of both tradable and nontradable goods, there is no presumption that free trade in goods and capital strictly equalizes real interest rates across countries, although such free trade is expected to narrow the differentials among real rates of interest. As figure 1.9 indicates, real interest rate differentials seem to have narrowed somewhat during the latter part of the 1980s.

1.3   Intertemporal Taxation and Direct Foreign Investment

Theoretical and empirical economic models can better analyze and explain *net* flows of funds across countries than *gross* flows, implemented through various means and financial intermediaries.[3] The net imports of capital (measured by the net surplus of the current account of the balance of payments) represent the amount of investment in the home country that is financed by net savings of the rest of the world. Similarly, the net exports of capital represent the amount of savings in the home country that finances investment in the rest of the world. In contrast, specific components of gross financial capital flows can easily substitute for one another, so they usually cannot indicate the direction and magnitude of the net flows of financial capital. For instance, direct foreign investment (in contrast with portfolio investment) that serves to acquire ownership in foreign corporations (at least 10 percent of the voting shares) or to expand already-owned foreign corporations is only a subset of the international flows of funds and therefore can only partially explain the capital formation in the foreign country. Direct foreign investment that is carried out by multinationals can easily be substituted for by portfolio investment (e.g., bond issues and loans) in the same way as domestic equity finance can easily be substituted for by domestic debt finance.

The interactions between taxes and multinationals raise several pertinent issues that are widely discussed in the context of international taxation.[4] First, there exists the issue of shifting taxable income from one country to another via transfer pricing, management fees, royalties, etc. Usually tax authorities handle the problem of transfer pricing by applying the so-called arm's length rule to the transactions conducted between a parent company and its subsidiary. According to this rule, one should establish prices that would have been charged if the interests of the parties were not related—that is, prices that would have been charged to (or by) a third party. In

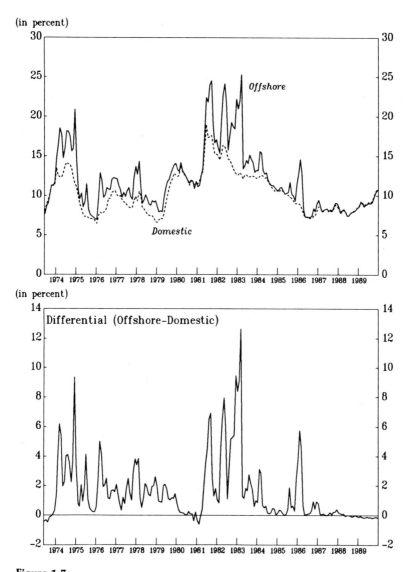

Figure 1.7
Domestic and offshore interest rates: France
Source: International Monetary Fund, Research Department: "The Determinants and Systemic Consequences of International Capital Flows," June 1990.
Domestic rate: Three-month interbank loan rate (OECD).
Offshore rate: Three-month Eurocurrency deposit bid rate.

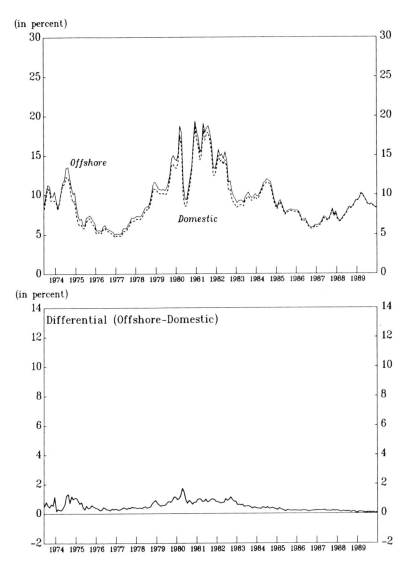

Figure 1.8
Domestic and offshore interest rates: United States
Source: See figure 1.7.
Domestic rate: Rate on negotiable three-month certificates of deposit, secondary market.
Offshore rate: Three-month Eurocurrency deposit bid rate.

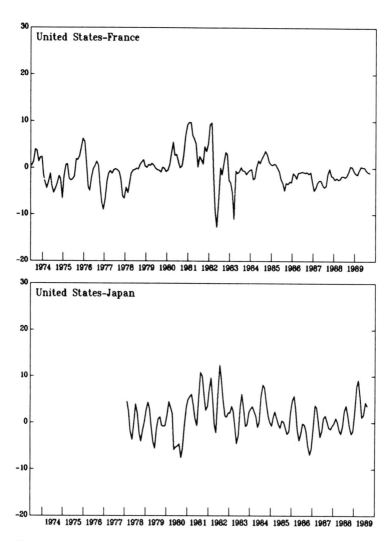

Figure 1.9
Real interest rate differentials (percent per annum)
Source: See figure 1.7.
This differential equals the difference between the real rate of interest on instruments denominated in each currency. The real interest rate in each country is defined as the three-month Eurocurrency deposit rate adjusted for the inflation (as measured by the consumer price index) which occurred during the subsequent three months.

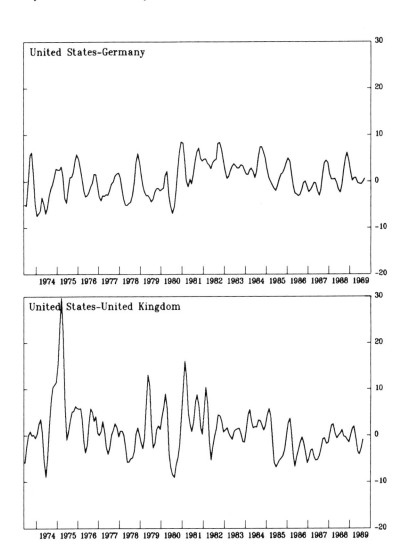

practice this rule is difficult to implement, because in many cases it is not possible to find equivalent transactions by unrelated parties. This is particularly true in the case of the pricing of flows of services derived from intangibles such as patents. Note also that transfer pricing can serve as a mechanism for capital flight. Second, because the income of a subsidiary is typically taxed at the source, by the host country, and also as a foreign-source income of the parent company by the country in which the parent company is incorporated, problems of *double taxation* arise. Foreign tax credits are employed to alleviate the double-taxation problem. Third, because most countries tax their domestic corporations on their foreign-source income only upon payments of dividends, it follows that a parent company can use the so-called dividend deferral to defer its domestic tax liability by postponing dividend payments of the foreign subsidiary.[5]

The issues of double taxation, capital flight, and tax deferral, that were discussed in the context of multinationals are fundamental in the general analysis of international allocation of savings and investments. Although the analysis in subsequent chapters does not address specifically the role of multinationals, the relevant issues are dealt with in a broader context in a framework suitable for the analysis of the determinants and effects of net international capital flows.

1.4   The Road Map

The process of integration of capital markets in the world economy is advancing rapidly. Within the integrated world economy, the structures of national tax systems and their interrelations exert profound effects on the volume and direction of capital flows and, thereby, on the location and destination of production, consumption, savings, and investment. The facts reported in this chapter motivate the choice of some of the subjects analyzed in this book. The next chapter provides basic definitions and concepts central to the analysis of international taxation. These concepts are relevant to the understanding of the effects of taxes on the international allocation of savings, investment, consumption, and production.

Part II lays out the analytical infrastructure to the book. It provides a concise, self-contained exposition of the modern theory of international intertemporal macroeconomics as well as a basic exposition of analytical interrelations among tax systems for economies that are open to international trade. These two expositions are then integrated into an analytical framework that can be viewed as our "workhorse model" for the analysis of optimal international taxation.

Part III is devoted to an analysis of the international spillovers of tax policies. It addresses two main issues, starting with the consequences of changes in the means of government finance between taxes and debt; that is, the effects of different time profiles of taxes. This issue is motivated by the experience of the past two decades, during which budgetary imbalances in the industrial countries have played a major role in affecting the world economy. Second, the effect of international tax harmonization is analyzed. This issue is motivated by the 1992 process of economic integration in Europe.

Part IV assesses the efficiency and distributional aspects of the tax design in the integrated world economy. In this context, we apply the workhorse model of optimal international taxation to the analysis of the effects of capital-market liberalization on the cost of public funds, capital flight, and tax competition.

Part V is the epilogue. It contains concluding remarks, suggested extensions, and a selected bibliography, based primarily on references to recent work on this fast-growing subject of international taxation in an integrated world.

2

Basic Concepts of International Taxation

The various ways national tax systems treat international flows of goods and capital may significantly affect the efficiency of resource allocation in the integrated world economy. Free movements of goods and capital across national borders have important implications for both direct and indirect taxation. A key issue of direct taxation (income taxation) is how the home country treats resident capital income originating abroad and nonresident capital income originating at home. A key issue of indirect taxation (value-added taxation) is whether the tax is applied to exports or imports of goods and services.

In international flows of capital and goods, each flow may be subject to two tax jurisdictions. An export of one country is, by definition, an import of another country. Thus, the possibility of double taxation is very real and has far-reaching implications for the direction and magnitude of the flows of capital and goods in the world economy. For instance, if the home country taxes its residents on their capital income originating in the foreign country, and the foreign country taxes nonresidents on their capital income originating in the foreign country, then such income is subject to *double taxation*. Such double taxation may apply also to exports and imports of goods and services. With unconstrained flows of capital and goods, double taxation typically gives rise to tax arbitrage that may undermine the viability of the international market equilibria.

In this chapter we analyze the basic principles of taxation of exports and imports of capital and goods. We describe some common practices and elaborate on their implications for double taxation, the viability of international market equilibria in a borderless world economy, and the efficiency of the international allocation (or location) of savings, investments, production and consumption.

2.1   Direct Taxation: Residence Principle vs. Source Principle

Basic Principles

Two common principles of international taxation that are the foundations of many national tax systems are the *residence principle* and the *source principle*. The residence principle uses the place of residency of the taxpayer as the basis for assessment of tax liabilities, whereas the source principle emphasizes the source of income as the basis for assessing tax liabilities. To explain these principles, it is convenient to employ the familiar home-country–foreign-country framework of international economics. According to the residence principle, residents of the country are taxed uniformly on their worldwide income, regardless of the source of that income (domestic or foreign). Similarly, nonresidents are not taxed by the home country on their income originating in that country. According to the source principle, income originating in the home country is uniformly taxed, regardless of the residency of the income recipient. In addition, residents of the home country are not taxed by the home country on their foreign-source income.[1]

Countries may obviously adopt mixtures of these two pure (polar) principles of international taxation. For instance, a country may apply the residence principle for capital income but the source principle for labor income. Alternatively, one principle may be applied to individual taxpayers and the other principle to corporate taxpayers. Likewise, the home country may tax its residents at a high rate on their domestic-source income and at a low rate on their foreign-source income, and tax nonresidents on their income originating at home at a rate lower than the one applied to residents.

Mixtures of the two pure principles, either within the same country or among different countries, may involve, in some way or another, double taxation (by the two countries) of the same income. However, such double taxation is frequently eliminated by a system of domestic tax credits for foreign taxes. It is worth noting that if all countries adhere to the *same* pure principle (either residence or source), there will be no double taxation. For instance, if both the home country and the foreign country adopt the residence principle, then all the four possible categories of income are taxed only once: income of the home country residents originating in the home country is naturally taxed only by the home country; income of residents of the home country originating abroad is taxed only by the home country; income of residents of the foreign country originating in the home country is taxed only by the foreign country; and income of residents of the foreign country originating in the foreign country is naturally taxed only by the foreign country.

The difference between the residence principle and the source principle may also be viewed as the difference between taxing the *net national product* (NNP) and taxing the *net domestic product* (NDP). If a country adheres to the residence principle, then the tax base in that country is its NNP, because, by definition, the NNP of a country is its residents' worldwide income (net of foreign taxes). Similarly, if a country adopts the source principle, then the tax base in that country is its NDP, because, by definition, the NDP is the income produced by all factors of production employed in that country, regardless of the residency of their owners.

If countries do not adopt the same principle, a system of tax credits can alleviate the problem of double taxation. For instance, suppose that the home country adopts the residence principle, and the foreign country adopts the source principle as the basis for assessing tax liabilities. Suppose further that the home country allows a credit against taxes paid in the foreign country. In this case if the foreign country's tax rate does not exceed the home country's rate, then the resident of the home country receives at home full credit against taxes paid abroad. In effect, the home country resident pays the same tax rate on domestic-source and foreign-source income. From the point of view of *tax incidence*, the tax credit effectively transforms the tax principle applied to residents of the home country to a residence principle applied to their (before-tax) worldwide income. The tax credit also brings the foreign country closer toward an effective source principle by reducing the combined tax rate (home and foreign) on nonresidents' income in the foreign country. However, in the foreign country a nonresident pays a higher tax rate (the home country rate) than a resident. It is relevant to note, however, that even though the home country effectively adopts the residence principle, the tax base for revenue purposes is not its NNP. The home country collects taxes according to its own rate on the domestic income of its residents but collects only the *difference* between the high home rate and the low foreign rate on the foreign-source income of its residents The tax base for the foreign country in this case is still the NDP even though the income produced in that country is not subject to a pure source taxation.

If, however, the foreign tax rate is higher than the domestic rate, then a resident of the home country often does not receive a refund for the excess foreign tax credit. (Italy is a notable exception.) Hence, the resident effectively pays the foreign tax rate on foreign-source income. In this case, therefore, the tax credit does not fully restore an effective residence taxation in the home country (even though it moves the home country closer to such a principle). It does, however, fully restore an effective source principle in the foreign country. In this case, too, the tax base for revenue purposes in the foreign country is exactly NDP, but in the home country the tax base is not equal to the NNP.

Common Practice

For tax purposes countries may treat individuals differently than corporations. In most of the industrialized countries, individuals are taxed according to the residence principle. That is, the home country taxes their foreign-source (capital) income while the foreign country usually exempts nonresidents (or withholds tax at relatively low rates, below 15 percent). As table 2.1 demonstrates, most countries tax the worldwide income of their resident corporations, but they tax also the income of nonresident corporations. A system of credits or deductions usually supplements the tax systems in these countries, and, in some cases, the source principle applies under a bilateral treaty. A few countries predominantly apply the source principle to their resident corporations by exempting their foreign-source income.

A *deduction* means that the tax paid abroad is deducted from taxable income in the home country, whereas a *credit* means that the tax paid abroad is deducted from the tax liability in the home country. A deduction thus affords a smaller relief for double taxation than a credit. For example, suppose that a corporation earns a gross income of 100 ECU in a foreign country on which 30 ECU are paid as a tax to the foreign government. Suppose further that the tax rate in the home country is 40 percent. Under a deduction system the tax liability of this corporation at home is a 40 percent tax on 70 ECU. That is, the corporation pays at home an additional tax of 28 ECU, ending up with a net income of 42 ECU. Under a credit system, however, the tax liability of this corporation in the home country is 40 percent of 100 ECU, which is 40 ECU. But the corporation receives a tax credit of 30 ECU and hence pays only 10 ECU to the home government, ending up with a net income of 60 ECU.

Feasible National Tax Systems

The possibility for a resident in one country to invest in other countries raises the issue of international tax arbitrage. Such arbitrage has important implications for the viability of equilibrium in the capital markets.

Table 2.1
Taxation of foreign-source capital income—selected countries

| Country | Individual | | Corporate | |
	Top individual tax rate (%)	Dominant tax principle	Top corporate tax rate (%)	Dominant tax principle
European Community:				
Belgium	55	R	43	S
Denmark	68	R	50	R (with credit)
France	53	R	39	S
Germany	56	R	56	R (with deduction)[a]
Greece	50	R	35	R (with credit)
Ireland	58	R	43	R (with credit or deduction)
Italy	50	R	46	R (with credit)[b]
Luxembourg	56	R	36	R (with credit)
Netherlands	72	R	36	R (with credit or deduction)[a]
Portugal	40	R	36	R (with credit)
Spain	56	R	35	R (with credit)
United Kingdom	60	R	35	R (with credit)
Canada	42–49[c]		38	
Japan	50		42	
United States	28–38[d]	R	34	R (with credit)

Sources: Lans Bovenberg and George Kopits, "Harmonization of Taxes on Capital Income and Commodities in the European Community," IMF, October 1989, and *Individual Taxes: A Worldwide Summary*, Price Waterhouse, 1989.
a. The source principle applies under treaties and for substantial participation in foreign companies.
b. With refund for excess foreign tax credit.
c. Including provincial taxes.
d. Including state taxes.

We consider again the standard two-country world (home and foreign) with perfect capital mobility and denote interest rates in the home and the foreign countries by r and r^*, respectively. In general, the home country may have three different effective tax rates that apply to interest income:

1. τ_{rD}—tax rate levied on residents on their domestic-source income;

2. τ_{rF}—effective tax rate levied on residents on their foreign-source income in addition to the tax already levied in the foreign country.

3. τ_{ND}—tax rate levied on nonresidents on their interest income originating in the home country.

Correspondingly, the foreign country may also have three tax rates, which we denote by τ^*_{rD}, τ^*_{rF}, and τ^*_{ND}. Note that $\tau_{rF} + \tau^*_{ND}$ and $\tau^*_{rF} + \tau_{ND}$ are *effective tax rates* on foreign-source income of the home country residents and of the foreign country residents, respectively, after tax credits and deductions have been taken into account. (If a refund is offered in the home country for excess foreign tax credits, then τ_{rF} is negative, and similarly for τ^*_{rF}). In what follows we assume that these tax rates apply symmetrically to both interest receipts and interest payments (i.e., we allow for deductibility of interest expenses, including tax rebates).

With complete integration of capital markets between the two countries (including the possibility of borrowing in one country in order to invest in the other country), arbitrage possibilities imply that

$$r(1 - \tau_{rD}) = r^*(1 - \tau^*_{ND} - \tau_{rF}), \tag{2.1}$$

and

$$r(1 - \tau_{ND} - \tau^*_{rF}) = r^*(1 - \tau^*_{rD}). \tag{2.2}$$

Equation (2.1) applies to the residents of the home country. It implies that in equilibrium these residents are indifferent between investing at home or abroad. If this equality was violated, then the home-country residents could borrow unlimited amounts in the low (net of tax) interest rate country and invest these borrowed funds in the high (net of tax) interest rate country, thereby generating unlimited profits. Similarly, equation (2.2), which applies to residents of the foreign country, rules out such unlimited profit opportunities to foreign residents.

Equations (2.1) and (2.2) form a linear and homogenous system in two unknowns (r and r^*). Hence, if the world capital market equilibrium is *viable* (in the sense that pretax interest rates are positive), then the tax rates in the two countries must fulfill the following constraint involving the tax rates of both countries:

$$(1 - \tau_{rD})(1 - \tau^*_{rD}) = (1 - \tau^*_{ND} - \tau_{rF})(1 - \tau_{ND} - \tau^*_{rF}). \tag{2.3}$$

The constraint, which involves tax rates of different tax jurisdictions, implies that even though the two tax authorities do not explicitly coordinate their tax systems, each nevertheless must take into account the tax system of the other.

Noteworthy is the fact that the two polar principles (the source and the residence principles) are examples of *feasible tax structures*, provided that the two countries adopt the same principle. To illustrate, we consider first the case in which both countries adopt the source principle. Because that principle implies that income is taxed only according to its source, regardless of residency, it follows that

$$\tau_{rD} = \tau_{ND'}, \qquad \tau^*_{rD} = \tau^*_{ND'}, \qquad \text{and} \qquad \tau_{rF} = \tau^*_{rF} = 0. \qquad (2.4)$$

Evidently, the joint constraint of equation (2.3) holds and therefore the world equilibrium is viable.

We consider next the case in which both countries adopt the residence principle. Because in this case income is taxed only according to the place of residency, regardless of its source, it follows that

$$\tau_{rD} = \tau^*_{ND} + \tau_{rF'}, \qquad \tau^*_{rD} = \tau_{ND} + \tau^*_{rF'}, \qquad \text{and} \qquad \tau_{ND} = \tau^*_{ND} = 0. \qquad (2.5)$$

Again, with these equalities the joint constraint in equation (2.3) holds, and world equilibrium is also viable.[2]

However, if the two countries do not adopt the same effective principle, then equation (2.3) need not hold, and therefore a viable equilibrium may not exist. To see this, suppose, for instance, that the home country adopts in effect the residence principle while the foreign country adopts in effect the source principle, so that

$$\tau_{rD} = \tau^*_{ND} + \tau_{rF'}, \qquad \text{and} \qquad \tau_{ND} = 0, \qquad (2.6)$$

and

$$\tau^*_{rD} = \tau^*_{ND'}, \qquad \text{and} \qquad \tau^*_{rF} = 0.$$

Hence, unless the foreign country levies no taxes whatsoever, so that $\tau^*_{rD} = \tau^*_{NF} = 0$ [recall that $\tau^*_{rF} = 0$ by (2.6)], the joint constraint in equation (2.3) does not hold. Of course, if one of the two countries does not employ one of the two pure principles, then, again, (2.3) need not hold.

These examples underscore the added constraints that integrated world capital markets impose on national tax structures. At the same time they also provide a rationale for either detailed international tax coordination or adherence to (the same) pure principle of international taxation.

Efficiency

In a world with international capital mobility the equality between saving and investment need not hold for each country separately but rather for world aggregate saving and investment. This separation raises the issue of the efficiency of the international allocation of the world investments and savings.

In a closed economy a tax on capital income drives just one wedge between the consumer-saver marginal intertemporal rate of substitution and the producer-investor marginal productivity of capital. In a world of open economies two additional types of distortions can be caused by capital income taxation: (1) international differences in intertemporal marginal rates of substitution (after-tax interest rates), which imply an inefficient allocation of world savings across countries, and (2) international differences in the marginal productivity of capital (before-tax interest rates), which imply an inefficient allocation of world investments across countries.

It is worth studying the implications of the two pure principles of taxation (residence and source) for the global allocation of savings and investments. Recall that according to the residence principle, residents are taxed on their worldwide income equally, regardless of whether the source of the income is domestic or foreign. Recall that at equilibrium a resident in any country must earn the same after-tax return, no matter to which country he or she chooses to channel savings (the rate-of-return arbitrage). If a country adopts the residence principle, by effectively taxing at the same rate capital income from all sources, then the before-tax return accruing to an individual in that country must be the same, regardless of which country is the source of that return. Thus, the marginal product of capital in that country will be equal to the world return to capital. If all countries adopt the residence principle, then capital-income taxation does not upset the equality of the marginal product of capital across countries. Formally, the residence principle, when in effect in the home and the foreign country, is specified in condition (2.5). Substituting this condition into the (after-tax) rate of return equalization within countries [that is, conditions (2.1) and (2.2)], yields the (before-tax) rate of return equalization between countries: $r = r^*$. However, if the tax rates are not the same in all countries, then the net returns accruing to savers in different countries vary (i.e., $(1 - \tau_{rD})r \neq (1 - \tau_{rD}^*)r^*$), and the international allocation of world savings is distorted.

According to the source principle, residents of a country are not taxed on their income from foreign sources, and foreigners are taxed at the same rate as residents on income from domestic sources. Now, suppose that all countries adopt this principle. Then, a resident of the home country earns in the foreign country the same net return as the resident of the foreign country earns in the foreign country. Since a resident in the home country must earn the same net return whether he or she channeled savings to the home country or to the foreign country, it follows that residents of all countries earn the same net return. Thus, intertemporal marginal rates of substitutions are equated across countries, implying that the international allocation of world savings is efficient. Formally, the source principle is specified by condition (2.4). Substituting this condition into the arbitrage conditions, (2.1) and (2.2), yields the (net of tax) rate-of-return equalization between residents of different countries: $r(1 - \tau_{rD}) = r^*(1 - \tau_{rD}^*)$. However, if the tax rates are not the same in all countries (i.e., $\tau_{rD} \neq \tau_{rD}^*$), then $r \neq r^*$, and the international allocation of the world stock of capital is not efficient.

The inefficiencies of the world aggregate investments or savings are depicted in figures 2.1 and 2.2. Suppose that the world stock of capital is given. In figure 2.1 this stock is depicted on the horizontal axis. The home country's capital, K, is measured in a rightward direction, starting at point 0, whereas the foreign country's capital, K^*, is measured in a leftward direction, starting at point 0^*. The curves labeled MPK and MPK^* describe the marginal products of capital in the home and the foreign country, respectively. Under the source principle, with different tax rates in the two countries, the before-tax rates of return, r and r^*, are not equal (even

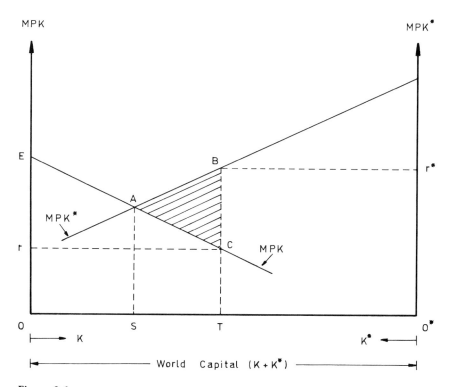

Figure 2.1
Allocation of world investment

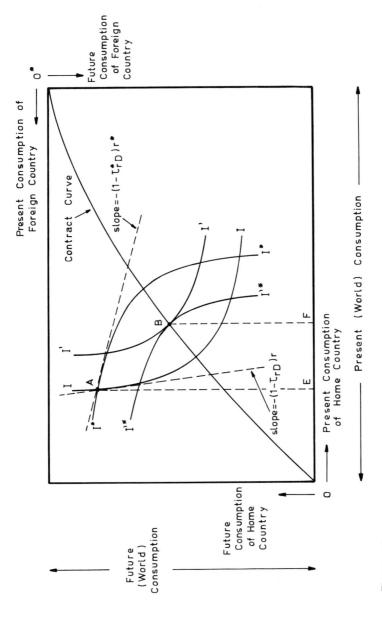

Figure 2.2
Allocation of world saving

though $(1 - \tau_{rD})r = (1 - \tau_{rD}^*)r^*)$. The equilibrium allocation of capital in this case will be at a point such as T, with a future (world) output loss of ABC. Under the residence principle, $r = r^*$, and the equilibrium allocation of the world stock of capital is at point S, where the world's future output is maximized, for the given stock of capital. (Obviously the equilibrium world stock of capital itself is different when the residence principle applies than when the source principle applies.)

The equilibrium allocation of world savings is depicted in figure 2.2. Suppose that the present world output is given. Suppose further that the world's total investment ($=$ savings) and the international distribution of investment have already been determined. Thus, aggregate (world) present and future consumption are given. Consider then the well-known Edgeworth box in figure 2.2, with a representative consumer for each country. Under the residence principle, with different tax rates in the two countries, the (net of tax) rates of interest are not equalized; that is, $(1 - \tau_{rD})r \neq (1 - \tau_{rD}^*)r^*$, even though $r = r^*$. Equilibrium in this case is at a point such as A, outside the contract curve. Global savings are inefficiently allocated between the representative residents of the two countries. Accordingly, if the home country resident saves less by increasing his or her present consumption by an amount EF while the foreign country resident saves more by the same amount, then the equilibrium can move to point B, where both residents are better off. Under the source principle, net-of-tax rates of interest are equalized in the two countries, and the equilibrium will be at point on the contract curve (such as point B). The allocation of global savings is efficient. (Obviously the equilibrium volume of world savings is generally different under the two modes of taxation.)

2.2 Indirect Taxation: Destination Principle versus Source Principle

Basic Principles

Apart from border taxes (e.g., tariffs), the international implications of indirect taxation lie primarily with the value-added tax (VAT). This broad-based tax is very common in Europe and other countries and serves as a major revenue source for governments. Table 2.2 describes concisely the major features of the VAT in the European Community. The table shows that the VAT provides between 13 percent and 27 percent of all tax revenues in those countries.

As the name suggests, the VAT is levied on the value-added of the firm. The administrative technique usually employed is to levy a tax on the full

Table 2.2
Value-added taxes in the European Community

Country	Year of introduction	Statutory rates[a]				Scope of zero rate	VAT as percent of tax revenue[b]	VAT as percent of GDP[b]
		Standard rate	Increased rate	Reduced rate				
Belgium	1971	19	25, 33	1, 6, 17	Newspapers	16.3	7.2
Denmark	1967	22	—	—	Newspapers, large ships and aircraft	26.9	
France[c]	1968	18.6	25	5.5	—	20.9	8.7
Germany, Fed. Rep. of	1968	14	—	7	—	13.1	3.8
Greece[d]	1987	16	36	3, 6	—	20.9	7.8
Ireland	1972	23	—	0, 5, 10	Wide range of items	18.9	8.0
Italy	1973	19	38	4, 9	Newspapers, some minor items	13.1	4.7
Luxembourg	1970	12	—	3, 6	—	13.3	6.0
Netherlands	1969	18.5	—	6	—	15.2	7.9
Portugal[e]	1986	17	30	8	Basic foods, newspapers, medicines, agricultural inputs	18.8	7.7
Spain	1986	12	33	6	—	16.0	5.3
United Kingdom	1973	17.5	—	0	Wide range of items	16.3	6.0

Sources: "EC: The Evolution of VAT Rates Applicable in Member States of the Community," *Intertax*, (1987/3); International Bureau of Fiscal Documentation, *Tax News Service*, various issues; IMF, *Government Finance Statistics Yearbook* (1989), and OECD, *Revenue Statistics of OECD Member Countries, 1966–88* (Paris, 1989).
a. As of July 1990.
b. Data for 1987.
c. France applies VAT rates of 2.1 percent to daily newspapers and some medicines, and 13 percent to sales and transfers of building land. Different VAT rates apply in Corsica.
d. Different rates apply in Dodecanese.
e. Different rates apply in the Azores and Madeira.

value of goods and services sold by the firm (i.e., to levy a tax on the revenue of the firm) and then to allow a credit (with a refund) for the taxes included in the prices of all the intermediate goods and *producible* services purchased by the firm (i.e., except for labor and capital services employed directly by the firm). Because the gross value-added of a firm is defined as revenue minus cost of intermediate goods and producible services, it follows that the tax is generally levied on the gross value-added of the firm. Because the sum of the gross value-added of all domestic firms is equal to gross domestic product (GDP), then, in principle, the VAT base is GDP.[3] There are, however, two major exceptions. The first exception concerns capital goods. They are treated as intermediate goods and thus are exempted from the tax base. This exception causes the base of VAT to be equal to GDP minus gross investment. The second exception concerns the treatment of exports and imports.

Analogous to the residence and source principles governing direct taxation, there are the destination and source principles in the case of VAT.[4] A country that employs the destination principle levies the VAT on all goods and services destined for final consumption in that country, regardless of the source of production. Therefore, exports are exempted, whereas imports are taxed.[5] Hence, the *destination-based* VAT is essentially a *consumption tax*. In contrast, a country that adopts the source principle levies the tax on all goods and services produced in that country, irrespective of their final destination. Therefore, exports are taxed, whereas imports are exempted. Hence, the *source-based* VAT is essentially a tax on GDP minus gross domestic investment.

Suppose a good is produced in the home country and then exported to a foreign market. Under the source principle the value-added would be taxed at home, regardless of the point of sale. Under the destination principle the value-added would be exempted from home tax if the good was shipped directly, and taxed immediately upon arrival in the foreign country, if that country also followed the destination principle. For exported goods with intermediate domestic value added and sales, the destination principle would call for a tax on initial sales of the intermediate goods and then a rebate of those taxes upon export of the final good.[6]

Common Practice

Currently, most countries apply the destination principle to their VAT systems. That is, they exempt exports and tax imports. To enforce this principle, most countries resort to border controls, where VAT is levied on imports, whereas exports are reported directly by the exporting firms. An exception is the Benelux countries, which do not have border controls among them. Still, the destination-based VAT is enforced through reporting by the importing firms. The European Community, which will eliminate fiscal frontiers in 1992, is currently scheduled to maintain the destination principle and to employ the Benelux model for administering this principle. However, the current agreement calls for the EC to shift to the source principle in 1997, with some kind of a clearinghouse for compensating or taxing member countries for revenue losses or gains resulting from the change in the VAT base. Even under this arrangement the EC will still maintain the destination principle vis-à-vis the rest of the world.

Feasible VAT Principles

Just as international capital flows dictate after-tax rate-of-return equalization within countries, free trade in goods and services dictates after-tax price equalization of goods within countries. This imposes some constraints on national VAT systems.

To clarify this point, we consider again a two-country world (home and foreign) with a free trade in goods and services. We denote by p the producer price of a certain tradable good in the home country, expressed in terms of a common (to both the home and the foreign country), untaxed numeraire, say labor (or capital).[7] In principle, the home country may apply three different (ad valorem) tax rates to the good:

1. τ_D—tax rate levied on the good if produced domestically and sold domestically;

2. τ_X—tax rate levied on exports of the good;

3. τ_M—*effective* tax rate levied on the imported good (in addition to the tax levied abroad).

Consider now a consumer in the home country who can purchase the good either from home production or from foreign production. If the good is produced in both countries, then the after-tax price to the home country consumer must be the same regardless of the country of production. That is,

$$p(1 + \tau_D) = p^*(1 + \tau_X^* + \tau_M), \tag{2.7}$$

where an asterisk stands for the foreign country. A similar after-tax price equalization condition applies for the consumer in the foreign country, that is,

$$p(1 + \tau_X + \tau_M^*) = p^*(1 + \tau_D^*). \tag{2.8}$$

Thus, if the good is produced and consumed in both countries, both equations (2.7) and (2.8) must hold. Since the VAT applies to all goods, then as long as there is at least one good that is produced and consumed in both countries, it follows that

$$(1 + \tau_D)(1 + \tau_D^*) = (1 + \tau_X^* + \tau_M)(1 + \tau_X + \tau_M^*). \tag{2.9}$$

Otherwise, the only solution to (2.7)–(2.8) is $p = p^* = 0$, which is impossible. Thus, a joint constraint involving the tax rates in the two countries is crucial for the existence of an equilibrium in which there is at least one good that is produced and consumed in both countries.

As with direct taxes, either of the polar principles, destination or source, meets the joint constraint (2.9) if adopted by both countries. For instance, if the destination principle is adopted by both countries, it is specified by

$$\tau_D = \tau_x^* + \tau_M, \quad \tau_D^* = \tau_x + \tau_M^*, \quad \text{and} \quad \tau_x = \tau_x^* = 0 \tag{2.10}$$

Similarly, if the source principle is adopted by both countries, it is specified by

$$\tau_D = \tau_X, \quad \tau_D^* = \tau_X^*, \quad \text{and} \quad \tau_M = \tau_M^* = 0. \tag{2.11}$$

It is straightforward to verify that the joint constraint (2.9) is satisfied if either (2.10) or (2.11) holds. However, as in the case of direct taxation, a mixture of the two polar principles (either by the same country or by the two countries) may violate the joint constraint (2.9) and consequently may be infeasible.[8]

Efficiency

Obviously, in a world with international trade in goods and services, the equality between production and consumption need not hold for each country separately but rather for world *aggregate* production and *aggregate* consumption. In a closed economy an excise tax drives a wedge between the producer price and the consumer price. In an integrated world economy two additional types of distortions are caused by a uniform, broad-based VAT. These distortions arise from (1) international differences in consumer marginal rates of substitution between commodities, which imply an inefficient allocation of world consumption and (2) international differences in producer marginal rates of transformation between commodities, which imply that world output is not efficiently produced.

If both countries adopt the destination principle, then (2.10) holds, and it follows from (2.7) and (2.8) that $p = p^*$ for all tradable goods. That is, the relative producer price between any tradable good (or all tradable goods grouped together as an aggregate consumption good) and labor (or capital) is equalized across countries. Profit maximization implies that the business sector equates the relative producer price between any tradable good and labor to the marginal rate of transformation between them (i.e., to the inverse of the marginal product of labor in the production of that tradable good). Hence, labor has the same marginal product in the production of any tradable good in both countries. That is, world aggregate production efficiency prevails: world production lies on the world aggregate production possibility frontier. However, if the VAT rates differ in the two countries, then the relative consumer price between any tradable good and leisure is not equated across countries, and the allocation of world consumption (of leisure and of tradable goods) is inefficient.

Similarly, if both countries adopt the source principle, equation (2.11) holds. It then follows from equations (2.7) and (2.8) that $p(1 + \tau_D) = p^*(1 + \tau_D^*)$ for all tradable goods. That is, the relative consumer price between any good and leisure is equalized across countries. Utility maximization implies that the relative consumer price between any tradable good and leisure is equated to the marginal rate of substitution between them. Hence, these marginal rates of substitution are equalized internationally. That is, the allocation of world consumption (of leisure and of tradable goods) is efficient. However, if the VAT rates are not the same in all countries, then the relative producer prices are not equalized internationally. That is, the marginal products of labor in the production of the same tradable good are not equalized internationally, and aggregate production is inefficient.

The inefficiencies of world allocation of production and consumption are depicted in figures 2.3 and 2.4. Under the source principle the relative consumer price of any tradable good (or all tradable goods grouped together into an aggregate consumption good), in terms of the numeraire leisure, is the same in the home and the foreign country. But the marginal products of labor in producing this good (denoted by MPL and MPL^* for the home and the foreign country, respectively) differ between the two countries. Figure 2.3 depicts the production inefficiency that arises in this case. Let 00^* be the total labor input employed in the production of the tradable good in the two countries. Let L and L^* be the labor input

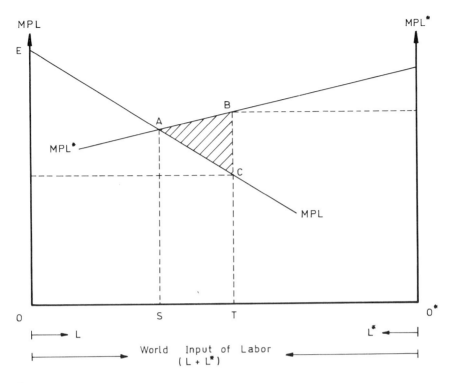

Figure 2.3
Allocation of world labor

employed in the production of the tradable good in the home and the foreign country, respectively. Suppose, for the sake of concreteness, that $MPL^* > MPL$, so that the allocation of world labor is at a point such as T. Recall that the consumer marginal rates of substitution between the tradable good and leisure are the same in the two countries. That is, the consumer marginal valuation of leisure in terms of the tradable good is the same in the two countries. Hence, if a representative consumer in the foreign country works for an additional unit of labor, and a representative consumer in the home country reduces his or her work effort by one unit, then an appropriate transfer of the tradable good (equaling the common marginal valuation of leisure) can be made from the representative consumer in the home country to the representative consumer in the foreign country that leaves both consumers indifferent. But, since the marginal product of labor is higher in the foreign country, these compensated changes in the labor supply increase total output of the tradable good, making it possible to increase the welfare of the consumer in both coun-

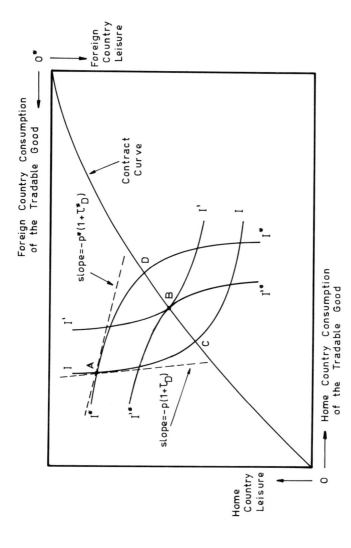

Figure 2.4
Allocation of world consumption

tries. This shows that world production of the tradable good is inefficient. In fact, the total output loss incurred at the inefficient point T is equal to the area of the triangle ABC.

Under the destination principle the marginal products of labor in the production of the tradable good are equalized across countries. But the marginal rates of substitution between the tradable good and leisure are not equalized internationally. The consumption inefficiency that arises in this case is described by the familiar Edgeworth box depicted in figure 2.4, where consumption of leisure and of the tradable good is represented by a point such as A, off the contract curve. Because the marginal product of labor is the same in both countries, increasing the labor supply of the home country and reducing the labor supply of the foreign country by the same amount will leave the total output of the tradable good unchanged. But then there exists a transfer of the tradable good from the foreign country to the home country to accompany these changes in the labor supply of each country that shifts the allocation to a point on the segment CD of the contract curve, making consumers in both countries better off.

Notice, nevertheless, that the aforementioned production and consumption inefficiencies, which are the hallmark of trade taxes such as an import tariff, do not exist *within* the set of tradable goods. As long as the VAT rate is *uniform* on all goods, these inefficiencies may arise only between the whole set of tradable goods (or any good within this set) and labor or leisure. To see this, consider any two tradable goods i and j. When the VAT rate is uniform, the consumer price ratio between these goods, $p_i(1 + \tau_D)/p_j(1 + \tau_D)$, is equal to the producer price ratio, p_i/p_j. Similarly, in the foreign country $p_i^*(1 + \tau_D^*)/p_j^*(1 + \tau_D^*) = p_i^*/p_j^*$. If both countries adopt the destination principle, then the producer price ratios are equal in the two countries (i.e., $p_i/p_j = p_i^*/p_j^*$), and it follows that the consumer price ratios are also equal (i.e., $p_i(1 + \tau_D)/p_j(1 + \tau_D) = p_i^*(1 + \tau_D^*)/p_j^*(1 + \tau_D^*)$). Thus, within the set of tradable goods both production and consumption are efficient. Similarly, if both countries adopt the source principle, then their consumer price ratios are equalized, and it follows that their producer price ratios are equalized, too. Again, within the set of tradable goods both production and consumption are efficient.

II

Principles of International
Macroeconomics and Taxation

3

International-Intertemporal
Macroeconomics

In this chapter we review basic elements of intertemporal open-economy macroeconomics. To motivate the discussion, we start in section 3.2 with a specification of a simple stylized two-period model of a small open economy that has free access to world capital markets and that produces and consumes a single aggregate tradable good. In this context we characterize the maximizing behavior of firms and households and determine the general equilibrium levels of investment, consumption, savings, and the various accounts of the balance of payments.[1]

The intertemporal disparities between the paths of consumption and income are reflected in debt accumulation and decumulation. To highlight the central motives underlying the determination of intertemporal allocations of debt, we introduce in section 3.3 three basic concepts: consumption smoothing, consumption tilting, and consumption augmenting. These concepts are useful for interpreting the role that capital markets play in facilitating the adjustments of consumption paths over time.

In section 3.4 we illustrate the usefulness of the three concepts by applying the stylized model to the analysis of supply shocks. In this context we analyze the effects of temporary (current or anticipated future) and permanent supply shocks on the levels of consumption, investment, and the trade balance.

In section 3.5 we extend the analysis of the small open economy to the familiar home-country–foreign-country model of the world economy. The analysis identifies the factors that determine the equilibrium level of the world rate of interest and the associated international and intertemporal distribution of trade imbalances. The key factors governing the equilibrium are the relation between the home and the foreign marginal saving propensities (reflecting differences between marginal rates of time preference), the relation between the home and the foreign percentage rates of growth of GDP, the percentage rate of growth of world GDP, and the initial distribution of world debt. The impact of the initial distribution is illustrated through an analysis of the effects of international transfers on the equilibrium level of the world rate of interest.

3.1 A Stylized Model

Let us consider a small open economy producing and consuming one aggregate tradable good and facing a given world rate of interest. The aggregation of goods into a single aggregate commodity is done to focus attention on intertemporal trade, that is, on international borrowing and lending. Obviously, in designing a model that is suitable for intertemporal analysis, we need to extend the single-period perspective into a multi-period setting. In the context of the stylized model we adopt the minimal framework of a two-period model.

We start by specifying the supply side of the model. The economy is endowed with an initial stock of capital, K_0, and a production function that depends on capital, $F_0(K_0)$. We assume that the production function exhibits positive and diminishing marginal returns.

The investment technology is assumed to exhibit increasing average as well as marginal costs of investment due to adjustment costs.[2] The latter, indicated by the coefficient $g \geq 0$, reflects installation, job reassignment, or training. To simplify we assume quadratic costs:

$$Z_0 = I_0\left(1 + \frac{\frac{1}{2}gI_0}{K_0}\right),$$

(3.1)

where I_0 is the level of investment, and Z_0 is the cost of investment. Average costs of investment, $1 + \frac{1}{2}gI_0/K_0$, fall short of the marginal costs of investment, $1 + gI_0/K_0$, implying increasing average costs. Putting it differently, there are diminishing returns to capital formation.

The capital stock in period one, K_1, is augmented by the investment that takes place in period zero, according to

$$K_1 = I_0 + K_0,$$

(3.2)

where for simplicity we ignore depreciation.[3]

The investment process modifies the intertemporal pattern of available outputs (GDP). Formally, output in period one, Y_1, is linked to the initial stock of capital, K_0, and the level of investment, I_0, through the production function

$$Y_1 = F_1(K_1) = F_1(I_0 + K_0).$$

(3.3)

Naturally, in the absence of investment the capital stock cannot be augmented, and future output is $Y_1 = F_1(K_0)$.

Firms are assumed to maximize the present value of profits. Formally, the firm's investment policy is determined by solving the maximization problem

$$\tilde{\pi} = \max_{I_0} \left\{ \alpha_1 [F_1(I_0 + K_0) + (I_0 + K_0)] - I_0 \left(1 + \frac{\frac{1}{2} g I_0}{K_0} \right) \right\}, \tag{3.4}$$

where $\alpha_1 = 1/(1 + r_0)$ denotes the present value or discount factor, and r_0 is the world rate of interest between periods one and zero. The formulation in (3.4) indicates that a unit of current investment, I_0, bears fruit, $F_1(I_0 + K_0)$, only in the subsequent period; this is reflected by the discounting in the profit function. Figure 3.1 illustrates the maximization problem and the firm's investment policy. In the absence of investment the output sequence is $(F_0(K_0), K_0 + F_1(K_0))$. This pair of outputs is denoted by point A, and the present value of this sequence of outputs is denoted by

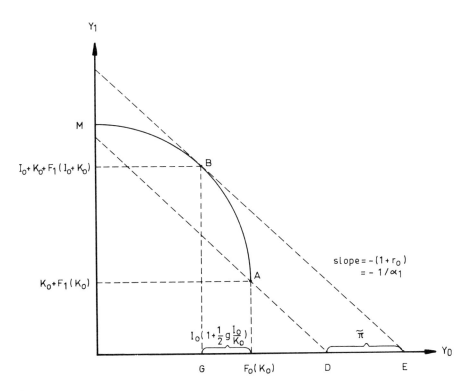

Figure 3.1
The determination of investment and profits

point D. The (absolute value of the) slope of the dashed line connecting points A and D is the intertemporal price $(1/\alpha_1) = 1 + r_0$. Point M represents the maximum level of investment, so that the domestic production that is allocated for present consumption is zero (i.e., $Z_0 = F_0(K_0)$). The schedule originating from point A and passing through point B specifies the transformation schedule linking current period production that is allocated for consumption with future period production that is allocated for consumption.

Diagrammatically, investment spending is measured in a leftward direction from $F_0(K_0)$. In the absence of investment, future profits are zero. Thus, the dashed line AD is a zero-profit locus. The profit-maximizing firm seeks to reach the highest isoprofit locus subject to its technological constraints. Point B in figure 3.1 represents the outcome of the firm's profit-maximizing investment policy. With such policy the present value of future profits, $\tilde{\pi}$, is measured by the distance DE, and the level of investment spending, Z_0, is measured by the distance from G to $F_0(K_0)$.

As is evident from figure 3.1, the firm will carry out positive investment only if the transformation function emerging at the initial endowment point, A, is steeper at that point than $1 + r_0$. At point B the present value of future profits is maximized, and the (absolute value of the) slope of the transformation function equals $1 + r_0$. More formally, we note from equation (3.4) that the first-order condition for profit maximization requires that

$$\frac{F_1'(I_0 + K_0) - gI_0/K_0}{q_0} = r_0, \tag{3.5}$$

where $q_0 = 1 + gI_0/K_0$ is the marginal adjustment cost. Diminishing returns, that is, $F_1''(I_0 + K_0) < 0$, and increasing marginal costs of adjustment, that is, $g > 0$, imply that a higher rate of interest lowers the profit-maximizing level of investment. In terms of figure 3.1, a higher rate of interest steepens the isoprofit loci and slides point B rightward along the transformation schedule toward point A. The new profit-maximization point is associated with a smaller level of investment.

We turn next to an analysis of the demand side of the model. Consider a representative consumer maximizing lifetime utility subject to budget constraints. The individual's resources are composed of the initial endowments, $F_0(K_0)$ and $K_0 + F_1(K_0)$, and profits, $F_1(I_0 + K_0) + (I_0 + K_0) - [F_1(K_0) + K_0]$, that firms distribute as dividends to share holders. These resources are used in the first period for consumption and saving. During the second (and last) period, total income is fully consumed. Hence, the first-period budget constraint is

$$C_0 = F_0(K_0) - Z_0 + B_0 - (1 + r_{-1})B_{-1}, \tag{3.6}$$

and the second-period budget constraint is

$$C_1 = F_1(K_0 + I_0) + (K_0 + I_0) - (1 + r_0)B_0. \tag{3.7}$$

In equations (3.6) and (3.7) C_0 and C_1 denote first- and second-period consumption; B_0 denotes first-period borrowing, which can be positive or negative; Z_0 denotes the initial investment spending corresponding to the losses of firms (negative dividends); and $(1 + r_{-1})B_{-1}$ is the historically given initial debt commitment of the representative individual corresponding to the economy's external debt. Finally, the term $-(1 + r_0)B_0$ in equation (3.7) indicates that in the second period individuals must repay debts incurred in the previous period. Obviously, in this two-period model the solvency requirement ensures that in the second period the individual does not incur new debt. Thus, in the final period all debt commitments are settled.

From national income accounting, the sum of consumption, investment, and the surplus in the current account of the balance of payments equals GNP. In terms of equation (3.6), GDP is $F_0(K_0)$, external debt payments are $r_{-1}B_{-1}$, GNP is $F_0(K_0) - r_{-1}B_{-1}$, and the current-account surplus (equal to the capital-account deficit) is $-(B_0 - B_{-1})$. Alternatively, the current-account surplus also equals savings ($F_0(K_0) - r_{-1}B_{-1} - C_0$) minus investment ($Z_0$). Hence, the specification in equation (3.6) conforms with national income accounting. Similar considerations apply to the second-period budget constraint in equation (3.7).

Because the representative individual has free access to world capital markets, he or she can lend and borrow freely subject to the world rate of interest, r_0. This access to capital markets implies that the individual's choices are constrained by a consolidated present-value budget constraint rather than two separate periodic budget constraints. To derive the consolidated constraint, we divide equation (3.7) by $(1 + r_0)$, add the resulting equation to equation (3.6), and obtain

$$C_0 + \alpha_1 C_1 = F_0(K_0) + \alpha_1[F_1(I_0 + K_0) + (I_0 + K_0)] - Z_0 - (1 + r_{-1})B_{-1}$$

$$\equiv W_0. \tag{3.8}$$

The right-hand side of equation (3.8) defines the value of wealth in period zero, W_0. The consolidated budget constraint highlights the fact that the key decisions that individuals make concern the choices of C_0 and C_1. Implicit in these decisions is the magnitude of new borrowing, B_0, which appears explicitly in the temporal budget constraints (3.6) and (3.7).

It is relevant to note that intertemporal solvency implies that the discounted sum of the periodic surpluses in the trade account must equal the sum of the principal plus interest payments on the historically given initial debt. The trade-balance surplus in each period equals GDP minus domestic absorption (consumption plus investment). Formally, using equations (3.6) and (3.7)—or equivalently using the consolidated equation (3.8)—we note that

$$(TA)_0 + \alpha_1 (TA)_1 = (1 + r_{-1})B_{-1}, \tag{3.9}$$

where $(TA)_i$ denotes the surplus in the trade balance in period $i = 0, 1$. Formally, $(TA)_0 = F_0(K_0) - C_0 - Z_0$, and $(TA)_1 = F_1(K_0 + I_0) + (K_0 + I_0) - C_1$. It follows therefore that the discounted sum of the periodic surpluses in the current account must equal the discounted sum of the trade balance surplus plus the discounted sum of the surplus in the debt-service account. Formally,

$$(CA)_0 + \alpha_1 (CA)_1 = (1 + r_{-1})B_{-1} + (DA)_0 + \alpha_1 (DA)_1, \tag{3.9a}$$

where $(CA)_i$ denotes the surplus in the current account (equal to GNP minus domestic absorption), and DA_i denotes the surplus in the debt-service account (equal to minus interest payments on previous period debt) in period $i = 0, 1$. Hence, in our two-period model $(DA)_0 = -r_{-1}B_{-1}$ and $(DA)_1 = -r_0 B_0$. Equation (3.9) reveals that in the absence of initial debt, a trade-balance surplus in a given period must equal (in present-value terms) the trade-balance deficits in all other periods taken as a whole. As illustrated by equation (3.9a), a similar property does not apply to the intertemporal pattern of the current account.

Let the representative individual's utility depend on the levels of consumption, and let his or her lifetime utility function be denoted by $U(C_0, C_1)$. As usual, we assume that the marginal utilities of consumption in each period are positive and that the marginal rate of substitution of consumption between two consecutive periods is diminishing along any given indifference curve (a quasi-concave U). The individual seeks to maximize lifetime utility subject to the consolidated lifetime budget constraint. Formally, the individual's maximization problem is

$$\tilde{U} = \max_{\{C_0, C_1\}} U(C_0, C_1), \tag{3.10}$$

subject to

$$C_0 + \alpha_1 C_1 = W_0.$$

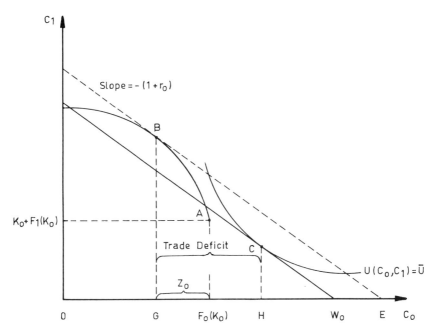

Figure 3.2
The general equilibrium of consumption, investment, and the trade balance

The solution to this maximization problem is shown in figure 3.2, which incorporates the relevant information from the firm's profit maximization problem of figure 3.1. In this figure, point E measures the discounted sum of current and future GDPs, minus investment (Z_0), and W_0 measures the value of wealth in period zero. That is, E measures $F_0(K_0) + \alpha_1[F_1(K_0 + I_0) + (K_0 + I_0)] - Z_0$, whereas W_0 measures $F_0(K_0) + \alpha_1[F_1(K_0 + I_0) + (K_0 + I_0)] - Z_0 - (1 + r_{-1})B_{-1}$. The horizontal distance between E and W_0 corresponds therefore to the initial external debt commitment $(1 + r_{-1})B_{-1}$. The maximized level of utility obtains at point C at the tangency of indifference curve $\bar{U} = U(C_0, C_1)$ with the budget line. The budget line in turn emerges from point W_0—corresponding to the value of wealth in period zero—and its slope (in absolute terms) equals $1/\alpha_1 = 1 + r_0$.

The equilibrium portrayed in figure 3.2 represents the general equilibrium of the small open economy incorporating both the profit maximization by firms and the utility maximization by households. The case shown in the figure corresponds to a situation in which period zero's absorption (consumption, OH, plus investment, $GF_0(K_0)$) exceeds that period's GDP, $F_0(K_0)$. As a result, the economy runs in period zero a trade-balance deficit that is equal to GH. Obviously, the corresponding current-account deficit is obtained by adding the debt service, $r_{-1}B_{-1}$, to the trade-balance deficit.

3.2 Three Determinants of Borrowing and Lending

The equilibrium pattern of consumption portrayed in figure 3.2 is associated with discrepancies between the periodic levels of consumption and incomes. The lack of a complete synchronization between the time series of consumption and income is reconciled by a reliance on the world capital markets. Accordingly, in obtaining the optimal time profile of consumption, individuals find it beneficial to incur debt during some periods of their life. In determining the extent of the optimal departure of the path of consumption from that of income, and thereby the optimal reliance on capital markets and debt accumulation, it is useful to identify three separate motives: the consumption-smoothing motive, the consumption-tilting motive, and the consumption-augmenting motive. These three motives govern the desired volume of borrowing and lending.

In introducing the three concepts we need to define the concept of the subjective discount factor, which plays a critical role in determining the intertemporal allocations. The subjective discount factor, δ, measures the marginal rate of substitution between consumption in two consecutive periods evaluated at the point of a flat time profile of consumption ($C_0 = C_1 = C$). Thus,

$$\delta = \frac{\partial U(C, C)/\partial C_1}{\partial U(C, C)/\partial C_0}. \tag{3.11}$$

The subjective discount factor, δ, is related to the subjective marginal rate of time preference, ρ, according to $\delta = 1/(1 + \rho)$.

To facilitate the exposition, we suppose that the subjective discount factor is fixed and that the utility function is

$$U(C_0, C_1) = U(C_0) + \delta U(C_1), \tag{3.12}$$

where U exhibits diminishing marginal utilities (i.e., U is concave). As is evident from the first-order condition of the consumer's maximization problem of equation (3.10), utility maximization implies an equality between the intertemporal marginal rate of substitution and the discount factor. Hence,

$$\frac{U'(C_0)}{\delta U'(C_1)} = \frac{1}{\alpha_1}. \tag{3.13}$$

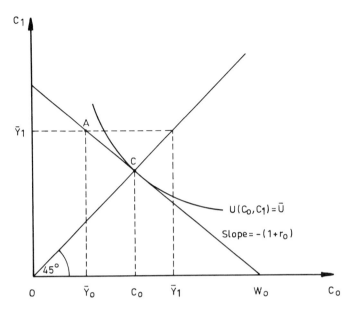

Figure 3.3
The consumption-smoothing effect
assumptions: $\rho = r_0$, $\bar{Y}_0 < \bar{Y}_1$, $F_1'(K_0) \leqslant r_0$

Armed with these preliminaries, we turn now to illustrate the basic concepts. To sharpen the exposition of each concept, we focus on special cases designed to isolate each factor separately. In all cases we assume that there is no initial debt. We consider first the consumption-smoothing motive. In figure 3.3 we assume that the subjective and the market discount factors are equal to each other (i.e., $\delta = \alpha_1$), that there is no investment, but that the periodic levels of income (endowments) differ from each other ($\bar{Y}_0 \equiv F_0(K_0) \neq K_0 + F_1(K_0) \equiv \bar{Y}_1$). In that case equilibrium consumption is described by point C along the $45°$ ray. As is evident, because of the equality between the subjective and the market discount factors, δ and α_1 (or equivalently, between the subjective rate of time preference, ρ, and the market rate of interest, r_0), individuals wish to smooth the time profile of consumption relative to the fluctuating levels of current income, and as seen in the figure, consumption (which is equal across periods) falls between $\bar{Y}_0$ and $\bar{Y}_1$. This consumption-smoothing motive is effected through borrowing in period zero and repaying the loan plus interest in the subsequent period.

We consider next the consumption-tilting motive. In figure 3.4 we assume that the subjective and the market discount factors differ from each

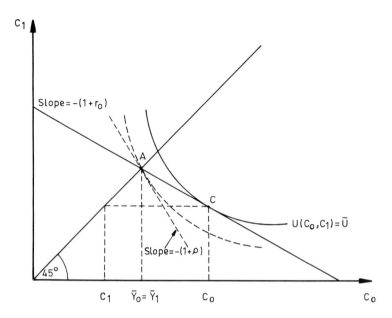

Figure 3.4
The consumption-tilting effect
assumptions: $\rho > r_0$, $\overline{Y}_0 = \overline{Y}_1$, $F_1'(K_0) \lessgtr r_0$

other (i.e., $\alpha_1 \neq \delta$), that there is no investment, and that the periodic levels of income (endowments) are equal (i.e., $\overline{Y}_0 = \overline{Y}_1$). In that case the equilibrium consumption point C does not lie along the $45°$ ray. In the case drawn, $\delta < \alpha_1$, so that the subjective rate of time preference (ρ) exceeds the world rate of interest (r_0). As a result, individuals facing a flat time profile of income wish to tilt the time profile of consumption toward period zero. This consumption-tilting motive is also effected through the world capital markets in which the individuals borrow in period zero and settle their debts in period one.

Finally, we consider the consumption-augmenting motive. In figure 3.5 we assume equality between the subjective and the market discount factors (i.e., $\delta = \alpha_1$) and between the periodic levels of income (endowments) so that $\overline{Y}_0 = \overline{Y}_1$; we also assume that there is positive investment, because $F_1'(K_0) > 1 + r_0$. In that case, equilibrium consumption is at point C. As seen, the investment opportunities, which tilt the time profile of income, augment the levels of consumption in each period without introducing variability to its time profile. As with the other cases, this consumption-augmenting motive is also effected through the world capital markets in which individuals borrow in period zero and repay debt commitment in

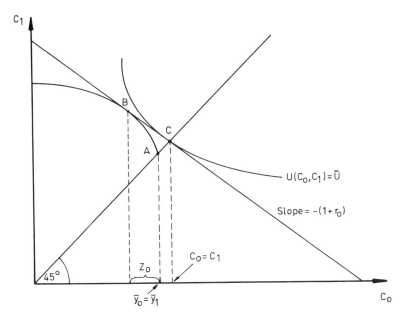

Figure 3.5
The consumption-augmenting effect
assumptions: $\rho = r_0$, $\overline{Y}_0 = \overline{Y}_1$, $F_1'(K_0) > r_0$

period one. As is evident, in the absence of international capital markets the investment carried out in period zero would have crowded out private-sector consumption in that period. Access to the world capital markets facilitates the augmentation of consumption at a rate that is uniform over time.

The assumptions needed to generate the pure consumption-smoothing, consumption-tilting, and consumption-augmenting effects are summarized in table 3.1. In all cases these motives are expressed through borrowing and lending in the capital market. Although we have isolated each of the three effects, in general, it is likely that the three motives coexist and interact in generating the equilibrium patterns of consumption, investment, and debt accumulation.

3.3 The Intertemporal Adjustment to Supply Shocks

In this section we illustrate the operation of the three factors in the context of adjustment to supply shocks. To analyze the equilibrium response to supply shocks and to highlight the intertemporal considerations involved in such an adjustment, we distinguish between temporary and permanent

Table 3.1
Assumptions generating pure consumption-smoothing, consumption-tilting, and consumption-augmenting effects

	Smoothing	Tilting	Augmenting
Discount	$\delta = \alpha_1$	$\delta \neq \alpha_1$	$\delta = \alpha_1$
Endowments	$\bar{Y}_0 \neq \bar{Y}_1$	$\bar{Y}_0 = \bar{Y}_1$	$\bar{Y}_0 = \bar{Y}_1$
Investment profitability	$F'_1(K_0) \leqslant r_0$	$F'_1(K_0) \leqslant r_0$	$F'_1(K_0) > r_0$

shocks and between current and anticipated future shocks. The supply shocks are reflected in either a change in the endowment, $(\bar{Y}_0, \bar{Y}_1)$, or a change in the technological coefficient governing investment, g. Throughout we consider positive supply shocks that increase the endowment bundle or improve the technology of investment. To facilitate the exposition in this discussion, we assume that the utility function $U(C_0, C_1)$ is homothetic. This assumption implies that for a given rate of interest the ratio of consumption in different periods is independent of the level of wealth.

Figure 3.6 illustrates the effects of supply shocks. To focus on the essentials, we assume that the historically given debt, B_{-1}, is zero; that the subjective rate of time preference, ρ, equals the rate of interest, r_0; that initially the endowments are uniformly distributed over time (so that $\bar{Y}_0 = \bar{Y}_1$), and that initially there is no profitable investment. In that case the initial equilibrium is described by point A along the $45°$ ray, and thus consumption in each period equals the corresponding level of the endowment. Hence, in the initial equilibrium the trade-balance deficit is zero. Furthermore, because there is no initial debt, the current account of the balance of payments is also balanced.

Consider first a permanent supply shock that raises the endowment in each period by the same proportion. In terms of figure 3.6 the new endowment is represented by point H. Because we have assumed that the utility function is homothetic, the consumption-expansion locus is the ray from the origin going through the initial equilibrium point. Hence, the new pattern of consumption coincides with the new endowment point H on the new higher budget line. In this case the permanent supply shock results in neither a surplus nor a deficit in the balance of trade. The supply shock yielding this outcome is referred to as a *neutral supply shock*.

Obviously, if the utility function is not homothetic, then the consumption-expansion locus would not be characterized by the $45°$ ray in figure 3.6; in that case a permanent supply shock is not neutral with respect to its effect on the current account of the balance of payments. For example, if

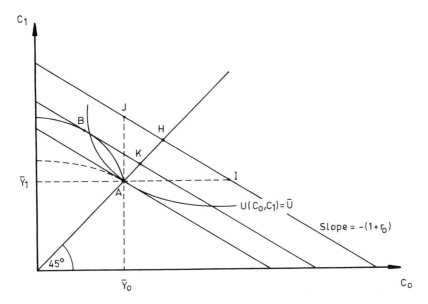

Figure 3.6
Supply shocks

the rate of time preference is high at low levels of wealth and falls as wealth rises, then the consumption-expansion locus is steeper than the $45°$ ray (it intersects point A in figure 3.6 from below), and a permanent positive supply shock induces a trade-account surplus in the early period.

We consider next a temporary supply shock that raises the endowment only in period zero to point I in figure 3.6. In the figure we have assumed that this temporary supply shock yields the same budget line as the one obtained in the previous case of a permanent shock. Because we are interested only in the qualitative effects of the various shocks, we make this assumption to simplify the diagrammatic exposition. With this shock, equilibrium consumption is described by point H. To bring about this pattern of consumption, the economy runs a surplus in its balance of trade equal to the difference between the new endowment in period zero (corresponding to point I) and the new consumption in period zero (corresponding to point H). Obviously the counterpart to this trade surplus is a trade deficit in the subsequent period in which consumption exceeds the endowment level.

Analogously, an expected future supply shock that raises the endowment in period one is illustrated by point J in figure 3.6 (which is again designed to yield the same budget as in the previous cases). As before, the consumption point is described by point H, and the economy runs a trade-balance deficit in period zero and a corresponding surplus in period one.

The key factor underlying the consumption response to the various supply shocks is the consumption-smoothing motive. Accordingly, the utility-maximizing consumers smooth the time profile of consumption and disregard the variability in the time profile of GDP. The mechanism that facilitates such consumption smoothing operates through the world capital market, and the variability of the stream of GDP is reflected in the time profile of the trade balance. If the (positive) supply shock is temporary, it leads to a trade-balance surplus in the period in which the shock occurs and to trade-balance deficits in all other periods. By analogy with our definition of a neutral (permanent) supply shock, we define a prolending supply shock as the situation in which the positive temporary shock occurs in the present, and we define a proborrowing supply shock as the situation in which the positive temporary shock is expected to occur in the future. Obviously the description of the shocks as being prolending or proborrowing is valid from the perspective of the current period.

The foregoing analysis examined the response of the economy to supply shocks that take the form of exogenous changes in the levels of GDP. Another possible (positive) supply shock may stem from a technological improvement in the process of investment. In terms of figure 3.6 suppose that under the initial technology the investment opportunities schedule is the dashed schedule emerging from point A. Because the marginal product of investment falls short of the rate of interest, no investment takes place at the initial equilibrium. The technological improvement is represented in figure 3.6 by the higher investment opportunities schedule emerging from point A and passing through point B. In that case, as shown earlier, the level of production is characterized by point B, and the level of consumption by point K. Thus, the current level of consumption rises even before the process of investment bears fruit. This represents both the consumption-smoothing and the consumption-augmenting effects. Following our previous definitions, this type of supply shock may be classified as a proborrowing shock.

3.4 The Determination of the World Interest Rate

In the previous sections the analysis of the stylized model treated the world rate of interest as given to the small open economy. In this section we analyze the determination of the equilibrium rate of interest in the world economy. For this purpose we consider the familiar home-country–foreign-country model. As usual, we designate all variables pertaining to the foreign economy by an asterisk.

In determining the world equilibrium intertemporal terms of trade (the rate of interest and the associated patterns of intertemporal trade (trade-account surplus or deficit), it is convenient to separate the effects of three distinct factors: international differences in subjective rates of time preference, international differences in GDP growth rates, and the growth rate of world output. In the exposition of these three factors we abstract from initial debt and from endogenous investment.

We consider first the role of the subjective rates of time preference. To isolate this factor, let us suppose that home and foreign endowments are stationary and equal to each other; that is, let $\bar{Y}_0 = \bar{Y}_1 = \bar{Y}_0^* = \bar{Y}_1^*$. Also, suppose that the home subjective rate of time preference exceeds the foreign rate, so that $\rho > \rho^*$. The equilibrium of the world economy is portrayed by the Edgeworth box in figure 3.7. In that figure the horizontal axis measures world GDP in period zero, $\bar{Y}_0 + \bar{Y}_0^*$, and the vertical axis measures the corresponding quantity for period one $\bar{Y}_1 + \bar{Y}_1^*$. By construction the box is squared, and the international and intertemporal distribution of world outputs is specified by point A, the midpoint along the diagonal OO^*. As usual, quantities pertaining to the home country are measured from point O as an origin, and quantities pertaining to the foreign country are measured from point O^* as an origin. At the initial endowment point A the slope of the domestic indifference curve, UU, equals one plus the domestic subjective rate of time preference $(1 + \rho)$, whereas the slope of the foreign indifference curve, U^*U^*, equals one plus the foreign subjective rate of time preference $(1 + \rho^*)$.

Because $\rho > \rho^*$, it follows that the equilibrium patterns of international and intertemporal consumption must be located to the southeast of point A, at a point like point B on the contract curve (the locus of tangencies between home and foreign indifference curves). At the equilibrium point B the rate of interest, r_0, is equalized across countries, and its magnitude must be bounded between the domestic and the foreign subjective rates of time preference; that is, $\rho > r_0 > \rho^*$. As is evident from a comparison of the patterns of consumption at point B with the patterns of GDPs at point A, in period zero the home country runs a deficit in its trade account while the foreign country runs a corresponding surplus of an equal magnitude. In the subsequent period this pattern of trade is reversed to ensure that the discounted sum of each country's trade balance is zero. This intertemporal pattern of international trade reflects the consumption-tilting effect operat-

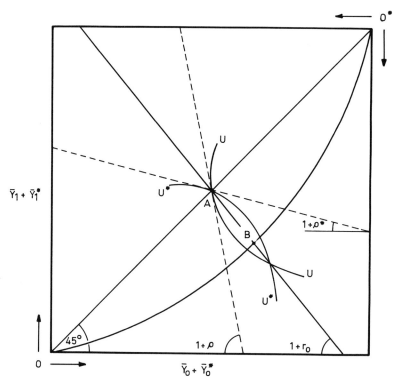

Figure 3.7
International differences in time preferences
assumptions: $\bar{Y}_0 = \bar{Y}_1 = \bar{Y}_0^* = \bar{Y}_1^*$, $\rho > \rho^*$

ing in each country. Hence, the less patient country (the country with the higher rate of time preference) runs a trade deficit in the early period.

We consider next the role of international differences in GDP growth rates. To isolate this factor, let us suppose that the home and the foreign subjective rates of time preference are equal to each other, so that $\rho = \rho^*$. Our previous analysis implies that in equilibrium the rate of interest equals the common value of the subjective rates of time preference; that is, $\rho = r_0 = \rho^*$. Let us suppose further that world output is stationary, so that $\bar{Y}_0 + \bar{Y}_0^* = \bar{Y}_1 + \bar{Y}_1^*$, but let the growth rate of the home country GDP exceed the foreign growth rate. We denote the percentage growth of GDP by θ, where $\theta = (\bar{Y}_1/\bar{Y}_0) - 1$, and a similar definition applies to the foreign growth rate, θ^*.

The equilibrium of the world economy is portrayed in figure 3.8, where the international and the intertemporal distributions of GDP are specified by point A. This point lies to the left of the diagonal OO^*, thereby

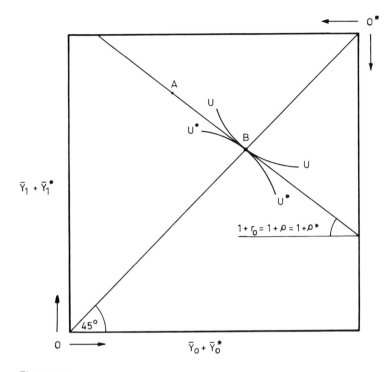

Figure 3.8
International differences in GDP growth rates
assumptions: $\rho = \rho^*$, $\bar{Y}_0 + \bar{Y}_0^* = \bar{Y}_1 + \bar{Y}_1^*$, $\theta > \theta^*$

reflecting the assumption that $\theta > \theta^*$. (Notice that because, by assumption, world output is stationary, it follows that $\theta > 0$, whereas $\theta^* < 0$). The international and intertemporal distribution of world equilibrium consumption is specified by point B. This point lies on the diagonal OO^*, thereby reflecting the assumptions that the world output is stationary and that $\rho = \rho^*$. As is evident, in this case the home country runs a trade deficit in the early period while the foreign country runs a corresponding surplus. Obviously this pattern of trade imbalances is reversed in the subsequent period. This intertemporal pattern of international trade reflects the consumption-smoothing effect operating in each country. Hence, the faster-growing country runs a trade deficit in the early period.

Finally, we consider the role of the rate of growth of world output. To isolate this factor we continue to assume that the domestic and foreign subjective rates of time preference are equal, so that $\rho = \rho^*$. We also assume that world output is growing at the percentage rate, θ, that is common to the percentage growth rate of each country's GDP. Thus, let

$\bar{Y}_1/\bar{Y}_0 = \bar{Y}_1^*/\bar{Y}_0^* = 1 + \theta$. The equalities between the home and the foreign marginal rates of time preference and between the home and the foreign growth rates imply that in this case the two factors analyzed here do not play a role in determining the rate of interest, nor do they determine the patterns of trade. If we assume that the home and the foreign utility functions are identical and homothetic, then we can specify the equilibrium without taking account of international differences in the levels of GDP.

The equilibrium of the world economy is shown in figure 3.9, in which point A describes the international and the intertemporal distributions of both GDP and consumption. Obviously, in that case, because of the equal-

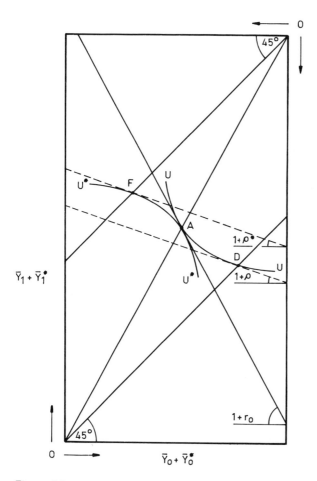

Figure 3.9
Growth of world output
assumptions: identical homothetic utility functions, $\rho = \rho^*$, $\theta = \theta^* > 0$

ity between the patterns of production and consumption in each country, there are no trade imbalances. The main point that is demonstrated by the figure concerns the equilibrium value of the world rate of interest. As shown, the equilibrium rate of interest (corresponding to the common slope of the home and the foreign indifference curves at point A) exceeds the home and foreign common subjective rates of time preference (corresponding to the slopes of the domestic and the foreign indifference curves at points D and F on the $45°$ lines). The difference between the equilibrium rate of interest and the rates of time preference rises with the growth rate of world GDP. Hence, the higher the growth rate of the world economy, the higher the equilibrium world rate of interest.

To derive the precise relation between the equilibrium rate of interest and the rate of growth of the world economy, we denote the consumption ratio C_1/C_0 by c and the intertemporal elasticity of substitution by σ, where

$$\sigma = \frac{\partial \log c}{\partial \log[(\partial U/\partial C_0)/(\partial U/\partial C_1)]} > 0. \tag{3.14}$$

Assuming that the elasticity of substitution is constant and using these notations, we observe from figure 3.9 that

$$\log c(A) = \log c(D) + \sigma[\log(1 + r_0) - \log(1 + \rho)], \tag{3.15}$$

where $c(A)$ and $c(D)$ are the consumption ratios in figure 3.9 at points A and D, respectively. Because point D lies on the $45°$ line, $c(D) = 1$. Further, because point A lies on the diagonal OO^*, it is evident that $c(A) = 1 + \theta$. It follows that $\log(1 + \theta) = \sigma \log[(1 + r_0)/(1 + \rho)]$; therefore,

$$(1 + r_0) = (1 + \rho)(1 + \theta)^{1/\sigma}. \tag{3.16}$$

This means that $1/\sigma$ is the equilibrium elasticity of the rate of interest with respect to the percentage rate of growth of world GDP. Hence, the positive association between the equilibrium rate of interest and the percentage rate of growth of world GDP decreases with the elasticity of substitution between the levels of consumption in two consecutive periods.

The foregoing analysis presumed that the growth of world output stemmed from an exogenous rise in the levels of the endowments. A similar analysis also applies to the case in which the growth of world output (evenly distributed across countries) arises from an improved availability of investment opportunities. In that case, figure 3.9 applies, except that the dimensions of the box are endogenous. Specifically, although in the previous case the dimensions of the box reflected the exogenously given growth rate of world GDP, $1 + \theta = \bar{Y}_1/\bar{Y}_0 = \bar{Y}_1^*/\bar{Y}_0^*$, in the present case they reflect the endogenously determined growth rate of GDP net of investment:

$$
\begin{aligned}
1 + \theta &= \frac{F_1(I_0(r_0) + K_0) + I_0(r_0) + K_0}{F_0(K_0) - I_0(r_0)(1 + (\frac{1}{2})gI_0(r_0)/K_0)} \\
&= \frac{F_1^*(I_0^*(r_0) + K_0^*) + I_0^*(r_0) + K_0^*}{F_0^*(K_0^*) - I_0^*(r_0)(1 + (\frac{1}{2})g^*I_0^*(r_0)/K_0^*)},
\end{aligned}
\tag{3.17}
$$

where $I_0(r_0)$ and $I_0^*(r_0)$ denote desired investment as a function of the rate of interest. The equilibrium rate of interest is determined as the solution to equations (3.16) and (3.17), and as before, in equilibrium there are no trade imbalances.

If investment opportunities are not distributed evenly between the two countries, then the two (endogenous) growth rates of GDP also differ from each other. In that case the total effect exerted by the investment opportunities on the rate of interest and on the patterns of trade reflects the considerations underlying the cases analyzed in figures 3.8 and 3.9. Specifically, suppose that the home country faces a more profitable set of investment opportunities than the foreign country. Then the (endogenously determined) growth rate of the home country's GDP, net of investment, exceeds the corresponding growth rate of the foreign economy, and the world rate of interest exceeds the subjective rate of time preference according to equation (3.16) in which the growth rate, θ, is now interpreted as the weighted average of the two countries' growth rates. The resulting patterns of trade are similar to those portrayed by figure 3.8, reflecting the general principle that the faster-growing country runs a trade deficit in the early period.

Up to now we have abstracted from the role that the historically given initial debt position plays in determining the equilibrium world rate of interest and the patterns of trade. To examine the consequences of the initial debt position, it is useful to compare an equilibrium without an initial debt commitment with another equilibrium in which the initial debt commitment of the home country is positive. Hence, we consider an initial zero-debt equilibrium that is disturbed by a transfer of $T = (1 + r_{-1})$ B_{-1} units of current output from the home to the foreign country. The effects of such a transfer are examined with the aid of figure 3.10, which is familiar from the famous transfer-problem analysis.[4]

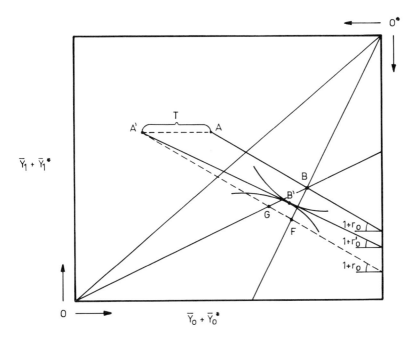

Figure 3.10
The effect of a redistribution of world debt
assumptions: $\partial c_0/\partial W_0 > \partial c_0^*/\partial W_0^*$, $\rho > \rho^*$

Suppose that at the initial equilibrium the international and intertemporal distributions of GDP are specified by point A and the corresponding distributions of consumption by point B. Analogous to our discussion of figure 3.7, this pattern of consumption reflects the assumption that the home marginal propensity to save falls short of the foreign marginal propensity. This difference between the two marginal saving propensities is reflected in the relative slopes of the home and foreign consumption-expansion loci, OGB and O^*BF, respectively. As shown in figure 3.10, at the initial equilibrium the rate of interest is r_0, and the two expansion loci are drawn for this rate of interest.

As a brief digression, we compute now the slopes of the expansion loci. Using the representative individual's maximization problem of equation (3.8), we obtain the implied demand functions for current and future consumption:

$$C_0 = C_0(\alpha_1, W_0),$$

(3.18)

$$C_1 = C_1(\alpha_1, W_0).$$

(3.19)

If we assume normality, we can invert equation (3.18) to read

$$W_0 = h(\alpha_1, C_0). \tag{3.20}$$

Substituting (3.20) into (3.19) yields

$$C_1 = C_1[\alpha_1, h(\alpha_1, C_0)]. \tag{3.21}$$

The slope of the consumption-expansion locus is obtained by differentiating equation (3.21) and noting that from (3.20) $\partial h/\partial C_0 = 1/(\partial C_0/\partial W_0)$. Thus,

$$\frac{dC_1}{dC_0} = \frac{\partial C_1/\partial W_0}{\partial C_0/\partial W_0} = \frac{1 - (\partial C_0/\partial W_0)}{\alpha_1(\partial C_0/\partial W_0)}, \tag{3.22}$$

where the second quality follows from the budget constraint in equation (3.10).

It follows that if the foreign and the home residents face the same rate of interest, then the differences between the slopes of their consumption-expansion loci depend only on the relations between their marginal propensities to consume (or save) out of wealth. Our previous analysis of figure 3.7 indicates that in the absence of world output growth there is also a unique relation between the equilibrium pattern of the two countries' consumption ratios (C_1/C_0 and C_1^*/C_0^*) and the difference between their subjective rates of time preference. Specifically, as illustrated by point B in figure 3.7, if $\rho > \rho^*$, then $(C_1/C_0) < (C_1^*/C_0^*)$, and vice versa. Hence, in the absence of growth the pattern of consumptions exhibited in figure 3.10, and the analysis of the effects of a redistribution of world debt that is carried out with the aid of the same figure, can also be characterized in terms of differences between the subjective rates of time preference rather than differences between the marginal propensities to save. Finally, we note that if the utility functions are homothetic, then the difference between the home and foreign marginal propensities to save depends only on the difference between their subjective rates of time preference. In that case, the general-equilibrium configuration exhibited by figure 3.7 is also applicable to a situation in which there is growth.

We consider now the effects of a transfer from the home to the foreign country. Following the transfer, the net endowments of the two countries are specified in figure 3.10 by point A', where the horizontal distance between A and A' equals the size of the transfer, T. The new endowment alters the patterns of demand in both countries, and since the two subjective rates of time preference differ from each other, the new pattern of demand alters the rate of interest. Specifically, following the transfer at the initial rate of interest, the home demand for current and future goods is described by point G, and the corresponding foreign demand is described by point F, where points G and F lie on the consumption-expansion loci associated with the initial interest rate. Obviously this pattern of world demand creates an excess supply of current-period goods and an excess demand for future-period goods. To eliminate this disequilibrium, the relative price of current goods in terms of future goods (i.e., the rate of interest) must fall. Put differently, world savings rise because the transfer redistributes wealth from the home country (with the low saving propensity) to the foreign country (with the high saving propensity). The fall in the rate of interest is necessary to eliminate excess savings in the world economy. Diagrammatically, the fall in the rate of interest from r_0 to r_0' raises the desired consumption ratios C_0/C_1 and C_0^*/C_1^* and alters accordingly the slopes of both the home and the foreign consumption-expansion loci. The new equilibrium obtains at point B', at which the slopes of the two countries' indifference curves are equal to $1 + r_0'$, where $r_0' < r_0$. As is evident, point B' must be located inside the triangle BGF. It follows that if the foreign rate of time preference exceeds the home rate, the contract curve in figure 3.10 would be located above the diagonal OO^*, and the transfer from the home to the foreign country would necessitate a rise rather than a fall in the world rate of interest.

It is relevant to note that as is typical in transfer-problem analyses, the relevant criterion determining the effect of a redistribution of world debt on the rate of interest involves a comparison between the home and the foreign marginal propensities to save rather than the average saving propensities. In fact, the initial endowment in figure 3.10 could have been placed to the southeast of point B along the extension of the line segment AB. The analysis of the effect of the transfer on the rate of interest remains intact as long as the home marginal propensity to save is smaller than the foreign marginal propensity, even though in that case the (positive) home average propensity to save exceeds the (negative) foreign average propensity to save.

4

Equivalence Relations in Taxation

This chapter is about equivalence relations among different combinations of fiscal instruments.[1] Taxes themselves may vary in many apparently significant respects, such as who pays them, what country collects them, when the taxes are collected, and whether the fiscal instruments are even thought of as taxes, yet many of these differences vanish with the households and firms. The resulting equivalences have an important bearing on the design and effectiveness of tax policy. They suggest that a given objective may be accomplished in a variety of ways, some perhaps more feasible or politically acceptable than others. Another implication, however, is that a tax policy may be subverted by the failure to coordinate such equivalent channels. These implications can have considerable economic significance, and there is ample evidence that they, as well as the equivalences themselves, are of prime relevance for policymaking.

For example, one fundamental equivalence we discuss is of combinations of trade-based (border) taxes on exports and imports and domestic taxes on production and consumption. A second equivalence concerns *direct* and *indirect* taxation. As Anthony Atkinson (1977) puts it, direct taxes are taxes that can be based on specific characteristics of individuals and households (e.g., marital status, number of dependents, or age) or businesses (e.g., type of industry). The main forms of direct taxes are personal and corporate income taxes, wealth taxes, and inheritance taxes. Indirect taxes are taxes based on *transactions* such as consumption, exports, or imports.

As we argue below, the relevance of these tax equivalences can be demonstrated using the economic integration of the countries of the European Community (EC). Among the goals of the 1992 process of economic integration in Europe is a harmonization of national tax systems, aimed at eliminating the adverse incentives for the movement of capital, goods, and production activity that may derive from the conflicting national objectives of independently designed national tax systems.

Economic integration obviously requires limits on the ability of countries to tax or subsidize exports or imports within the integrated community. In addition, in recognition of the relevance of domestic taxation to export and import incentives, two types of domestic indirect taxation are dealt with in the harmonization provisions. As indicated in chapter 2, an important indirect tax used in the EC is the value-added tax (VAT) that applies to the domestic consumption of goods and services. As demonstrated in table 2.2, the coverage, rates, and method of calculation of such taxes vary extensively among the member countries. The difference in tax rates gives rise to incentives to move reported sales from high-tax to low-tax countries. Because of differences in tax base definitions, some sales across national borders may be taxed in more than one country. The harmonization proposals would attack these problems by reducing the extent of tax rate variation and standardizing the tax base definition. In addition, the excise duties currently levied at very different rates among countries on specific commodities such as alcoholic beverages, cigarettes, and gasoline would be entirely harmonized at uniform tax rates for each commodity.

The apparent motivation for these provisions is that they will facilitate the elimination of fiscal frontiers within the EC. This exclusive focus on indirect taxation is also found in the provisions of the General Agreements on Tariffs and Trade, (GATT), which restrict tax-based trade barriers. The discussion in this chapter implies, however, that there is little theoretical basis for such an approach. Just as domestic and trade-based indirect taxes have similar effects that require coordination, so too do direct and indirect taxes.

To provide the intuition for certain tax equivalences, we begin with a simple model in which many different types of tax policy are assumed to be the same and then show the conditions under which some of these very basic equivalences carry over to much more refined models that are better suited for guiding policy actions.

4.1 One-Period Model

We consider a one-period model of a small open economy with a single representative consumer. The country produces two goods in domestically owned industries, and both goods are consumed domestically. One good, X, is exported as well as being domestically consumed. The other good, M, is imported as well as being domestically produced. Each good is produced using two factors of production, labor, L, and capital, K. Let C_i be the domestic consumption of good i; L_i and K_i the levels of labor and capital allocated to industry i, respectively; w and r the factor returns of labor and capital, respectively; and π_i the pure profits generated for the household sector by industry i, ($i = X, M$). Let the world price of the export good be normalized to unity, with the relative world price of the imported good equal to p_M. In the absence of taxes the household's budget constraint is

$$C_X + p_M C_M = wL_X + wL_M + rK_X + rK_M + \pi_X + \pi_M. \tag{4.1}$$

Equation (4.1) states, simply, that spending equals income.

This budget constraint may be derived in an alternative way via the production and trade sectors of the economy. Starting with the production sector accounts, which require that production in sector i, Z_i, equal factor payments plus profits, we obtain

$$p_i Z_i = wL_i + rK_i + \pi_i, \qquad (i = X, M). \tag{4.2}$$

To this we add the requirement that trade must be balanced; that is, exports must equal imports:

$$p_M(C_M - Z_M) = Z_X - C_X. \tag{4.3}$$

Equation (4.3) is a requirement imposed by the model's single-period assumption. No country will be willing to "lend" goods to the rest of the world by running a trade surplus, because there will be no subsequent period in which the debt can be repaid via a trade deficit. Using equation (4.2) in equation (4.3) yields equation (4.1), which can then be viewed as the overall budget constraint of the economy.

Let us now introduce to this model a variety of taxes including consumption taxes, income taxes, and trade taxes. In practice, consumption taxes may take a variety of forms, including retail sales taxes and VATs on consumption goods. In this simple model, with no intermediate production, the two types of taxes are identical. One could also impose a direct consumption tax at the household level. Although there has been considerable theoretical discussion of personal consumption taxes, no country has yet adopted such a tax.

Simple Equivalences

Let the tax on good i be expressed as a fraction τ_i of the producer price. (A basic and familiar feature concerning excise taxes is that it is irrelevant whether the tax is paid by the producer or the consumer). The tax appears on the left-hand side of the budget constraint (4.1), and the export good's domestic consumer price becomes $1 + \tau_x$, and the import good's domestic consumer price becomes $(1 + \tau_M)p_M$. The producer domestic prices are $p_x = 1$ and p_M, respectively.

The first very simple equivalence to note is that the taxes could also be expressed as fractions (τ_i', $i = X, M$) of the consumer prices, in which case the consumer prices would become $p_i/(1 - \tau_i')$. This distinction is between a tax, τ, that has a *tax-exclusive* base and one, τ', that has a *tax-inclusive* base. If $\tau' = \tau/(1 + \tau)$, then the two taxes have identical effects on the consumer and producer and provide the same revenue to the government. Yet, when tax rates get reasonably high, the nominal difference between tax-exclusive and tax-inclusive rates becomes quite substantial. A tax-inclusive rate of 50 percent, for example, is equivalent to a tax-exclusive rate of 100 percent.

We consider now income taxes on profits and returns to labor and capital. Rather than raising consumer prices, these taxes reduce the resources available to consume. In practice, such taxes are assessed both directly and indirectly. There are individual and business income taxes, but also payroll taxes, for example. By the national income identity, a uniform VAT on all production is simply an indirect tax on domestic factor incomes, both payrolls and returns to capital and profits.

We note, as in the case of consumption taxes, that it does not matter whether the supplier of a factor, in this case the household, or the user, in this case the firm, must actually remit the tax. A factor tax introduced in equation (4.2) or (4.1) has the same effect. The same point holds in regard to tax-exclusive versus tax-inclusive tax bases. We also observe from inspection of (4.1) that a uniform tax on income is equivalent to uniform tax on consumption. Each tax reduces real income. Imposition of a tax-inclusive consumption tax at rate τ divides the left-hand side of (4.1) by the factor $(1 - \tau)$, whereas a tax-inclusive income tax (the way an income tax base is normally defined) at the same rate multiplies the right-hand side of (4.1) by $(1 - \tau)$. Because dividing one side of an equation by a certain factor is equivalent to multiplying the other side by the same factor, the equivalence between a uniform consumption tax and a uniform income tax is established in a one-period model.

Despite their simplicity, these basic equivalences are useful in understanding the potential effects of various policies. For example, the EC tax harmonization provisions would narrow differences in rates of VAT among member countries, but these provisions say nothing about income taxes. But our results suggest that a uniform consumption tax or any type of uniform income tax would be equivalent to a uniform VAT. Thus, a country with a VAT deemed too high could accede to the provisions of the harmonization process by lowering its VAT and raising other domestic taxes, with no impact on its own citizens or on the citizens of other countries. We must conclude that either these proposals have not taken adequate account of simple equivalences or that the simple equivalences may break down in more complicated situations, a possibility we explore next.

International Trade Equivalences

We turn now to taxes explicitly related to international trade. We say *explicitly*, of course, because an obvious theme of this chapter is to recognize the equivalences that make some policies, not specifically targeted at trade, perfect substitutes for others that are.

Tax-based trade policies may involve border taxes, such as tariffs on imports or export subsidies, but may also be industry-specific taxes aimed, for example, at making trade-sensitive industries more competitive. It is well known that quantity restrictions may in some cases be used to replicate the effects of trade-based taxes. The most familiar case is the use of import quotas instead of tariffs. Other alternatives to explicit tax policies are discussed later.

The first equivalence we note among trade-based tax policies is between taxes on exports and taxes on imports. One might imagine that these policies would work in opposite directions, because the first appears to encourage a trade deficit (a decline in exports not of imports), whereas the second appears to discourage one. However, it must be remembered that this one-period model *requires* balanced trade. Hence, there can be no trade deficit or surplus; only the *level* of balanced trade may be influenced. Once this is recognized, the equivalence of these two policies can be more rapidly understood; each policy discourages trade by driving a wedge between the buyer's and seller's prices of one of the traded goods. This is the well-known Lerner's symmetry proposition.[2]

Algebraically, the equivalence is straightforward. An import tax at a tax-exclusive rate of τ causes the domestic price of the imported good to equal the world price, p_M, multiplied by the factor $1 + \tau$. Note that because the import tax does not apply to the domestic producer, then $p_M(1 + \tau)$ is the domestic price not only for the consumer but also for the domestic producer. If we denote by w and r the equilibrium factor returns to labor and capital, respectively, the four-tuple

$$(p_M(1 + \tau), 1, w, r) \tag{4.4}$$

is an equilibrium domestic price vector with an import tax at a tax-exclusive rate of τ. On the other hand, an export tax at the same tax-exclusive rate of τ causes the exporting firm to receive only $1/(1 + \tau)$ for every unit of the export good sold at the export price of one. The rest, $\tau/(1 + \tau)$, equals what the tax exporters must pay, which is the tax rate times the net price received, $1/(1 + \tau)$. Note that $1/(1 + \tau)$ becomes also the domestic price of the export good, as an exporter can either sell domestically or abroad and must therefore receive the same net price at home and abroad. Multiplying the price vector (4.4) by $1/(1 + \tau)$, we obtain another price vector

$$\left(p_M, \frac{1}{(1 + \tau)}, w', r' \right), \tag{4.5}$$

where $w' = w/(1 + \tau)$, and $r' = r/(1 + \tau)$. Notice that the price vectors (4.4) and (4.5) represent the same *relative* prices. As only relative prices matter for economic behavior, the two price vectors, (4.4) and (4.5), support the same equilibrium allocation. Put differently, multiplying p_M on the left-hand side of the household's budget constraint by $1 + \tau$ (an import tax) is equivalent to multiplying all other prices in that equation (and the profits π_M and π_X) by $1/(1 + \tau)$ (an export tax). Thus, the equivalence between an import tax at a tax-exclusive rate of τ [which generates the equilibrium price vector (4.4)] and an export tax at the same tax-exclusive rate of τ [which generates the equilibrium price vector (4.5)] is established.

It is important to point out that this symmetry of trade taxes makes no assumption about whether the taxing country is small or large, that is, whether its policies can affect the relative world price of the two goods. The equivalence indicates that these two policies are really one.

Equivalences Between Trade and Domestic Policies

The next class of policy equivalences we study is between trade policies and combinations of domestic policies. We have already shown that an import tariff at a tax-exclusive rate τ causes the domestic price of the imported good to equal the world price, p_M, multiplied by the factor $1 + \tau$. We also noted that $p_M(1 + \tau)$ is the domestic price for both the consumer and the producer. If instead of an import tax at a tax-exclusive rate of τ, the government imposes an excise (consumption) tax at the same tax-exclusive rate of τ, then the consumer price of the import good becomes $p_M(1 + \tau)$, but the producer price remains the world price of p_M. However, the producer will be indifferent between the import tax [which generates a producer price of $p_M(1 + \tau)$] and the excise tax (which generates a producer price of only p_M) if the excise tax is accompanied by a subsidy at a rate τ to domestic production that raises the price for the producer back to $p_M(1 + \tau)$. An immediate implication is that one cannot control tax-based trade barriers without also controlling domestic taxes and that controlling only domestic sales or consumption taxes alone is still not enough.[3] It is possible to convert a perfectly domestic sales tax into an import tariff by subsidizing domestic production of the commodity in question at the rate of consumption tax already in place.

4.2 Multiperiod Model

Many of the equivalences just demonstrated hold in very general models. Even those that do not may "break down" in much more limited ways than one might think. Furthermore, the conditions under which such equivalences do fail provide insight into the channels through which different tax policies operate. Perhaps the most important extension of the simple model we have used is the addition of several periods during which households may produce and consume. This permits the appearance of saving, investment, and imbalances of both the government and trade accounts, the "two deficits."

In fact, we may go quite far toward such a model simply by reinterpreting the previous one. We consider once again the basic model of equations (4.1)–(4.3). We originally interpreted this as a one-period model, with capital and labor as primary factors supplied to the production process and p_M, w, and r the one-period relative prices of imports, labor, and capital. Let us suppose, instead, that we wished to consider a multiperiod economy. What would the budget constraint of a household choosing consumption and labor supply over several periods look like? From chapter 3 we know that the household planning no bequests would equate the present value of its lifetime consumption to the present value of its lifetime labor income plus the initial value of its tangible wealth. What is this initial wealth? It equals the present value of all future profits plus the value of the initial capital stock. The value of the initial capital stock, in turn, may also be expressed as the present value of all future earnings on that capital. Thus, we may replace expression (4.1) with

$$PV(C_X + p_M C_M) = PV(wL_X + wL_M) + PV(rK_X + rK_M) + PV(\pi_X + \pi_M),$$
$$(4.6)$$

where $PV(\ )$ represents the present value of a future stream rather than a single period quantity, K_i is the initial capital stock of industry i, and L_i and π_i are the flows of industry i's labor input and profits in period i.

In (4.6) we have made the transition to a multiperiod budget constraint. Note that this budget constraint no longer requires that income equal consumption in any given period, only that lifetime income (from labor plus initial wealth) equal lifetime consumption, in present value. Thus, there may be saving in some periods and dissaving in others.

Similar adjustments are needed to equations (4.2) and (4.3) to complete the transition to a multiperiod model. Just as a household need not balance its budget in any given year, a country need not have balanced trade in any given year. Over the entire horizon of the model, however, trade must be balanced in present value, following the argument used for balance in the one-period model. That is, each country will give up no more goods and services, in present value, than it receives. The dates of these matching exports and imports may be different, of course, and this is what causes single-period trade deficits and surpluses. Thus, equation (4.3) becomes

$$PV[p_M(C_M - Z_M)] = PV(Z_X - C_X). \tag{4.7}$$

The last equation in need of reinterpretation is (4.2). The natural analogue in the multiperiod context is

$$PV(p_i Z_i) = PV(wL_i) + PV(rK_i) + PV(\pi_i) \qquad (i = X, M), \tag{4.8}$$

which says that the present value of output in each industry equals the present value of the streams of payments to labor and profits plus the payments to the *initial* capital stock. However, this condition requires further explanation, because one might expect returns to all capital over time, and not just the initial capital stock, to appear on the right-hand side of the expression.

The explanation is that new investment and its returns are subsumed by the "final form" relationship between final outputs and primary inputs given in (4.8). Stated differently, Z_i is interpreted as the output that is available for final uses outside the production sector, that is, Z_i is output that is available for either domestic consumption or exports. We may think of capital goods produced after the initial date and then used in production as intermediate goods. Normal production relations represent each stage of production. In a two-period model, for example, we would depict first-period capital and consumption as being produced by initial capital and first-period labor, and second-period consumption as being produced by initial capital plus capital produced during the first period, and second-period labor. Inserting the first-period production relation into the second-period production relation allows us to eliminate first-period capital from the equation, giving us a single "final form" relating each period's consumption to each period's labor input and the initial stock of capital. This approach may be applied recursively in the same manner for multiperiod models, leading to the type of relationship given in (4.8). In fact, if the capital goods produced in one industry are used in the other, then (4.8) does not hold for each industry separately—only when the two conditions are summed together. This is still consistent with conditions (4.6) and (4.7).

Given the similarity of the multiperiod model (4.6)–(4.8) and the single-period model (4.1)–(4.3), it is not surprising that several of the one-period equivalences carry over to the multiperiod model. First, a permanent tax on consumption is equivalent to a permanent tax on labor income plus profits plus the returns to the initial capital stock. A permanent consumption tax at a tax-exclusive rate of τ causes expression (4.6) to become

$$PV[(1 + \tau)(C_X + p_M C_M)] = PV(wL_X + wL_M) + PV(rK_X + rK_M)$$

$$+ PV(\pi_X + \pi_M). \tag{4.9}$$

Multiplying this equation by $1 - \tau' = 1/(1 + \tau)$, we obtain:

$$PV(C_X + p_M C_M) = PV[(wL_X + wL_M)(1 - \tau')] + PV[(rK_X + rK_M)(1 - \tau')]$$

$$+ PV[(\pi_M + \pi_X)(1 - \tau')]. \tag{4.10}$$

Equation (4.10) is obtained from (4.6) when a permanent tax at a tax-inclusive rate of τ' is imposed on labor income plus profits plus the returns to the initial stock of capital. Thus, the equivalence between the latter tax and a consumption tax is established. Clearly, this equivalence holds only if the tax rates are *constant* over time, so that the tax terms can be taken outside the present value operators $PV(\ )$. One may be tempted to interpret this result as showing that consumption taxes and income taxes are equivalent in multiperiod models with saving, but it is important to recognize that the type of income tax imposed here is not the income tax as normally conceived. The tax here is on wage income plus capital income attributable to initial wealth. It excludes from the tax base the income attributable to capital generated by saving done during the model's periods. Were such income also taxed, there would be an additional change to both sides of (4.6): the present-value operator, $PV(\ )$, which aggregates future streams of income and consumption, would now be based on the after-tax interest rate, $r(1 - \tau')$, rather than on the market interest rate, r. Transferring resources from one period to a subsequent one would now increase the household's tax burden. Indeed, this *double taxation* of saving has traditionally been emphasized in distinguishing income taxation from consumption taxation.

On the other hand, it is also no longer true that labor-income taxation and consumption taxation are equivalent. The equivalence we have uncovered is between consumption taxation, and labor-income taxation *plus* taxes on profits and the returns to the initial capital stock. This distinction between consumption taxes and labor-income taxes has been misleadingly termed a "transition" issue by some, because only the capital income from initial assets is concerned. However, such income is large, even in present value. For example, if the economy's capital to output ratio is 3, and the ratio of output to consumption is 1.5 (realistic values for the United States), then a permanent consumption tax of, say, 20 percent, which attaches 20 percent of these assets' flows and hence 20 percent of their value, will raise additional revenue equal to 90 percent ($0.2 \times 3 \times 1.5$) of one year's consumption.

The equivalence between export and import taxes also carries over to the multiperiod case. Inspection of (4.7) shows that the imposition of a permanent import tariff at rate τ multiplies the terms inside the present-value operator on the left-hand side by $(1 + \tau)$, whereas an export tax divides each of the terms inside the present-value operator on the right-hand side by $(1 + \tau)$. Again, if the tax rates are constant over time, one may take them outside the present-value operators, and the logic of the one-period model then applies. Clearly, the equivalence would not hold for time-varying tax rates. For example, a single-period import tax would be expected not only to discourage trade overall but also to shift imports to other periods. Likewise, an export tax would not only discourage trade but also shift exports to other periods. Thus, one would expect the first policy to lead to a greater trade surplus *in the period of taxation* than the second.

A similar outcome for temporary taxation would hold in the previous case of consumption taxes and taxes on labor income plus returns to initial assets. It has been argued that a VAT should be more favorable to the development of trade surpluses because of its use of the destination principle rather than the origin principle of taxation. Indeed, for a one-period tax, this will be so, because a one-period consumption tax (destination-based VAT) will shift consumption to other periods, whereas a one-period income tax will shift production to other periods.

Thus, the primary requirements for the basic one-period equivalences to carry over to the multiperiod context are that rates be permanent and the returns to savings not be taxed. (Even the basic equivalences depend on our implicit assumption that there are no additional nominal constraints on the system—for example, that it is just as easy for a real wage reduction to be accomplished through a fall in the nominal wage as a rise in the price level.) Yet, it is unrealistic to assume that governments wish to keep taxes constant over time or that, even if they did, they could bind themselves to do so. Likewise, the taxation of new saving and investment plays an extremely important role not only in the domestic policy context but also increasingly in the international area, as world capital markets become more integrated and the transactions and information costs to investment abroad decline. It is important that we go beyond the previous analysis to consider the effects of changing tax rates and the taxation of saving and investment.

4.3 Tax Equivalences in a Two-Period Model and Cash-Flow Taxation

To allow a tractable treatment of more general tax policies and yet maintain the dynamic aspect of the multiperiod model, we consider a two-period model with a single consumption good, no pure profits, and fixed labor supply, with the input in each period normalized to unity. In such a model there can no longer be exports and imports in the same period, but issues of trade can still be discussed because there can be exports in one period and imports in another. Because we wish to consider time-varying tax policies and capital-income taxation, we must explicitly treat capital accumulation, including foreign as well as domestic investment. This is most easily exposited by representing separately the budget constraints the household faces in each of the two periods, taking account of first-period savings decisions.

In the absence of taxes the household's budget constraints in periods zero and one for this model are

$$C_0 = w_0 + \rho_0 K_{D0} + \rho_0^* K_{F0} - K_{D1} - K_{F1}, \tag{4.11}$$

$$C_1 = w_1 + \rho_1 K_{D1} + \rho_1^* K_{F1}, \tag{4.12}$$

where C_i is period i consumption, w_i is the wage in period i, ρ_i is the return to capital in the home country in period i, ρ_i^* is the return to capital in the foreign country in period i, K_{Di} is the stock of domestic capital owned by the household in period i, and K_{Fi} is the stock of foreign capital owned by the household in period i. In terms of the multiperiod model previously considered, K_{D0} and K_{F0} are stocks of initial capital. Capital fully depreciates in each period. There are no adjustment costs of investment. The only savings decisions involve the levels of second-period capital purchased.

Now let us introduce taxes to this model. In addition to the consumption taxes and labor income taxes discussed previously, we consider several taxes on capital income. We make three important distinctions with respect to these capital-income taxes: whether they are assessed at home or abroad, whether they are assessed on the firm or the household, and whether they apply to capital investment or capital income. These three binary distinctions give rise to eight types of capital-income tax. Although such a number of tax instruments may seem excessive, each of these taxes has different economic effects, and all have significant real-world representations. Indeed, there are still important restrictions implicit in this characterization.

The eight instruments are denoted τ_{RD}, τ_B, τ_{RF}, τ_{NB}^*, τ_{HS}, τ_I, τ_{RFC}, and τ_I^*. The first four apply to capital income, and they may be different in periods zero and one. The last four apply to capital investment and hence are relevant only in period zero. We now define each of these taxes and offer real-world examples:

τ_{RD} —   household-level domestic tax on income from domestic investment; taxes on interest and dividend income from domestic sources;

τ_B —   firm-level domestic tax on income from domestic investment; domestic corporate income taxes;

τ_{RF} —   household-level domestic tax on income from foreign investment; taxes on interest and dividend income from foreign sources (net of foreign tax credits);

τ_{NB}^* —   firm level foreign tax on income from foreign investment; foreign corporate income taxes;

τ_{HS} —   household-level domestic rate of deduction for domestic investment;

τ_I —   firm-level domestic rate of deduction for domestic investment; domestic investment tax credit;

τ_{RFC} —   household-level domestic rate of deduction for foreign investment; tax-deductible pension saving abroad;

τ_I^* —   firm-level foreign rate of deduction for foreign investment; foreign investment tax credit;

Note that the two tax instruments denoted by an asterisk are applied by foreign governments to investment and capital income owned by the domestic household in the foreign countries. This tax classification scheme does not include domestic taxes on foreign corporate income. For simplicity we assume that all investment abroad is portfolio investment by domestic households rather than foreign direct investment by corporations. We adopt this restriction not because foreign direct investment is unimportant empirically (for this is not the case) but because the effects of taxation on foreign investment can be described adequately using the instruments already specified. Likewise, we ignore the fact that such portfolio income may in some countries be taxed by the host country at the individual as well as firm levels before being repatriated.

In any particular country several of these eight capital tax instruments might be absent. For example, if a country integrated its personal and corporate income tax systems, a policy often recommended but never fully adopted, all separate firm-level taxes would vanish. If a country's tax rules called for taxation of foreign-source capital income, the tax rate τ_{RF} could be low or even zero if the home country credited foreign taxes on such income. In such a scheme the tax on foreign-source income is:

$$\tau_{RF} = \frac{(\tau - \tau^*)}{(1 - \tau^*)},$$

where τ and τ^* are the statutory rates of income tax in the home and foreign countries, respectively. Thus, if $\tau = \tau^*$, $\tau_{RF} = 0$.

To introduce these taxes into the budget constraints (4.11) and (4.12) in a realistic manner, we need one additional element of notation. Most countries that tax household capital income emanating from firms do so only on a *realization* basis. Households are taxed on dividends and interest received, but not on corporate retained earnings. This has important implications concerning the cost of capital and the market value of corporate assets. To represent the fact that retained earnings are not taxed at the household level, we let R_0 and R_0^* be earnings retained in period 0 by domestic and foreign corporations owned by domestic households and assume that household-level taxes on corporate income are levied on earnings net of these values.

Letting τ_{Ci} be the tax-exclusive consumption tax rate and τ_{Li} the labor income tax in period i, we may rewrite the budget constraints (4.11) and (4.12) to account for the capital-income tax treatment just considered:

$$(1 + \tau_{C0})C_0 = (1 - \tau_{L0})w_0 + (1 - \tau_{RD0})[(1 - \tau_{B0})\rho_0 K_{D0} - R_0]$$
$$+ (1 - \tau_{RF0})[(1 - \tau^*_{NB0})\rho^*_0 K_{F0} - R^*_0]$$
$$- (1 - \tau_{HS})[(1 - \tau_I)K_{D1} - R_0]$$
$$- (1 - \tau_{RFC})[(1 - \tau^*_I)K_{F1} - R^*_0], \tag{4.13}$$

and

$$(1 + \tau_{C1})C_1 = (1 - \tau_{L1})w_1 + (1 - \tau_{RD1})(1 - \tau_{B1})\rho_1 K_{D1}$$
$$+ (1 - \tau_{RF1})(1 - \tau^*_{NB1})\rho^*_1 K_{F1}. \tag{4.14}$$

Despite its apparent complexity, this system is useful in demonstrating a variety of tax equivalences.

We begin with a special case. Suppose there are no taxes at the firm level, and that tax rates that apply to deductions for investment at home and abroad, τ_{HS} and τ_{RFC}, equal the corresponding taxes on investment income, τ_{RD} and τ_{RF}, respectively. The budget constraints (4.13) and (4.14) then become

$$(1 + \tau_{C0})C_0 = (1 - \tau_{L0})w_0 + (1 - \tau_{RD0})(\rho_0 K_{D0} - K_{D1})$$
$$+ (1 - \tau_{RF0})(\rho^*_0 K_{F0} - K_{F1}), \tag{4.15}$$

and

$$(1 + \tau_{C1})C_1 = (1 - \tau_{L1})w_1 + (1 - \tau_{RD1})\rho_1 K_{D1} + (1 - \tau_{RF1})\rho^*_1 K_{F1}. \tag{4.16}$$

Note that in this case the consumption tax in each period is equivalent to a combination of taxes in the same period at the same rate on labor income, domestic capital income, and foreign capital income, net of domestic and foreign investment. This is a new result, but it is closely related to one derived in the previous section. If, in addition, we assume that the tax rates are constant over time, and the rates of return ρ_1 and ρ^*_1 are equal (as would be the case if foreign and domestic investments were taxed at the same rate and investors chose to hold each), we may combine (4.15) and (4.16) to obtain

$$(1 + \tau_C)\left(C_0 + \frac{C_1}{\rho_1}\right) = (1 - \tau_L)\left(w_0 + \frac{w_1}{\rho_1}\right)$$
$$+ (1 - \tau_{RD})\rho_0 K_{D0} + (1 - \tau_{RF})\rho^*_0 K_{F0}, \tag{4.17}$$

which gives the previous multiperiod result, confirming the equivalence of a constant consumption tax to taxes at the same rate on labor income and the income from initial assets.

Even when tax rates differ across periods, we have identified an important period-by-period equivalence between consumption and income taxes. A consumption tax can be replicated by a tax on labor income plus taxes on domestic plus foreign capital income, net of new investment. This is in no way inconsistent with our previous intuition that a consumption tax does not impose a tax on new savings: a constant tax on capital income, net of investment, imposes no tax in present value on the income from new investment. Although the entire return from such investment is taxed, its entire cost is deducted at the same rate. Thus, the government is simply a fair partner in the enterprise (although because of its passive role in the actual operation of the firm it is sometimes called a "sleeping" partner). Only income from capital already in place at the beginning of period one is subject to a true tax, and this tax was previously seen to be part of the income tax—equivalent scheme.

These foreign and domestic taxes on capital income less investment are sometimes called *cash-flow* taxes, because they are based on net flows from the firm. In the case of the foreign tax, the cash-flow tax is a tax on net capital inflows. In this sense it is equivalent to a policy of taxing foreign borrowing and interest receipts and subsidizing foreign lending and payments of interest. In the domestic literature on taxation much has been made of the equivalence between labor-income taxes plus business cash-flow taxes and consumption taxes. But in an open economy this equivalence also requires the taxation of cash flows from abroad; otherwise, the destination-based consumption tax will include an extra piece that is absent from the tax on labor and domestic capital income net of domestic investment.

We turn next to issues related to the level of capital-income taxation, business versus household. In the real world, some payments by firms to suppliers of capital are taxed only at the investor level, without being subject to a business-level tax. These are interest payments, which are treated as tax-deductible business expenses. Other payments—dividends —are typically either partially deductible or not deductible at all. One may think of the tax rates τ_B and τ_{NB}^* as representing weighted-average tax rates of the positive tax rate on dividends and the zero tax rate on interest. (Again, it is typical for the *individual* tax rates on these two forms of capital income to differ, but not as significantly. We ignore such differences in our model.)

One would expect these tax provisions to affect firms' incentives with respect to retained earnings, R and R^*. Indeed, it is clear from the budget constraint (4.13) that the optimal policy will be to maximize (minimize) R if $\tau_{RD} > (<) \tau_{HS}$; likewise, for foreign investment R^* should be maximized (minimized) if $\tau_{RF} > (<) \tau_{RFC}$. In the "normal" case that savers do not receive a full immediate deduction for funds supplied to the firm, firms will retain earnings until constrained from doing so. This would presumably be when they had financed all their investment, $(1 - \tau_I)K_{D1}$, or exhausted all available internal funds, $(1 - \tau_B)\rho_0 K_{D0}$. Were τ_{RD} to equal τ_{HS}, households would be indifferent: payments made to them by the firm and then immediately sent back would have no tax consequences. Following the same logic, a more generous rate of savings deduction would lead firms to distribute as much as possible to allow savers the opportunity to return the funds and reduce their net taxes. The lower limit on retentions would be zero, as dividends cannot be negative.

We thus have three cases domestically (and analogously three cases with respect to foreign savings):

(a) $\tau_{RD} > \tau_{HS}$ and $R = \min[(1 - \tau_I)K_{D1}, (1 - \tau_B)\rho_0 K_{D0}]$;

(b) $\tau_{RD} = \tau_{HS}$ and $\min[(1 - \tau_I)K_{D1}, (1 - \tau_B)\rho_0 K_{D0}] > R > 0$;

(c) $\tau_{RD} < \tau_{HS}$ and $R = 0$.

For each of these cases we may substitute the optimal value of R into equation (4.13) to obtain a budget constraint in which R does not explicitly appear. In the normal case (a) and the intermediate case (b) this procedure yields

$$(1 + \tau_{C0})C_0 = (1 - \tau_{L0})w_0$$

$$+ (1 - \tau_{DS0})[(1 - \tau_{B0})\rho_0 K_{D0} - (1 - \tau_I)K_{D1}]$$

$$+ (1 - \tau_{FL0})[(1 - \tau_{NB}^*)\rho_0^* K_{F0} - (1 - \tau_I^*)K_{F1}], \qquad (4.13')$$

where

$$\tau_{DS} = \begin{cases} \tau_{HS} & \text{if } (1 - \tau_{B0})\rho_0 K_{D0} < (1 - \tau_I)K_{D1} \\ \tau_{RD} & \text{if } (1 - \tau_{B0})\rho_0 K_{D0} > (1 - \tau_I)K_{D1} \end{cases}$$

$$\tau_{FL} = \begin{cases} \tau_{RFC} & \text{if } (1 - \tau_{NB}^*)\rho_0^* K_{F0} < (1 - \tau_I^*)K_{F1} \\ \tau_{RF} & \text{if } (1 - \tau_{NB}^*)\rho_0^* K_{F0} > (1 - \tau_I^*)K_{F1}. \end{cases}$$

The value of τ_{DS} depends on whether the firm is in a regime in which it is paying dividends at the margin and hence financing marginal investment from retained earnings, τ_{RD}, or not paying dividends and financing new investment through issues of new shares, τ_{HS}. In either case, however, the behavior of the optimizing firm induces a household-level cash-flow tax. This implies that the economy may be closer to cash-flow taxation than might appear from the statutory tax treatment of household capital income. In particular, the *effective* tax burden on capital income at the household level is zero in present value, even if there are dividends and $\tau_{RD} > \tau_{HS}$. This is another equivalence, of existing systems of household capital income taxation to household cash-flow taxation.

A final equivalence involving the two levels of capital income taxation is *between* taxes at the two levels. In a variety of situations a tax at the firm level is equivalent to one at the household level. Consider, for example, the case in which all capital income taxes are cash-flow taxes. This is like the situation considered in equation (4.15) but with cash-flow business taxes added. In this case the first-period budget constraint is

$$(1 + \tau_{C0})C_0 = (1 - \tau_{L0})w_0 + (1 - \tau_{RD0})(1 - \tau_{B0})(\rho_0 K_{D0} - K_{D1})$$

$$+ (1 - \tau_{RF0})(1 - \tau_{B0}^*)(\rho_0^* K_{F0} - K_{F1}). \qquad (4.13'')$$

[The second-period budget constraint (4.14) is unaffected.] It is clear from this equation that it is irrelevant from the household's viewpoint whether taxes are collected from firms or individuals. The tax rate τ_B is a perfect substitute for τ_{RD}, and τ_B^* is one for τ_{RF}. In the first case, with both taxes collected by the same government, the equivalence is complete; the government is indifferent as well. In the second case this would not be so, unless a tax treaty existed that directed capital income taxes collected on specific assets to specific countries regardless of who actually collected the taxes.

Even in the domestic case, the taxes might *appear* to have different effects due to their different collection points. For example, measured rates of return from the corporate sector would be net of tax were the taxes collected from firms, but gross of tax were they collected from households.

4.4   Present-Value Equivalences

In discussing cash-flow taxation, we have made a point that has a more general application: that tax policies may change the timing of tax collections without changing their burden, in present value. A constant-rate cash-flow tax exerts no net tax on the returns to marginal investment, giving investors an initial deduction equal in present value to the ultimate tax on positive cash flows the investment generates.

In our two-period model, a cash-flow tax at a constant rate collects revenue equal in present value only to the cash flows from the first-period capital stock. Thus, an initial wealth tax on that stock would be equivalent from the viewpoint of both household and government. For example, consider the simple case with no firm-level taxes and constant tax rates examined previously. This is the example in which the first-period and second-period budget constraints can be combined as in the multiperiod model of the previous section. These three budget constraints (first-period, second-period, and combined) are under cash-flow taxation (assuming that $\rho = \rho^*$):

$$(1 + \tau_C)C_0 = (1 - \tau_L)w_0 + (1 - \tau_{RD})(\rho_0 K_{D0} - K_{D1})$$

$$+ (1 - \tau_{RF})(\rho_0^* K_{F0} - K_{F1}), \tag{4.15'}$$

$$(1 + \tau_C)C_1 = (1 - \tau_L)w_1 + (1 - \tau_{RD})\rho_1 K_{D1} + (1 - \tau_{RF})\rho_1^* K_{F1}, \tag{4.16'}$$

and

$$(1 + \tau_C)\left(C_0 + \frac{C_1}{\rho_1}\right) = (1 - \tau_L)\left(w_0 + \frac{w_1}{\rho_1}\right)$$

$$+ (1 - \tau_{RD})\rho_0 K_{D0} + (1 - \tau_{RF})\rho_0^* K_{F0} \tag{4.17'}$$

Here, if the terms K_{D1} and K_{F1} appearing in the first- and second-period budget constraints were no longer multiplied by $1 - \tau_{RD}$ and $1 - \tau_{RF}$, respectively, cash-flow tax would be replaced by a first-period tax on the returns to existing capital—a wealth tax—yet there would be no impact at all on the household's combined budget constraint. Its *measured* saving would be affected, but not its consumption.

Just as measured household saving would be affected, so also would there be apparent differences between the levels of government debt in the two cases. In the cash-flow tax case the government's revenue would be lower in the first and higher in the second period, and it would have a bigger first-period budget deficit. At the same time, firm values would be lower, to account for the larger impending second-period cash-flow tax payments. Indeed, these differences exactly offset each other. One could imagine the cash-flow tax policy as being a combination of the wealth tax policy plus a decision by the government to lend in the first period and force firms to accept loans of equal value at the market interest rate, to be repaid in the next period. Firms would require fewer funds from the household sector, leaving households just enough extra money to purchase the bonds floated by the government under the cash-flow taxation.

Thus, the explicitly measured government debt is not an accurate indicator of policy, because it may vary considerably between the two equivalent situations. One may think of the "forced loans" of the cash-flow tax system as being off-budget assets that cause the deficit to be overstated, assets that can be brought on budget by recalling the loans, paying back the debt, and shifting to the wealth tax.[4]

One can imagine many similar examples of present-value equivalences, none of which go beyond the bounds of the realistic tax policies we have already considered. The government can arbitrarily change the measured composition of a household's wealth between government debt and tangible capital (and indeed between government debt and human capital, through changes in the time pattern of labor-income taxation) simply by introducing offsetting levels of debt and forced loans attached to these other assets. This is true whether or not the asset owners are domestic residents or not. Foreign owners of a domestic corporation that is suddenly hit with a cash-flow tax on *new* investment (i.e., excluding the wealth-tax effect on preexisting capital) will spend less of their funds on the domestic firms and the remainder on other assets—quite possibly the government debt—but not on the country's external debt, that is, the aggregate value of domestic assets owned by foreigners.

It is noteworthy that the government's ability to shift such asset values of foreigners is more circumscribed than its ability with respect to domestic residents. It cannot, for example, cause a reduction in the value of a foreigner's human capital offset by a loan to the foreigner (by cutting labor-income taxes today and raising them in the future), because it cannot tax the foreigner's labor income. All adjustments with respect to external debt must be through the tax treatment of foreign-owned domestic assets.

5

Optimal International Taxation

The analysis of taxes is complex and has various ramifications in all sectors of the economy. Neither the efficiency aspects nor the incidence aspects of taxes can be fully understood without resorting to a general-equilibrium analysis of consumers, producers, the foreign sector, and the government. As the preceding chapter demonstrates, many seemingly different tax instruments can be shown by a proper general-equilibrium analysis to be in fact equivalent, or altogether redundant. This chapter lays out a general-equilibrium model that is in some version or another necessary for a rigorous economic analysis of international taxation. The model serves as the workhorse of the normative analysis in this book.

The organization of the chapter is as follows. In section 5.1 we incorporate the details of the tax structure into the basic intertemporal model of chapter 3. In this context we pay special attention to the formulation of the business sector. This formulation highlights the differential role that taxes play in influencing the economic decisions of households and firms.

Section 5.2 addresses the issue of optimal taxation. Assuming that the government wishes to use its tax policy to maximize the level of welfare of consumers, we examine the resultant optimal tax structure. In this context we focus on the determination of the optimal set of tax instruments, in particular those pertaining to income from capital from domestic and from foreign sources. The analysis also yields conclusions regarding the desirability of free international capital flows.[1]

5.1 Analytical Framework

We consider a stylized model of an open economy with emphasis on the fiscal (tax-expenditure) branch of the government. To highlight the interactions between fiscal factors, savings and investment decisions, international capital flows, and the like, in the simplest possible fashion, we cast our economy in a two-period model with one composite consumption-investment good. Output is produced with a conventional constant returns-to-scale production function with two factors of production, labor and capital. We focus our analysis on four sectors: the domestic household sector, the domestic business sector, the government sector, and the foreign sector. For simplicity we assume that international capital flows consist of debt rather than equity transactions.

The Household Sector

Consider a representative household (or individual) who lives for two periods: the present period (period zero) and the future period (period one). In each period the individual is endowed with a given amount of time that can be allocated between leisure and work effort (labor supply). The individual also owns the domestic firm.

In period zero the individual consumes C_0 units of the consumption good and supplies ℓ_0 units of labor. If we normalize the endowment of time to unity, it follows that the consumption of leisure is $1 - \ell_0$. The individual may extend loans to the government, L_G^H; to the domestic business sector, L_B^H; and to foreign borrowers, L_F^H. Throughout, we use the convention that L_i^j indicates lending by entity j (the superscript) to entity i (the subscript), where H stands for "household", G for "government", B for "business", and F for "foreign." If the individual borrows from any of these entities, then the corresponding variable is negative. However, in our model we abstract from the financial sector and thus assume that the business sector cannot extend loans; accordingly, L_B^H cannot be negative. With no initial debt, the individual's resources in period zero consist of the value of the endowment of time, and dividend income. Thus, the budget constraint in period zero is given by:

$$(1 + \tau_{C0})C_0 + (1 - \tau_{\ell0})(1 - \ell_0)w_0 + L_G^H + L_B^H + L_F^H$$

$$= (1 - \tau_{\ell0})w_0 + (1 - \tau_{D0})D_0 \qquad (5.1)$$

where w_t denotes the pretax wage rate in period t, τ_{Ct} denotes the rate of tax on consumption in period t, $\tau_{\ell t}$ denotes the rate of tax on wage income in period t, D_t denotes dividend income in period t, τ_{Dt} denotes the rate of tax on dividend income in period t, and where $t = 0,1$. Note that being tax inclusive, $(1 - \tau_{\ell0})w_0$ is the consumer price of leisure.

In the next period the representative household consumes C_1 units of the composite good and $1 - \ell_1$ units of leisure. In that period the household resources consist of the value of the time endowment, the loan repayments (principal and interest), and dividend income. Because period one is also the last period, the firm is liquidated at the end of that period. Last-period dividends consist therefore of three components: profits from period one, retained profits from period zero, and the value of the capital stock at the end of period one. Thus, the budget constraint in period one is given by

$$(1 + \tau_{C1})C_1 + (1 - \tau_{/1})w_1(1 - \ell_1)$$

$$= (1 - \tau_{/1})w_1 + [1 + (1 - \tau_{rD0})r_0](L_G^H + L_B^H)$$

$$+ [1 + (1 - \tau_{rF0})r_0^*]L_F^H + (1 - \tau_{D1})D_1, \tag{5.2}$$

where r_0 denotes the domestic rate of interest linking periods zero and one; r_0^* denotes the world rate of interest (net of taxes levied abroad) linking periods zero and one; τ_{rD0} denotes the rate of tax on interest income from domestic sources; and τ_{rF0} denotes the rate of tax on interest income from foreign sources.

With no loss of generality, we assume that the government borrows domestically at the same rate of interest as the business sector and that the same tax rate applies to the interest earned by the household from these two sources. Because of arbitrage, any difference in the tax treatment of these two sources of income would be offset by a difference in the gross (before tax) rates of interest. Furthermore, arbitrage also implies that the net rates of return on financial investments from domestic and foreign sources must equal each other:

$$(1 - \tau_{rD0})r_0 = (1 - \tau_{rF0})r_0^*. \tag{5.3}$$

Thus, we can aggregate all forms of lending (or borrowing) by the household sector into $L^H \equiv L_G^H + L_B^H + L_F^H$.

With these considerations we can rewrite the two budget constraints (5.1)–(5.2) as

$$(1 + \tau_{C0})C_0 + (1 - \tau_{/0})w_0(1 - \ell_0) + L^H = (1 - \tau_{/0})w_0 + (1 - \tau_{D0})D_0 \tag{5.1a}$$

and

$$(1 + \tau_{C1})C_1 + (1 - \tau_{/1})w_1(1 - \ell_1)$$

$$= (1 - \tau_{/1})w_1 + [1 + (1 - \tau_{rF0}^*)r_0^*]L^H$$

$$+ (1 - \tau_{D1})D_1. \tag{5.1b}$$

Because the individual has free access to the capital market, economic behavior is constrained by the lifetime budget constraint, in present value. This constraint requires that the present value of lifetime consumption not exceed lifetime income (wealth). Accordingly, we multiply equation (5.1b) by the (net of tax) discount factor from period one to period zero,

$$\alpha_1^H \equiv [1 + (1 - \tau_{rF0})r_0^*]^{-1},\tag{5.4}$$

and add the result to (5.1a). This yields

$$(1 + \tau_{C0})C_0 + (1 + \tau_{C1})\alpha_1^H C_1 + (1 - \tau_{\ell 0})w_0(1 - \ell_0)$$
$$+ (1 - \tau_{\ell 1})\alpha_1^H w_1(1 - \ell_1)$$
$$= (1 - \tau_{\ell 0})w_0 + (1 - \tau_{\ell 1})\alpha_1^H w_1 + (1 - \tau_{D0})D_0$$
$$+ (1 - \tau_{D1})\alpha_1^H D_1.\tag{5.5}$$

The left-hand-side of the lifetime budget constraint (5.5) represents the after-tax present value of lifetime consumption of goods and leisure. The right-hand side represents the wealth of the individual (W_0). Wealth in turn consists of the discounted sum of the after-tax value of the time endowment as well as the discounted sum of net capital income. In this setup, lendings (or borrowings) do not appear as an explicit variable. However, we can still derive indirectly the amount of lendings from this budget constraint by recalling that lendings are equal to the difference between current-period income and consumption. Thus,

$$L^H = (1 - \tau_{\ell 0})w_0\ell_0 + (1 - \tau_{D0})D_0 - (1 + \tau_{C0})C_0.\tag{5.6}$$

The utility function is specified as

$$u(C_0, 1 - \ell_0, G_0, C_1, 1 - \ell_1, G_1).\tag{5.7}$$

As usual, the arguments in the utility function are ordinary consumption, leisure, and government spending, G, in each of the two periods. Consumption demand and labor supply are determined by maximizing the utility function (5.7) subject to the lifetime budget constraint (5.5), taking as given the levels of public consumption, G_0 and G_1, as well as the time pattern of dividend income, D_0 and D_1. Equation (5.6) then determines the supply of lendings (or the demand for borrowings). These demands and supplies are, as usual, functions of all after-tax prices and wealth:

$$p_{C0} = 1 + \tau_{C0} \qquad \text{(price of present consumption);}\tag{5.8}$$

$$p_{\ell 0} = (1 - \tau_{\ell 0})w_0 \qquad \text{(price of present leisure);}\tag{5.9}$$

$$p_{C1} = (1 + \tau_{C1})\alpha_1^H \qquad \text{(price of future consumption)}; \tag{5.10}$$

$$p_{\ell 1} = (1 - \tau_{\ell 1})\alpha_1^H w_1 \qquad \text{(price of future leisure)}; \tag{5.11}$$

$$W_0 = p_{\ell 0} \cdot 1 + (1 - \tau_{D0})D_0 + (1 - \tau_{D1})\alpha_1^H D_1 + p_{\ell 1} \cdot 1. \tag{5.12}$$

The demand and supply functions depend also on government's spendings, G_0 and G_1. The maximized value of the utility function (the indirect utility function) depends therefore on the preceding prices, wealth, and government spendings. It is denoted by v and provides a measure of welfare that depends on after-tax prices, wealth, and government spendings:

$$v(p_{C0}, p_{\ell 0}, p_{C1}, p_{\ell 1}, W_0, G_0, G_1), \tag{5.13}$$

where

$$v(\cdot) \equiv u(C_0(\cdot), 1 - \ell_0(\cdot), G_0, C_1(\cdot), 1 - \ell_1(\cdot), G_1).$$

The Business (Production and Investment) Sector

The domestic business sector is aggregated into a single competitive firm. The production technology available to the firm is described by a standard constant returns-to-scale production function that depends on labor and capital:

$$Y = F(K, \ell), \tag{5.14}$$

where Y denotes output. As usual, we assume that the marginal products of capital, F_K, and of labor, F_ℓ, are positive and diminishing. To simplify the notation, we also assume that the same technology is available in each period.

The firm possesses an initial stock of capital, K_0, and by investing in the present period can augment this stock in the future. There is, however, some cost involved in adjusting the stock of capital (due to installation, job reassignment, training, etc.). This feature is captured by an investment technology exhibiting a quadratic cost of adjustment, as follows:

$$Z_0 = I_0 \left(1 + \frac{\frac{1}{2}gI_0}{K_0}\right), \qquad (g \geq 0), \tag{5.15}$$

where I_0 is the level of investment and Z_0 is the cost of investment. In this setup the average cost of investment is $1 + (\frac{1}{2})gI_0/K_0$, whereas the marginal cost of investment is $1 + gI_0/K_0$. Notice that the marginal cost of investment exceeds the average cost by the amount $(\frac{1}{2})gI_0/K_0$, implying that the average cost function is increasing. That is, there are diminishing returns to capital formation. Assuming that capital depreciates at the rate $\theta > 0$, the firm's stock of capital in the future, K_1, is given by

$$K_1 = I_0 + (1 - \theta)K_0. \tag{5.16}$$

The representative firm hires labor in each period and invests in period zero (from borrowing or retained earnings) to maximize the discounted sum of the net cash flows accruing to its owners. Reflecting the owners' preferences, the firm decides to apply the owners' rate of discount (namely, $\alpha_1^H = [1 + (1 - \tau_{rF0})r_0^*]^{-1} = [1 + (1 - \tau_{rD0})r_0]^{-1}$). Thus, the firm aims to maximize V_0:

$$V_0 \equiv (1 - \tau_{D0})D_0 + (1 - \tau_{D1})\alpha_1^H D_1. \tag{5.17}$$

We refer to the cash flows D_0 and D_1 as "dividends" and to the corresponding personal taxes τ_{D0} and τ_{D1} as "dividend taxes."

The firm must decide on both its *financing* policies (such as cash holdings, retained earnings, or dividends) and *production-investment* policies (such as labor employment, production level, and capital formation).

In period zero the firm decides how much labor, ℓ_0, to employ; how much output, $F(K_0, \ell_0)$, to produce; and how much investment in physical capital, I_0, to make. In addition, the firm chooses how many dividends to distribute, D_0; how many funds to borrow from domestic sources, L_B^H, and from abroad, L_B^*; and how much working capital (cash), R_0, to hold.[2]

Because in our model we assume perfect foresight and unconstrained capital market transactions, the choice between debt and equity plays no meaningful role in the absence of taxes (the familiar Modigliani-Miller theorem). In the presence of taxes the net returns on the two kinds of investment are still equalized when they coexist, and short-selling is allowed. Therefore, we ignore the possibility that the firm issues new equity and assume that the entire level of investment of the firm (physical and financial) is financed through borrowing and retained earnings.

As is evident, the firm minimizes its finance costs by borrowing in markets where the pretax interest rates are lowest. We assume that there is no differential tax treatment of interest deductibility for interest paid domestically or interest paid abroad (and we later show that it is indeed efficient not to have such a differential treatment). Thus, if the domestic and the foreign rates of interest are equal ($r_0 = r_0^*$), the firm is indifferent between borrowing domestically or from abroad. If, however, the domestic rate of interest lies below the foreign rate (i.e., $r_0 < r_0^*$), then the firm borrows only from the domestic household sector. The opposite holds for the case in which $r_0 > r_0^*$.

In carrying out its financial operations the firm is subject to institutional constraints that directly affect its borrowing and dividend policies. As was already mentioned, our nonbanking firm cannot lend; this restriction implies that

$$L_B^H \geqslant 0 \qquad \text{and} \qquad L_B^* \geqslant 0. \qquad (5.18)$$

Due to its inability to lend, the firm cannot engage in arbitrage between the domestic and foreign credit markets in case the two interest rates are not equal to each other. For the sake of concreteness we assume that the domestic rate of interest, r_0, does not exceed the corresponding foreign rate, r_0^*. In that case we may, with no loss of generality, assume that the firm borrows only domestically, so that $L_B^* = 0$.

The second institutional constraint concerns the firm's dividend policy. We assume that the firm may not borrow to pay dividends. (This regulatory constraint is commonplace.) In other words, dividends should not exceed profits. Formally, in period zero this constraint can be written as:

$$D_0 \leqslant \pi_0 \equiv (1 - \tau_{B0})[F(K_0, \ell_0) - w_0\ell_0 - \theta K_0 - (Z_0 - I_0)], \qquad (5.19)$$

where τ_{Bt} is the business or corporate tax in period $t = 0, 1$. As indicated by equation (5.19), after-tax profits, π_0, consist of the value of sales (output) net of the wage bill, deprecation allowances, and the cost of adjustment associated with investment, $Z_0 - I_0$; all net of the business tax.

The firm's budget (cash flow) constraint in period zero is

$$L_B^H + (1 - \tau_{B0})[F(K_0, \ell_0) - w_0\ell_0 - \theta K_0 - (Z_0 - I_0)] + \theta K_0$$

$$\geqslant D_0 + I_0 + R_0. \qquad (5.20)$$

This constraint simply states that the uses of funds by the firm (the right-hand side) cannot exceed the sources of funds (the left-hand side). Because depreciation costs that were deducted from gross sales for tax purposes do not affect the firm's cash flow, we add them to the left-hand side of equation (5.20) along with the amount that the firm borrows from the domestic household sector (L_B^H). We assume that the depreciation rate allowed for tax purposes is the true depreciation rate, θ. Dividend distribution, D_0, physical investment, I_0, and working capital, R_0, constitute the uses of funds by the firm.

Alternatively, the firm's budget constraint can also be written as

$$L_B^H + \pi_0 \geqslant D_0 + (I_0 - \theta K_0) + R_0, \qquad (5.20')$$

indicating that the sum of dividends and the net additions to physical and working capital [the right-hand side of equation (5.20′)] may not exceed the sum of net borrowings and after-tax profits.

In the final period (period one) the firm is liquidated. Hence, the firm's net wealth is distributed to the owners. (As indicated earlier, we refer to such distributions as dividends.) Thus, the amount that is distributed in period one includes also the firm's capital left after all debt is repaid. That is,

$$D_1 \leqslant (1 - \tau_{B1})[F(K_1, \ell_1) - w_1\ell_1 - r_0 L_B^H - \theta K_1] + \theta K_1$$

$$- L_B^H + (1 - \theta)K_1 + R_0. \tag{5.21}$$

As before, the term in the square brackets on the right-hand side of (5.21) indicates the profits of the firm, π_1. We note that in period one interest costs, $r_0 L_B^H$, are deducted from gross sales. Again, depreciation costs, θK_1, that were deducted from gross sales for tax purposes are added back to the cash flow of the firm. Notice that the entire stock of capital after depreciation, $(1 - \theta)K_1$, and the working capital held from period zero, R_0, are also available for distribution in period one.

The firm's objective is to choose its dividend policy, (D_0, D_1), investment policy, (I_0, R_0), borrowing policy, L_B^H, and employment policy, (ℓ_0, ℓ_1), so as to maximize its market value, V_0. In carrying out this maximization, the firm is subject to the institutional and budget constraints, equations (5.19)–(5.21). There are also the constraints that D_0, D_1, I_0, L_B^H, and R_0 should not be negative. The detailed derivation of the optimal policy for the firm is relegated to the appendix. In what follows we describe the main features of the optimal policy and provide an economic interpretation.

Starting with the borrowing decisions, it is evident that the firm will not borrow to hold cash as long as the after-tax (business tax) rate of interest exceeds the corresponding return on working capital (assumed to be zero in our case). Also, because the firm is not allowed to borrow to distribute the funds as dividends, we conclude that the firm borrows *only* to invest in physical capital.

Suppose that the firm does borrow. In that case its optimal investment rule takes one of the following two forms. First, if profits exceed dividends, so that $D_0 < \pi_0$ in equation (5.19), then the investment process is entirely *internal* to the firm in the sense that the firm's decision does not impinge on the household (owner) constraints. In this case the investment rules depend *only* on the tax characteristics of the firm and not the household sector. The investment rule for the firm is

$$\frac{(1 - \tau_{B0})gI_0}{K_0} = \alpha_1^B (1 - \tau_{B1})(F_K - \theta - r_0),\tag{5.22}$$

where $\alpha_1^B = [1 + (1 - \tau_{B1})r_0]^{-1}$ is the discount factor faced by the firm.

This rule states that the firm invests up to a point where the marginal adjustment cost (net of the business tax) equals the discounted value of the marginal product of capital, net of depreciation and interest cost, and adjusted for business taxes (at the rate prevailing when the returns to investment materialize). The discounting is performed by employing the business discount factor, α_1^B.

Second, if all profits are distributed as dividends, so that $D_0 = \pi_0$ in equation (5.19), then the investment rule impinges on the household constraint. In that case, therefore, optimal investment depends also on the tax characteristic of the individual. Accordingly, the rule for optimal investment becomes

$$\frac{(1 - \tau_{D0})(1 - \tau_{B0})gI_0}{K_0} = \alpha_1^H (1 - \tau_{D1})(1 - \tau_{B1})(F_K - \theta - r_0).\tag{5.23}$$

A comparison of this rule with the investment rule in equation (5.22) reveals two basic differences. First, if the dividend constraint is binding, so that dividends equal profits, then the firm's investment rule employs the household's discount factor (adjusted by the household's tax rate), α_1^H, instead of the business discount factor (adjusted by the business tax rate), α_1^B. Second, the household dividend taxes (τ_{D0} and τ_{D1}) are applied to both the marginal cost and the net marginal benefits associated with the investment. The household tax characteristics appear in the firm's optimal investment rule, because an additional investment in physical capital adds to the adjustment cost and thus lowers profits. Since all profits are distributed as dividends, the rise in investment forces an intertemporal shift in the distribution of dividends by substituting dividend distribution from the present to the future; this alters the time profile of the tax liabilities of the household (the owner). Due to the interdependence of the investment process and the dividend-distribution process, the former cannot be entirely internal to the firm. Rather, it involves factors external to the firm, such as the tax characteristics of the household sector.

The foregoing analysis presumed that the firm *does* borrow. As a result, the firm does not find it profitable to hold low-return working capital. Suppose next that the firm does *not* borrow. As before, the investment rule takes one of two forms depending on whether or not all profits are distributed as dividends. If some profits are retained, so that $D_0 < \pi_0$, then the investment rule for the firm is

$$\frac{(1 - \tau_{B0})g I_0}{K_0} = (1 - \tau_{B1})(F_K - \theta). \tag{5.24}$$

Accordingly, at the optimum, the after-tax marginal adjustment cost is just covered by the after-tax marginal product of capital, net of depreciation. In this case, as before, the investment process is governed by factors that are entirely internal to the firm.

A comparison of this rule with the one presented in equation (5.22) reveals that when the firm finances physical investment internally by drawing on noninterest working capital rather than by issuing interest-bearing debt, then the market rate of interest governing both the interest cost and the discount factor plays no role. With the absence of discounting the investment rule is also independent of the tax structure if the business tax rate remains constant over time.

If, on the other hand, all profits are distributed, so that $D_0 = \pi_0$, then the optimal investment rule is

$$\frac{(1 - \tau_{D0})(1 - \tau_{B0})g I_0}{K_0} = \alpha_1^H (1 - \tau_{D1})(1 - \tau_{B1})(F_K - \theta). \tag{5.25}$$

This rule is analogous to the one presented in equation (5.23) except for the absence of the interest cost, reflecting the fact that the firm relies on its noninterest working capital.[3]

Finally, the demand for labor in each period is given by the standard conditions equating the marginal product of labor to the pretax real wage:

$$F_\ell(K_0, \ell_0) = w_0, \tag{5.26}$$

and

$$F_\ell(K_1, \ell_1) = w_1. \tag{5.27}$$

These rules do not depend directly on the tax rates, although, of course, the various taxes do affect the equilibrium gross values of wages and the marginal products themselves.

The Government Sector

The government provides free of charge pure public goods, G_0 and G_1, in periods zero and one, respectively. To finance its spending, the government employs various personal taxes on consumption, labor income, dividend income, and interest income as well as business taxes. As usual, if tax revenues do not match spendings period by period, the government borrows or lends in either the domestic or the world capital markets.

We denote by L_F^G the amount that the government lends abroad. (L_F^G can be negative, indicating borrowing). With no initial debt the budget constraint faced by the government in period zero is

$$\tau_{C0}C_0 + \tau_{/0}w_0\ell_0 + \tau_{D0}D_0 + \tau_{B0}\pi_0 + L_G^H = G_0 + L_F^G. \tag{5.28}$$

The budget constraint simply states that the revenues from taxes on consumption, $\tau_{C0}C_0$, labor income, $\tau_{/0}w_0\ell_0$, dividend income, $\tau_{D0}D_0$, and business profits, $\tau_{B0}\pi_0$, plus the amount borrowed from the domestic household sector, L_G^H, equals spending on the public good, G_0, and government lending abroad, L_F^G.

A similar budget constraint pertains to period one:

$$\tau_{C1}C_1 + \tau_{/1}w_1\ell_1 + \tau_{D1}D_1 + \tau_{B1}\pi_1$$
$$+ \tau_{rD0}r_0(L_G^H + L_B^H) + \tau_{rF0}r_0^*L_F^H + L_F^G(1 + r_0^*)$$
$$= G_1 + L_G^H(1 + r_0). \tag{5.29}$$

In the final period (period one) the government repays its loan from the domestic household sector—principal and interest $[(1 + r_0)L_G^H]$—and is paid back the loan it extended to the foreign sector—principal and interest $(L_F^G(1 + r_0^*))$. In addition to the revenues from taxes on consumption, labor income, "dividend" income, and business profits, the government also obtains revenue from taxing domestic and foreign interest income of the domestic household sector $(\tau_{rD0}r_0(L_B^H + L_G^H) + \tau_{rF0}r_0^*L_F^H)$.

Because the government has free access to the world capital market, it is constrained by a single lifetime budget constraint. Therefore, the discount factor applicable to the government is $\alpha_1^G \equiv (1 + r_0^*)^{-1}$.

Multiplying (5.29) by α_1^G and adding the product to (5.28) yields

$$\tau_{C0}C_0 + \tau_{/0}w_0\ell_0 + \tau_{D0}D_0 + \tau_{B0}\pi_0$$
$$+ \alpha_1^G\{(\tau_{C1}C_1 + \tau_{/1}w_1\ell_1 + \tau_{D1}D_1 + \tau_{B1}\pi_1)$$
$$+ (\tau_{rD0}r_0L_B^H + \tau_{rF0}r_0^*L_F^H) + [r_0^* - (1 - \tau_{rD0})r_0]L_G^H\}$$
$$= G_0 + \alpha_1^G G_1. \tag{5.30}$$

The expressions appearing in equation (5.20) are self-explanatory, except for the term $[r_0^* - (1 - \tau_{rD0})r_0]L_G^H$. This term appears on the revenue side because the government borrows domestically at a net (of tax) rate of

$(1 - \tau_{rD0})r_0$ and lends abroad at a rate of r_0^*. Hence, its net revenue is $r_0^* - (1 - \tau_{rD0})r_0$, on each unit.

Equilibrium

Households and firms are assumed to behave competitively. Accordingly, in shaping their plans they behave as price-takers. These plans specify the actions to be taken throughout the planning horizon. With such a forward-looking view, any price in any period may affect supply and demand in all periods. Also, under the assumption of perfect foresight (self-fulfilling expectations), an equilibrium is reached when the various prices simultaneously clear all markets in all periods. In the absence of unexpected shocks the equilibrium (market-clearing) path of prices determined in the initial period for the entire horizon continues to clear the markets with the passage of time.

Specifically, the consumption-demand function (C_0 and C_1), the labor-supply function (ℓ_0^S and ℓ_1^S), and the function indicating the supply of lending ($L^{HS} = L_B^{HS} + L_G^{HS} + L_F^{HS}$)—all determined by the household sector —depend on the after-tax prices, (5.8)–(5.11), wealth, (5.12), and government's spendings. At the same time the business sector determines its demand functions for labor, ℓ_0^D, ℓ_1^D, for investment, $Z_0 = I_0 + (\frac{1}{2})gI_0^2/K_0$, for working capital, R_0, and for borrowing, L_B^{HD}, and the supply of output, Y_0^S, Y_1^S. These behavioral functions are derived from the firm's maximizing conditions (equations (5.45)–(5.51) in the Appendix) and its cash-flow institutional constraints (equations (5.42)–(5.44) in the Appendix). The firms demand and supply functions depend on the *pretax* wage rates (w_0, w_1), the owner's (the household's) tax-adjusted discount factor (α_1^H), the firm's tax-adjusted discount factor (α_1^B), the tax rates on business profits (τ_{B0} and τ_{B1}) and the tax rates levied on dividend income (τ_{D0} and τ_{D1}).

Similarly, the dividends paid by the firm (D_0 and D_1) are also functions of these variables.

Formally, the labor-market equilibrium requires that

$$\ell_0^S = \ell_0^D \tag{5.31}$$

$$\ell_1^S = \ell_1^D. \tag{5.32}$$

Likewise, equilibrium in the goods market in period zero requires that

$$C_0 + Z_0 + R_0 + G_0 + L = Y_0^S, \tag{5.33}$$

where

$$L = L^{HS} - (L_G^{HD} - L_F^{GD}) - L_B^{HD}.$$

As indicated, L denotes the country's net lending abroad. It consists of the household supply of lending, L^{HS}, the government's net lending (negative borrowing), $-(L_G^{HD} - L_F^{GD})$, and the business sector net lending (negative borrowing), $-L_B^{HD}$. In equation (5.33) the country's net lending was substituted for net exports. Analogously, goods-market equilibrium in period one requires that

$$C_1 + G_1 - (1 + r_0^*)L = Y_1^S + (1 - \theta)K_1 + R_0, \qquad (5.34)$$

where, being the final period, period-one supply includes current production, Y_1^S, and the net stocks of physical capital, $(1 - \theta)K_1$ (where $K_1 = (1 - \theta)K_0 + I_0$) and working capital, R_0.

In addition to the market-clearing conditions for labor and goods, the equilibrium conditions also include the interest arbitrage condition (5.3), repeated here for convenience:

$$(1 - \tau_{rD0})r_0 = (1 - \tau_{rF0})r_0^*. \qquad (5.3)$$

Finally, given these equilibrium conditions, the government budget constraints can be omitted by Walras's law[4].

5.2   Optimum Taxation and Efficiency

The aim of the government is to use its policy instruments so as to maximize the level of welfare of the household sector. The set of policy instruments that can be used to achieve this objective includes the provision of public goods, tax rates on business and on households (consumption and income taxes—including taxes on labor income, interest income from domestic and foreign sources, and dividend income), as well as finance policies, including domestic and foreign borrowing and lending. In setting its policy instruments, the government must take account of the fact that households and firms react to the incentives embedded in the tax structure. Accordingly, the whole structure of the economy including the equilibrium prices and quantities as well as the various tax bases reflects the details of public finance. In view of the many interactions among the household sector, the business sector, and government policy, the design of optimal taxation (which at the same time maintains government budget solvency) is extremely complex. This complexity is amplified by the fact that in providing and financing its services the government operates in the marketplace alongside the private sector and, by its very actions (i.e., the use of distortionary taxes), distorts the decisions of the private sector. It follows therefore that the design of the optimal tax structure must be carried out within the analytical framework of a *second-best* world.

Perhaps the most-general and best-known result in the theory of optimum taxation is the *aggregate production efficiency theorem* first developed by Peter Diamond and James Mirrlees (1971) and later extended by Mirrlees (1972) and by Sadka (1977). As indicated by this theorem, optimum taxation requires the economy to operate on its consumption possibility frontier. This requirement is remarkable in view of the various tax wedges that separate marginal rates of transformation in production from the corresponding marginal rates of substitution in consumption. The condition necessary for the attainment of this result is that all commodities (including labor) and all profits and rents be taxable; in particular, depending on the government's budgetary needs, these profits and rents may be fully taxed away.

A formal proof of this theorem can be found in the works cited. A heuristic derivation is offered here. Notice that a commodity tax (including labor) is equal to the difference between the consumer price and the producer price of that commodity. Therefore, when there are no restrictions on the government's ability to impose taxes (except no individual lump-sum taxes), the choice of tax policy can be viewed as a choice between a consumer price vector and a producer price vector. In addition, the government is free to choose a set of taxes on pure profits and rents. The objective of the government is to maximize a social welfare function that depends on individual (indirect) utilities. These utilities depend on (1) consumer prices and (2) after-tax pure profits and rent, which affect individuals' net incomes. Before-tax pure profits and rents depend on producer prices.

Therefore, the optimal tax policy is obtained when the government chooses consumer and producer price vectors and a set of taxes on pure profits and rents so as to maximize the (indirect) social welfare function, subject to the constraint that the aggregate consumption bundle induced by these choice variables is feasible in the sense that it is within the aggregate consumption possibility *set*. The Diamond-Mirrlees efficiency theorem states that the optimal policy must induce an aggregate consumption bundle that lies on the *frontier* of this set. For if the consumption bundle does not lie on the frontier, the government can slightly lower the consumer price of certain goods and improve welfare. Such a consumer price change generates a change in the aggregate consumption bundle. The latter can be matched by a change in the production-cum-import (export) bundle, upon an appropriate change in the producer price vector. In general, producer prices affect before-tax pure profits and rents. However, because unrestricted taxes on pure profits and rents are allowed, the government can ensure that the small change in before-tax pure profits and rents is not transmitted to the level of after-tax pure profits and rents and therefore does not affect the individual's utilities. Therefore, only the initial reduction in one of the consumer prices affects (increases) social welfare. Thus, an aggregate consumption bundle that does not lie on the aggregate consumption possibility frontier is inefficient. This is the essence of the aggregate production efficiency result.

Our model economy conforms to the conditions of the aggregate production efficiency theorem. Therefore, it follows that with optimum government policy the economy operates on its consumption possibility frontier. We therefore turn to the derivation of this frontier.

There are six final commodities in the economy (three in each period $t = 0, 1$): leisure, $1 - \ell_t$, private consumption C_t, and public consumption G_t. The consumption possibility frontier, reflecting the production-investment technology and the resource constraint,[5] is

$$C_0 + \frac{C_1}{1 + r_0^*} + G_0 + \frac{G_1}{1 + r_0^*}$$

$$= F(K_0, \ell_0) + \frac{F((1 - \theta)K_0 + I_0, \ell_0)}{1 + r_0^*}$$

$$+ \frac{(1 - \theta)[I_0 + (1 - \theta)K_0]}{1 + r_0^*} - \frac{r_0^*}{1 + r_0^*}R_0 - I_0 - \frac{\frac{1}{2}gI_0^2}{K_0}. \tag{5.35}$$

The right-hand side of (5.35) represents the present value of the economy's net production of the single all-purpose good. Aggregate production efficiency prevails if an increase in the consumption of any one of the six final commodities ($C_0, C_1, G_0, G_1, 1 - \ell_0, 1 - \ell_1$) can be achieved only by reducing consumption of at least one other commodity. Therefore, an optimal policy aims to maximize the right-hand side of the resource constraint. This maximization treats K_0 as exogenous and is carried out with respect to the intermediate, nonconsumable goods, R_0 and I_0, which do not appear as arguments in the household's utility function. Obviously, because leisure is consumable, the optimal policy does not maximize net production with respect to leisure inputs ($1 - \ell_0$ and $1 - \ell_1$).

To minimize the opportunity interest cost of holding working capital the optimal policy sets the level of working capital, R_0, at zero. That is,

$$R_0 = 0. \tag{5.36}$$

This result reflects the structure of our frictionless economy in which working capital does not play a productive role. Likewise, maximization with respect to I_0 (assuming interior solution) yields

$$\frac{gI_0}{K_0} = (1 + r_0^*)^{-1}[F_K(K_1, \ell_1) - \theta - r_0^*]. \tag{5.37}$$

As indicated by this optimal investment rule, investment is carried out up to the point where the marginal cost of adjustment [the left-hand side of equation (5.37)] equals the discounted value of net benefits [the right-hand side of equation (5.37)].

We turn now to the question of what policy tools (or tax structure) are needed in order to sustain the aggregate efficiency rules (5.36) and (5.37). Consider the plausible case in which the firm borrows to invest. Because (as shown earlier) the firm in this case does not hold working capital, it follows that (5.36) holds. With zero holdings of working capital, the investment rule of the firm is given by either equation (5.22) [the case in which the dividend constraint in equation (5.19) is not binding] or by equation (5.23) (the case in which the constraint is binding). As should be evident, however, with lump-sum dividend income it is optimal to first tax this income away (because it would not entail a distortion). It follows that the constraint in equation (5.19) is not binding; therefore, in what follows we focus on equation (5.22).[6]

Employing the arbitrage condition in equation (5.3), we see that the firm's investment rule (5.22) satisfies the economywide efficiency rule (5.37) if, and only if, the following equalities hold:

$$\frac{(1 - \tau_{B1})[F_K - \theta - r_0^*(1 - \tau_{rF0})(1 - \tau_{rD0})^{-1}](1 - \tau_{B0})^{-1}}{1 + r_0^*(1 - \tau_{B1})(1 - \tau_{rF0})(1 - \tau_{rD0})^{-1}}$$

$$= \frac{gI_0}{K_0} = \frac{F_K - \theta - r_0^*}{1 + r_0^*}. \tag{5.38}$$

In the absence of cost of adjustment in investment the conditions in (5.38) imply that the *residence principle* is a necessary condition for efficiency. Indeed, if $g = 0$, the expression on the extreme right-hand side in equation (5.38) vanishes, so that $F_K - \theta - r_0^* = 0$. Because the expression on the extreme left-hand side of equation (5.38) also vanishes, it follows (assuming that the business tax rates are not fully confiscating) that the residence principle must hold. That is,

$$\tau_{rD0} = \tau_{rF0}. \tag{5.39}$$

Equation (5.39) implies that the residence principle must hold. As is evident in this case, the domestic and the world rates of interest are equal, so that

$$r_0 = r_0^*. \tag{5.40}$$

The preceding analysis assumed that investment is not subject to cost of adjustment. If, however, $g > 0$ in condition (5.38), then the residence principle still applies as long as there are no business taxes (so that $\tau_{B0} = \tau_{B1} = 0$).[7] Of course, if business taxes are not zero, then, as is evident from condition (5.38), the residence principle ceases to be a necessary condition for efficiency in the presence of investment cost of adjustment.

The determination of optimal taxation is shown diagrammatically in figure 5.1. For given values of initial capital, K_0, and labor inputs, ℓ_0 and ℓ_1, the economy can produce present (private and public) consumption $(C_0 + G_0)$ and future (private and public) consumption $(C_1 + G_1)$ according to the transformation schedule ABM. Point A represents zero investment in physical capital. In this case the domestic production of private and public consumption in period zero is $F(K_0, \ell_0)$, and the corresponding output in period one is $(1 - \theta)^2 K_0 + F[(1 - \theta)K_0, \ell_1]$. Point M represents a situation in which all resources in period zero are allocated to investment. Accordingly, domestic production of investment in period zero is $F(K_0, \ell_0)$, and there is no production of private and public consumption. Given the world rate of interest, r_0^*, the intermediate point B represents the efficient level of production. At this point the slope of the transformation schedule ABM, which represents the domestic marginal rate of transformation between present and future consumption [namely, $(F_K - \theta - r_0^*)/(gI_0/K_0)$] equals the world marginal rate of transformation between present and future consumption (namely, $1 + r_0^*$). The (private and public) consumption possibility frontier is given by the line NBQ. Subtracting from this consumption frontier a vector of public consumptions (G_0, G_1) yields the private consumption possibility frontier $N'Q'$. Measured in terms of present goods, the difference between the two frontiers is the discounted sum of public consumption, $G_0 + G_1/(1 + r_0^*)$. At the optimum, the household sector consumes C_0 and C_1. This vector of private consumption lies along the private-consumption possibility frontier (point C), where the intertemporal marginal rate of substitution equals the intertemporal consumer price ratio, p_{c0}/p_{c1}. Evidently, the tax-inclusive relative price, p_{c0}/p_{c1}, may differ from the undistorted world intertemporal relative price, $1 + r_0^*$. Thus,

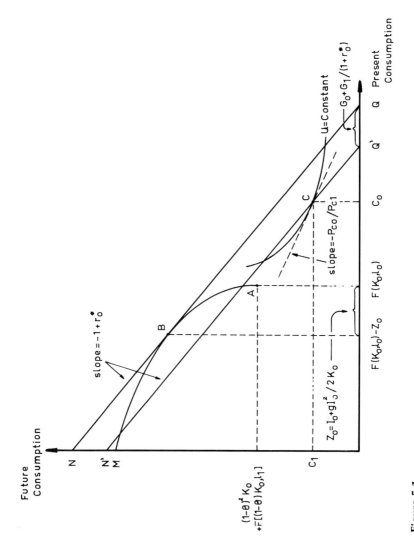

Figure 5.1
Optimal taxation: production efficiency and production-consumption inefficiency

the optimal policy is typically characterized by production-consumption inefficiency.

An important implication revealed by this diagrammatic analysis is that the optimal policy should make no restrictions on international capital flows. Such restrictions force the domestic economy to invest-produce at a point other than point B. Such distorted production would obviously be suboptimal, because (private and public) consumption would be suppressed to a point below the production possibility frontier, QBN.

5.3   Appendix: Taxes and the Behavior of the Firm

The representative firm maximizes the discounted sum of dividends accruing to its owner (shareholder). In doing so, and representing its owner's interest, the firm uses the owner's tax-adjusted rate of discount (namely, $\alpha_1^H = [1 + (1 - \tau_{rF0})r_0^*]^{-1} = [1 + (1 - \tau_{rD0})r_0]^{-1})$.

In period zero, the firm decides how much labor to employ (ℓ_0), how much output to produce [$F(K_0, \ell_0)$], and how much to invest in physical capital (I_0). In addition, the firm chooses how many dividends to distribute (D_0), how much to borrow (L_B^H), and how much working capital to hold (R_0).

In period one (the final period) the firm faces a similar production decision [i.e., a choice of ℓ_1 and, consequently, $F(K_1, \ell_1)$]. Because the firm is liquidated at the end of this period, it distributes its entire net worth as dividends (D_1).

Denoting the discounted sum of the firm's outflow to its owner by V_0, the firm aims to maximize V_0, where

$$V_0 = (1 - \tau_{D0})D_0 + (1 - \tau_{D1})\alpha_1^H D_1. \tag{5.41}$$

An added institutional restriction is that dividends in period zero cannot exceed the firm's profit in that period, that is,

$$D_0 \leqslant (1 - \tau_{B0})[F(K_0, \ell_0) - w_0\ell_0 - \theta K_0 - (Z_0 - I_0)]. \tag{5.42}$$

The firm's budget (cash-flow) constraint in period zero is

$$L_B^H + (1 - \tau_{B0})[F(K_0, \ell_0) - w_0\ell_0 - \theta K_0 - (Z_0 - I_0)] + \theta K_0$$
$$\geqslant D_0 + I_0 + R_0. \tag{5.43}$$

The "dividends" (D_1) in period one are restricted by

$$D_1 \leqslant (1 - \tau_{B1})[F(K_1, \ell_1) - w_1\ell_1 - \theta K_1 - r_0 L_B^H] + K_1 + R_0 - L_B^H. \tag{5.44}$$

Because $Z_0 = I_0 + g I_0^2 / 2K_0$, and $K_1 = K_0(1 - \theta) + I_0$, we can rewrite the constraints (5.42)–(5.43) as:

$$(1 - \tau_{B0}) \left[F(K_0, \ell_0) - w_0 \ell_0 - \theta K_0 - \frac{g I_0^2}{2K_0} \right] - D_0 \geqslant 0, \tag{5.42'}$$

$$L_B^H + (1 - \tau_{B0}) \left[F(K_0, \ell_0) - w_0 \ell_0 - \theta K_0 - \frac{g I_0^2}{2K_0} \right]$$

$$+ \theta K_0 - D_0 - I_0 - R_0 \geqslant 0 \tag{5.43'}$$

and

$$(1 - \tau_{B1})[F((1 - \theta)K_0 + I_0, \ell_1) - w_1 \ell_1 - \theta(1 - \theta)K_0 - \theta I_0]$$

$$- \frac{L_B^H}{\alpha_1^B} + (1 - \theta)K_0 + I_0 + R_0 - D_1 \geqslant 0. \tag{5.44'}$$

The firm chooses D_0, D_1, I_0, L_B^H, R_0, ℓ_0, and ℓ_1 so as to maximize V_0 subject to the constraints (5.42')–(5.44') and the relevant nonnegativity constraints on D_0, I_0, L_B^H, and R_0. The rest of the nonnegativity constraints (e.g., $D_1 \geqslant 0$) are typically not binding and therefore ignored. In performing this maximization, the firm behaves competitively and takes as given the market values of wages, rates of interest, and so forth.

The Lagrange multipliers associated with the constraints (5.42')–(5.44') are denoted by $\delta_{D0} \geqslant 0$, $\delta_0 \geqslant 0$, and $\delta_1 \geqslant 0$, respectively. Likewise, the Lagrange multipliers associated with the nonnegativity constraints are denoted by $\beta_{D0} \geqslant 0$, $\beta_{I0} \geqslant 0$, $\beta_L \geqslant 0$, and $\beta_{R0} \geqslant 0$, respectively. We assume (as usual) that $\delta_0 > 0$ and $\delta_1 > 0$, so that the constraints on the cash flows of the firm in periods zero and one are strictly binding. The necessary first-order conditions are

$$(1 - \tau_{D0}) - \delta_{D0} - \delta_0 + \beta_{D0} = 0, \tag{5.45}$$

$$(1 - \tau_{D1})\alpha_1^H - \delta_1 = 0, \tag{5.46}$$

$$\frac{-(\delta_{D0} + \delta_0)(1 - \tau_{B0})g I_0}{K_0} - \delta_0 + \delta_1(1 - \tau_{B1})[F_K(K_1, \ell_1) - \theta]$$

$$+ \delta_1 + \beta_{I0} = 0, \tag{5.47}$$

$$\delta_0 - \frac{\delta_1}{\alpha_1^B} + \beta_L = 0, \tag{5.48}$$

$$-\delta_0 + \delta_1 + \beta_{R0} = 0, \tag{5.49}$$

$$(\delta_0 + \delta_1)(1 - \tau_{B0})[F_\ell(K_0, \ell_0) - w_0] = 0, \tag{5.50}$$

and

$$\delta_1(1 - \tau_{B1})[F_\ell(K_1, \ell_1) - w_1] = 0. \tag{5.51}$$

These conditions can be used to determine the firm's optimal financial and production investment policies. We consider first the decision concerning the holding of working capital. If the firm holds working capital, then $\beta_{R0} = 0$. It follows from (5.49) that $\delta_0 = \delta_1$, and from (5.48) that $\beta_L = -\delta_1(1 - 1/\alpha_1^B) > 0$. The latter inequality holds because $\alpha_1^B < 1$. We conclude therefore, by the complementary slackness condition, that $L_B^H = 0$, so that the firm will never borrow to hold working capital. If the firm holds working capital, then investment in physical capital should not be more attractive at the margin. This conclusion follows from (5.47) and (5.49), which imply that

$$\frac{(1 - \tau_{B0})gI_0}{K_0} + \frac{(\delta_{D0}/\delta_0)(1 - \tau_{B0})gI_0}{K_0} \geqslant (1 - \tau_{B1})(F_K - \theta) \tag{5.52}$$

(assuming that $I_0 > 0$, so that $\beta_{I0} = 0$).

It is relevant to note that the tax rates applicable to the household sector are absent from (5.52). This feature reflects the fact that the choice between holding of working capital and physical investment does not directly affect the flow of cash out of the firm.

Given that the firm holds working capital, we consider first the case in which the upper limit on dividend distribution is not binding (i.e., $\delta_{D0} = 0$). In this case (5.52) states that at the margin of choice between investment in working and physical capital, the firm does not incur any actual or opportunity cost of interest and therefore the rate of interest is absent from (5.52). At the margin the after-tax marginal product of capital (net of depreciation) just covers the after-tax marginal adjustment cost. Hence, physical investment is equally attractive to working capital. If, on the other hand, $\delta_{D0} > 0$ and hence the upper limit constraint on dividend distribution is binding, then the cost of investment includes also the shadow price of that constraint, because by investing in physical capital, the firm reduces the level of profit available for distribution in period zero, via the adjustment cost. Condition (5.52) shows that in this case, again, working capital is as attractive at the margin as physical capital.

We consider next the margin of choice between working capital and dividend distribution in period zero. If the firm chooses to hold working capital rather than distribute dividends, then the individual tax rate in period one must be sufficiently lower than in period zero to compensate for the postponement of dividends, given the owner's positive rate of time preference. Accordingly,

$$1 - \tau_{D0} < (1 - \tau_{D1})\alpha_1^H. \tag{5.53}$$

To see that indeed $D_0 = 0$, we note that $\delta_0 = \delta_1$ (because $\beta_{R0} = 0$). With positive holding of working capital it follows from (5.45) and (5.46) that

$$(1 - \tau_{D0}) - \delta_1 + \beta_{D0} = (1 - \tau_{D1})\alpha_1^H. \tag{5.54}$$

If (5.53) holds, then $-\delta_{D0} + \beta_{D0} > 0$. Hence, $\beta_{D0} > \delta_{D0} \geqslant 0$, and, by the complementary slackness condition, $D_0 = 0$. If the inequality sign in (5.53) is reversed, then the firm reaches the upper-limit constraint on dividend distribution. To see this, we note that if the inequality sign in (5.53) is reversed, then $-\delta_{D0} + \beta_{D0} \leqslant 0$, so that $\delta_{D0} > \beta_{D0} \geqslant 0$. Hence, the upper-limit constraint on dividend distribution is binding.

We have already seen that the firm will never borrow to hold working capital. In what follows we show that the firm will also never borrow to distribute dividends concurrently. To see this, notice that the cash-flow constraint (5.43) must obviously hold with equality. Hence, it follows from (5.42) and (5.43) that

$$L_B^H \leqslant I_0 - \theta K_0 + R_0. \tag{5.55}$$

The expression on the right-hand side of (5.55) represents the increase in the firm's net worth, which consists of the increase in physical capital, $I_0 - \theta K_0$, and the holding of working capital, R_0. Thus, (5.55) states that borrowing must not exceed the increase in the firm's net worth; that is, the firm is not allowed to borrow to distribute dividends. We therefore conclude that the firm will borrow only to invest in physical capital.

We turn next to the investment rule of the firm. Suppose for the sake of concreteness that the firm borrows (i.e., $\beta_L = 0$) and makes a positive investment (i.e., $\beta_{I0} = 0$). It then follows from (5.45)–(5.48) that

$$\frac{[(1 - \tau_{D0}) + \beta_{D0}](1 - \tau_{B0})gI_0}{K_0} = (1 - \tau_{D1})\alpha_1^H(1 - \tau_{B1})(F_K - \theta - r_0). \tag{5.56}$$

There are two possibilities. If the upper-bound constraint on the distribution of dividends, equation (5.42′), is not binding, then $\delta_{D0} = 0$. In this case it follows from (5.45), (5.46), and (5.48) that

$$(1 - \tau_{D0}) + \beta_{D0} = \frac{(1 - \tau_{D1})\alpha_1^H}{\alpha_1^B}. \tag{5.57}$$

Substituting (5.57) into (5.56) yields

$$\frac{(1 - \tau_{B0})gI_0}{K_0} + \alpha_1^B(1 - \tau_{B1})r_0 = \alpha_1^B(1 - \tau_{B1})(F_K - \theta). \tag{5.58}$$

This rule is equation (5.22). It states that the firm invests up to a point where the sum of the marginal adjustment cost (net of business tax) and the discounted interest cost equals the (after business tax) discounted marginal product of capital, net of depreciation. The discounting is performed by employing α_1^B, the discount factor applicable to the business sector rather than the household sector. Notice that the investment rule does not depend on the individual tax rates (τ_{D0} and τ_{D1}) nor on the individual discount factor (α_1^H). The reason is that investment is entirely internal to the firm: the firm borrows to invest, without affecting at all its ability to pay dividends [recall that constraint (5.42′) is not binding].

In the alternative case in which the upper-bound constraint on dividend distribution is binding, $D_0 > 0$, $\delta_{D0} \geqslant 0$, and $\beta_{D0} = 0$. Hence, the investment rule becomes

$$\frac{(1 - \tau_{D0})(1 - \tau_{B0})gI_0}{K_0} + (1 - \tau_{D1})\alpha_1^H(1 - \tau_{B1})r_0$$

$$= (1 - \tau_{D1})\alpha_1^H(1 - \tau_{B1})(F_K - \theta), \tag{5.59}$$

which is equation (5.23). The difference between this investment rule and the preceding one is that in (5.59) the individual tax rates (τ_{D0} and τ_{D1}) appear, and the individual discount factor (α_1^H) replaces the business discount factor (α_1^B). In the present case, by investing in physical capital, the firm reduces the profits available for distribution in period zero (due to the adjustment cost incurred in that period), which forces a reduction in dividend distribution. In other words, investment causes a shift of dividends from period zero to period one.

Summing up the investment decision, the firm has two instruments to increase its net worth: holding of working capital and investment in physical capital. We have seen that when the firm holds working capital, it does not borrow, and the rule guiding investment decision is shown in (5.52). Alternatively, when the firm does not hold working capital and borrows to invest, then it follows rule (5.58) if the constraint on dividend distribution is not binding, or (5.59) otherwise.

Finally, to specify the firm's production-labor employment decision we turn to the last two first-order conditions, (5.50)–(5.51). These conditions yield the conventional rules for labor demand in each period, indicating that labor should be employed up to the point where its marginal product equals the real wage:

$$F_\ell(K_0, \ell_0) = w_0 \qquad\qquad (5.60)$$

and

$$F_\ell(K_1, \ell_1) = w_1. \qquad\qquad (5.61)$$

As is evident by the use of the pretax wage rates and the absence of business taxes in these equations, the tax structure does not have a *direct* effect on the employment-production decisions, although of course, it affects these decisions *indirectly* through the general-equilibrium adjustments.

III

International Spillovers of
Tax Policies

6

Deficits with Lump-Sum Taxation

Normally, taxes and expenditures are viewed as the major ingredients of fiscal policy. Nevertheless, in a non-Ricardian economy, as is the real-world economy, budget deficits per se play a significant role. Indeed, budget deficits are the key fiscal policy instruments in traditional macroeconomics and public policy discussions. This chapter and the one that follows lay out the formulations for the macroeconomic analysis of budget deficits in the world economy.

The analytical framework developed in this chapter focuses on the pure wealth effects of budget deficits. To highlight the essential mechanisms we allow for a difference between the horizon of the private and the public sector and a more refined commodity aggregation than in previous chapters, distinguishing between tradable and nontradable goods. The incorporation of nontradable goods into the model permits a reexamination of the consequences of budget deficits on the real exchange rate as they operate through the mechanism of the pure wealth effect. Assuming lump-sum taxes, the analysis of the pure wealth mechanism is different from the one carried out in chapter 7, where we allow for distortionary taxes, thereby focusing on the substitution effects of budget deficits.

6.1 The Model

The model provides insights into the interactions among fiscal policies, interest rates, real exchange rates, and the comovements of private-sector consumption. To deal with the real exchange rate we assume that each country produces internationally tradable and nontradable goods.

For a meaningful analysis of budget deficits we depart from the Ricardian equivalence proposition and introduce a "myopic" element as in Blanchard (1985) and Frenkel and Razin (1987).[1] Accordingly, there are overlapping generations of rational individuals, but due to mortality each individual has a finite horizon. The coefficient of "myopia" reflects the finiteness of the horizon. Suppose that γ is the probability that an individual survives from one period to the next, and let $\gamma < 1$. The magnitude of γ (< 1) influences savings in two ways. First, it introduces a risk premium $(1 - \gamma)$ that raises the rate of interest applicable to individuals, $\rho = r + (1 - \gamma)$. Hence, it affects current wealth through the heavier discounting of future disposable incomes. Second, it lowers the effective saving propensity from the subjective discount factor δ (in the absence of mortality) to $\gamma\delta$.

To study the effect of the myopic element it is convenient to adopt Yaari's (1965) formulation according to which because of uncertain lifetime all loans require in addition to regular interest a purchase of life insurance. In case of death the estate is transferred to the life-insurance company, which, in turn, guarantees to cover outstanding debts. It is assumed that there are a large number of individuals and insurance companies; therefore, competition among insurance companies implies that the percentage insurance premium equals the probability of death. The present-value factor, which is composed of one-period rates of interest compounded from period zero up to period t, is denoted by α_t. Therefore, α_t/α_{t+1} equals $(1 + r_t)$, where r_t denotes the market rate of interest from period t to period $t + 1$. Analogously, $\gamma^t/\gamma^{t+1} = 1/\gamma$ equals one plus the ratio of the life-insurance premium $(1 - \gamma)$ to the survival probability (γ). It follows that the *effective* interest rate faced by individuals is $(\gamma^t/\gamma^{t+1})(\alpha_t/\alpha_{t+1}) - 1 = [(1 + r_t)/\gamma] - 1$. This is the effective cost of borrowing relevant for individual decision making.[2]

Population is normalized so that at birth every cohort consists of one individual who is assumed to be born without debt. Due to death the size of each cohort of age t becomes γ^t; therefore, at each point in time the aggregate size of population is $1/(1 - \gamma)$. Disposable income is assumed to be the same across all individuals regardless of age, so per capita income equals $(1 - \gamma)$ times aggregate disposable income.

Under the assumptions that the utility function is logarithmic and that the subjective discount factor, δ, is constant, it can be shown [see, for example, Frenkel and Razin (1986c)] that the aggregate consumption function (which is derived from individuals' maximization of expected utility) is

$$C_t = (1 - \gamma\delta)W_t, \qquad C_{nt} = \frac{\beta_n C_t}{p_{nt}}, \qquad \text{and} \qquad C_{xt} = (1 - \beta_n)C_t, \qquad (6.1)$$

where C_t denotes aggregate consumption, W_t denotes aggregate private wealth, C_{nt} and C_{xt} denote consumption of nontradable and tradable goods, respectively, β_n denotes the relative share of consumption of nontradables in current spending, and p_{nt} denotes the relative price of nontradables in terms of tradables in period t. [In equation (6.1) and henceforth all quantities are measured in per capita terms.][3]

Government budgets are intertemporally balanced, and government commitments are honored. Hence, government debt (at the beginning of period zero) equals the present value of current and future budget surpluses, and the discount rate applicable to government debt is the world rate of interest, r. To simplify, we divide the horizon into two: the current period and the future period. All quantities pertaining to the current period are indicated by a zero subscript, and the paths of the exogenous variables are assumed stationary across future periods.

6.2   A Two-Country World Equilibrium

Equilibrium necessitates that in the current period, world output of tradable goods is demanded, and the discounted sum of future outputs of tradable goods equals the discounted sums of future demands. Likewise, in each country current- and future-period outputs of nontradable goods must be demanded. In what follows we outline the complete two-country model. The aggregate consumption functions at home and abroad are $C_t = (1 - s)W_t$, and $C_t^* = (1 - s^*)W_t^*$, where the propensities to save, s and s^*, are equal to $\gamma\delta$ and $\gamma\delta^*$ (where the survival probability, γ, is assumed to be equal across countries). Home and foreign private wealth are defined as

$$W_0 = (\overline{Y}_{x0} + p_{n0}\overline{Y}_{n0} - T_0) + \frac{\gamma}{R - \gamma}(\overline{Y}_x + p_n\overline{Y}_n - T)$$

$$- (1 + r_{-1})(B_{-1} - B_{-1}^g),\tag{6.2}$$

and

$$W_0^* = (\overline{Y}_{x0}^* + p_{n0}^*\overline{Y}_{n0}^* - T_0^*) + \frac{\gamma}{R - \gamma}(\overline{Y}_x^* + p_n^*\overline{Y}_n^* - T^*)$$

$$- (1 + r_{-1})(B_{-1}^* - B_{-1}^{*g}),\tag{6.3}$$

where $\overline{Y}_n$ and $\overline{Y}_x$ denote the endowment flows of nontradables and tradables, respectively. Thus, equations (6.2) and (6.3) express wealth as the sum of the present values of current and future disposable incomes plus net asset positions. In these equations the term $\gamma/(R - \gamma)$ denotes the present value of an annuity (commencing at period $t = 1$) evaluated by using the discount factor relevant for private decision making, γ/R, where $R =$

$1 + r$. The term B^g_{-1} indicates the size of the government's debt (both external and internal) at period -1, and B_{-1} indicates the national external debt at period -1. Thus, $B_{-1} - B^g_{-1}$ is equal to the size of the private-sector debt (to the government and to foreigners). T_0 and T are lump-sum taxes, which can be negative.

The market-clearing conditions for the domestic nontradable goods require that

$$\beta_n (1 - s) W_0 (p_{n0})^{-1} = \overline{Y}_{n0} - \beta_n^g (1 - \gamma_s^g) G(p_{n0})^{-1},$$ (6.4)

and

$$\beta_n \left[sW_0 + \frac{1 - \gamma}{R - 1} \frac{R}{R - \gamma} (\overline{Y}_x + p_n \overline{Y}_n - T) \right] (p_n)^{-1}$$

$$= \frac{1}{R - 1} [\overline{Y}_n - \beta_n^g \gamma_s^g G(p_n)^{-1}],$$ (6.5)

where G denotes the discounted sum of government spending, β_n^g denotes the relative share of nontradables in government spending, and γ_s^g indicates the government's intertemporal spending patterns. Equation (6.4) specifies the equilibrium condition in the current-period market. Equation (6.5) states that the discounted sum of domestic demand for future nontradable goods equals the discounted sum of future supply net of government absorption. The term in the square brackets on the left-hand side of this equation consists of two expressions. The expression sW_0 represents the per capita savings of the population present in $t = 0$; these savings ultimately must be spent on future goods. The second expression represents the per capita wealth of those who will be born in all future periods from $t = 1$ onward; this wealth will be spent on future goods. To verify that this is indeed the meaning of the second expression, we note that $\overline{Y}_x + p_n \overline{Y}_n - T$ is the disposable income of each individual at the time of birth, and its product with $R/(R - \gamma)$ is the present value of such an annuity. Therefore, the term $[R/(R - \gamma)](\overline{Y}_x + p_n \overline{Y}_n - T)$ denotes each individual's wealth at the time of birth, and since by our normalization the size of each cohort at birth is one individual, this term also represents the cohorts' wealth at birth. Because in each period in the future there is a new cohort whose wealth at birth is computed similarly, the discounted sum of all future cohorts' wealth (as of period $t = 1$) is obtained by multiplying the term $[R/(R - \gamma)](\overline{Y}_x + p_n \overline{Y}_n - T)$ by $R/(R - 1)$, which denotes the present value of an annuity (commencing at $t = 1$), evaluated by using the world interest rate. The resulting expression is then discounted to the present (period $t = 0$) by dividing by R, which yields $[R/(R - 1)(R - \gamma)](\bar{Y}_x + p_n\bar{Y}_n - T)$. Multiplying this term by $(1 - \gamma)$ converts this aggregate wealth into the corresponding per capita wealth.

Analogously, equation (6.6) and (6.7) describe the corresponding equilibrium conditions in the foreign markets for nontradable goods:

$$\beta_n^*(1 - s^*)W_0^*(p_{n0}^*)^{-1} = \bar{Y}_{n0}^* - \beta_n^{*g}(1 - \gamma_s^{*g})G^*(p_{n0}^*)^{-1},\qquad(6.6)$$

and

$$\beta_n^*\left[s^*W_0^* + \frac{1 - \gamma}{R - 1}\frac{R}{R - \gamma}(\bar{Y}_x^* + p_n^*\bar{Y}_n^* - T^*)\right](p_n^*)^{-1}$$

$$= \frac{1}{R - 1}[\bar{Y}_n^* - \beta_n^{*g}\gamma_s^{*g}G^*(p_n^*)^{-1}].\qquad(6.7)$$

Finally, the equilibrium conditions in the world market for tradable goods are specified in equations (6.8) and (6.9), where the first of the two pertains to the current period, and the second pertains to the discounted sums of demand and supply in all future periods:

$$(1 - \beta_n)(1 - s)W_0 + (1 - \beta_n^*)(1 - s^*)W_0^*$$

$$= \bar{Y}_x - (1 - \beta_n^g)(1 - \gamma_s^g)G + \bar{Y}_x^* - (1 - \beta_n^{*g})(1 - \gamma_s^{*g})G^*\qquad(6.8)$$

and

$$(1 - \beta_n)\left[sW_0 + \frac{1 - \gamma}{R - 1}\frac{R}{R - \gamma}(\bar{Y}_x + p_n\bar{Y}_n - T)\right]$$

$$+ (1 - \beta_n^*)\left[s^*W_0^* + \frac{1 - \gamma}{R - 1}\frac{R}{R - \gamma}(\bar{Y}_x^* + p_n^*\bar{Y}_n^* - T^*)\right]$$

$$= \frac{1}{R - 1}[\bar{Y}_x - (1 - \beta_n^g)\gamma_s^g G + \bar{Y}_x^* - (1 - \beta_n^{*g})\gamma_s^{*g}G^*].\qquad(6.9)$$

The system of equations (6.2) through (6.9) can be solved for the equilibrium values of the home and foreign current-period wealth, W_0 and W_0^*, respectively, current and future prices of nontradable goods (the inverse of the corresponding real exchange rates), p_{n0}, p_{n0}^*, p_n, p_n^*, and for the world rate of interest, $R - 1$. As usual, the eight-equation system (6.2) through (6.9) is linearly dependent, and thus, by Walras's law, one of these equations can be left out. In what follows we leave out equation (6.2) specifying the equilibrium value of domestic wealth.

We can now reduce the complete model to two basic equilibrium conditions. To focus on the role of domestic tax policy, we assume that $G = G^* = T_0^* = T^* = 0$. These conditions state that the world markets for tradable goods clear in both the current period as well as in the (consolidated) future period. These equations, derived explicitly in the Appendix, are reduced-form equations—they incorporate the requirement that in each country and in all periods the markets for nontradable goods clear too. Accordingly,

$$(1 - \beta_n)(1 - \gamma\delta)W_0 + (1 - \beta_n^*)(1 - \gamma\delta^*)W_0^*(R) = \bar{Y}_x + \bar{Y}_x^*, \tag{6.10}$$

$$(1 - \beta_n)\left[\gamma\delta W_0 + \frac{(1 - \gamma)R}{(R - 1)(R - \gamma)}I(R, W_0, T)\right]$$

$$+ (1 - \beta_n^*)\left[\gamma\delta^* W_0^*(R) + \frac{(1 - \gamma)R}{(R - 1)(R - \gamma)}I^*(R)\right]$$

$$= \frac{1}{R - 1}(\bar{Y}_x + \bar{Y}_x^*), \tag{6.11}$$

where we replaced s and s^* by $\gamma\delta$ and $\gamma\delta^*$, respectively. Equation (6.10) states that the sum of world private demand for current tradable goods equals world supply. In this equation $(1 - \beta_n)(1 - \gamma\delta)W_0$ is the home country's private demand, and $(1 - \beta_n^*)(1 - \gamma\delta^*)W_0^*$ is the corresponding foreign demand. The foreign wealth is expressed as a negative function of the rate of interest, reflecting the role of the latter in discounting future incomes and in influencing the real exchange rate used to evaluate the income streams. It is noteworthy that this reduced-form functional dependence of wealth on the rate of interest is not shown explicitly for the domestic wealth, because we have omitted the explicit domestic-wealth equation (6.2) by Walras's law. This choice makes the equilibrium determination of domestic wealth (along with the world rate of interest) the focus of the subsequent analysis.

The second reduced-form equation (6.11) states that the discounted sum of domestic and foreign demands for future tradable goods equals the discounted sum of future world supply. The first term is the product of the consumption share of tradable goods $(1 - \beta_n)$ and total domestic future consumption. The latter equals the sum of the savings of those alive in period zero, $\gamma\delta W_0$, and the discounted sum of the demand for future goods of those who will be born in the future and whose disposable income in each period is I. This reduced-form future disposable income (in terms of tradable goods) is expressed as a decreasing function of future taxes, T, and an increasing function of the future relative price of nontradable goods. The latter in turn depends negatively on R (through its effect on future wealth of those yet unborn) and positively on W_0 (through its effect on the demand of those alive). An analogous interpretation applies to the foreign disposable income, I^*. The dependence of I^* on R reflects only the assumption that foreign taxes are zero and incorporates the negative dependence of W_0^* on R. In the absence of nontradable goods, $\beta_n = \beta_n^* = 0$, $I(R, W_0, T) = \bar{Y}_x - T$, $I^*(R) = Y_x^*$, $\bar{Y}_n = 0$, and $W^*(R) = Y_x^* + Y_x^*/(R - 1) - (1 + r_{-1})(B_{-1}^* - B_{-1}^{*g})$.

Equations (6.10) and (6.11) yield the equilibrium values of the home country's initial wealth, W_0, and the world rate of interest, $r = R - 1$, for any given values of the parameters. In equilibrium the demand for nontradable goods $\beta_n(1 - \gamma\delta)W_0(p_{n0})^{-1}$ equals the supply, $\bar{Y}_n$. Hence, the equilibrium price (the inverse of the real exchange rate) is

$$p_{n0} = \frac{\beta_n(1 - \gamma\delta)W_0}{\bar{Y}_n}. \tag{6.12}$$

The equilibrium of the system is analyzed by means of figure 6.1. The PP schedule drawn in panel I of figure 6.1 shows combinations of r and

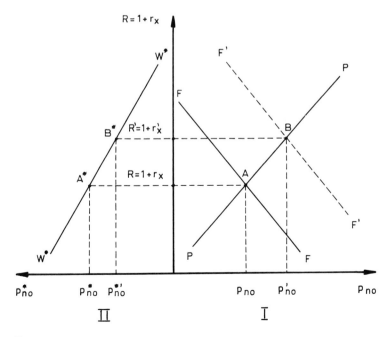

Figure 6.1
Budget deficits, the real exchange rate, and the real interest rate

p_{n0} that clear the market for present tradable goods. It is positively sloped, because a rise in the rate of interest lowers foreign demand (by lowering W_0^*), and a rise in p_{n0} raises domestic demand (by raising W_0). The future tradable-goods market clears along the FF schedule. This schedule is negatively sloped, because a rise in the rate of interest creates an excess demand for future tradable goods that must be offset by a fall in W_0 (and therefore p_{n0}). Panel II of the figure shows the negative relation between the equilibrium rate of interest and the foreign relative price of nontradable goods. This relation is based on equation (6.13), which is the foreign-country analogue to equation (6.12):

$$p_{n0}^* = \frac{\beta_n^*(1 - \gamma\delta^*)}{\overline{Y}_n^*} W_0^*(R).$$
(6.13)

The equilibrium of the system is shown by point A in panel I and point A^* in panel II of figure 6.1. Accordingly, the current equilibrium relative price of domestic tradable goods is p_{n0}, the foreign equilibrium relative price is p_{n0}^*, and the corresponding equilibrium rate of interest is r. In what follows we analyze the effects of a domestic budget deficit on the world rate of interest and on the equilibrium real exchange rates. The formal derivations of the results are contained in the Appendix.

6.3   Budget Deficits

A domestic budget deficit arising from a current tax cut necessitates a corresponding rise in future taxes, T. As seen from equation (6.11), the rise in future taxes lowers future domestic disposable income, I, and thereby lowers the demand for future goods. For a given world rate of interest the fall in demand can be eliminated by a rise in W_0. As implied by equation (6.12), the rise in W_0 is associated with a rise in p_{n0}. Thus, the FF schedule shifts to the right, to FF. As is evident, the horizontal shift of the FF schedule is proportional to $(1 - \gamma)$; if $\gamma = 1$, the position of the schedule as well as the characteristics of the initial equilibrium remains intact (the Ricardian equivalence case). In general, as indicated in panel I, the new equilibrium obtains at point B with a higher rate of interest, a higher domestic price of nontradable goods, p_{n0}, and a higher level of domestic wealth and consumption. The new equilibrium is indicated in panel II by point B^*, where it is seen that the higher rate of interest lowers foreign wealth and consumption and reduces the foreign relative price of nontradable goods. Thus, on the basis of the correlations between domestic and foreign private-sector spending and between domestic and foreign real exchange rates, the international transmission of the budget deficit is negative. As an interpretation, we note that the wealth effect induced by the domestic budget deficit creates an excess demand for present tradable goods, resulting in a rise in their intertemporal relative price—the rate of interest. Likewise, it creates an excess demand for domestic nontradable goods and an excess supply of foreign nontradable goods. These excess demands and supplies alter the temporal relative price of these goods—the real exchange rates.

6.4   Conclusions

In this chapter we analyzed the consequences of budget deficits on the real exchange rate operating through the mechanism of the pure wealth effect. To focus on this mechanism rather than the mechanism of substitution effects, we assumed that all taxes are nondistortionary. In that case the finiteness of the horizon implies that budget deficits induce a positive wealth effect.

Our analysis of the two-country case focused on the consequences of budget deficits on the domestic and the foreign real exchange rates. In this case the international transmission mechanism operates through the effects of the budget deficit on the world rate of interest. Accordingly, the wealth effect induced by the budget deficit raises the domestic demand for present-period goods and thereby lowers the domestic real exchange rate and raises the world rate of interest. The rise in the world rate of interest transmits the effects of the domestic deficit to the rest of the world: it lowers the foreign spending and raises the foreign real exchange rate. Accordingly, the budget deficit induces negative cross-country correlations between the levels of private-sector spending as well as between the real exchange rates.

The pattern of the cross-country correlations between real exchange rates and the effects of budget deficits on the world rate of interest reflect the mechanism of the pure wealth effect set in place in the absence of distortionary taxes.

6.5   Appendix: Real Exchange Rates in a Two-Country World

In this appendix we first derive the reduced-form equations (6.10) and (6.11). Throughout we omit equation (6.2) by Walras's law. Using equations (6.4) and (6.6) and solving for the future values of production of nontradable goods yields

$$p_n \bar{Y}_n = A[(R-1)sW_0 + \frac{(1-\gamma)R}{R-\gamma}(\bar{Y}_x - T)], \qquad (6.14)$$

$$p_n^* \bar{Y}_n^* = A^*[(R-1)s^*W_0^* + \frac{(1-\gamma)R}{R-\gamma}(\bar{Y}_x^* - T^*)], \qquad (6.15)$$

where

$$\theta = \frac{\beta_n^g \gamma_s^g G}{p_n \bar{Y}_n}, \; \theta^* = \frac{\beta_n^{*g} \gamma_s^{*g} G^*}{p_n^* \bar{Y}_n^*}$$

$$A = \frac{\beta_n}{(1-\theta) - \beta_n(1-\gamma)R/(R-\gamma)},$$

$$A^* = \frac{\beta_n^*}{(1-\theta^*) - \beta_n^*(1-\gamma)R/(R-\gamma)}.$$

The requirement that in equilibrium there is positive consumption of non-tradable goods that command a positive price imposes the feasibility condition according to which

$$A \geqslant 0, \qquad A^* \geqslant 0. \qquad (6.16)$$

Substituting (6.15) and equation (6.5) into equation (6.2) yields

$$W_0^* = D^*\left[\bar{Y}_x^* - T_0^* + \frac{\gamma}{R-\gamma}\left(1 + A^*\frac{(1-\gamma)R}{R-\gamma}\right)(\bar{Y}_x^* - T^*)\right.$$

$$\left. + (1 + r_{-1})(B_{-1}^{*g} + B_{-1})\right], \qquad (6.17)$$

where

$$D^* = (1-\theta^*)\left\{(1-\theta^*) - \beta_n^*\left[\frac{(R-1)\gamma s^*}{(1-\theta^*)(R-\gamma) - \beta_n^*(1-\gamma)R}\right.\right.$$

$$\left.\left. + \frac{1-s^*}{1-\theta^*}\right]\right\}^{-1}.$$

The requirement that in equilibrium wealth is positive imposes the additional feasibility constraint according to which

$$D^* \geqslant 0.$$

Substituting equation (6.17) into equation (6.18) yields

$$(1 - \beta_n)(1 - s)W_0 + (1 - \beta_n^*)D^* \left\{ \bar{Y}_x^* - T_0^* \right.$$

$$+ \frac{\gamma}{R - \gamma} \left[1 + A^* \frac{(1 - \gamma)R}{R - \gamma} \right] (\bar{Y}_x^* - T^*)$$

$$\left. + (1 + r_{-1})(B_{-1}^{*g} + B_{-1}) \right\}$$

$$= \bar{Y}_x - (1 - \beta_n^g)(1 - \gamma_s^g)G + \bar{Y}_x^* - (1 - \beta_n^{*g})(1 - \gamma_s^{*g})G^*. \quad (6.19)$$

Substituting equations (6.14) and (6.15) for $p_n \bar{Y}_n$ and $p_n^* \bar{Y}_n^*$ into equation (6.9) yields

$$(1 - \beta_n) \left[sW_0 + \frac{(1 - \gamma)R}{(R - 1)(R - \gamma)} \left\{ A(R - 1)sW_0 \right. \right.$$

$$+ \left[1 + A \frac{(1 - \gamma)R}{R - \gamma} \right] (\bar{Y}_x - T) \right\} \right] + (1 - \beta_n^*) \left[s^*W_0^* \right.$$

$$+ \frac{(1 - \gamma)R}{(R - 1)(R - \gamma)} \left\{ A^*(R - 1)s^*W_0^* \right.$$

$$+ \left[1 + A^* \frac{(1 - \gamma)R}{R - \gamma} \right] (\bar{Y}_x^* - T^*) \right\} \right]$$

$$= \frac{1}{R - 1} [\bar{Y}_x - (1 - \beta_n^g)\gamma_s^g G + \bar{Y}_x^* - (1 - \beta_n^{*g})\gamma_x^{*g}G^*]. \quad (6.20)$$

The system of equations (6.17), (6.19), and (6.20) can be used to solve for the equilibrium vlaues of W_0, W_0^*, and R.

To derive the more compact formulation of the reduced-form equilibrium conditions of the text, we focus on the role of domestic tax policy by assuming that $G = G^* = T_0^* = T^* = 0$. We first note that for a given value of the parameters the equilibrium value of foreign wealth shown in equation (6.13) can be expressed implicitly as

$$W_0^* = W_0^*(R), \qquad \frac{\partial W_0^*}{\partial R} < 0. \quad (6.21)$$

Equation (6.21) expresses foreign current wealth as a negative function of the rate of interest. This reduced-form relationship incorporates the equilibrium conditions in the markets for current and future nontradable goods. The negative dependence on the rate of interest reflects the role of the rate of interest in discounting future incomes and in influencing the real exchange rates used to evaluate the income streams. Next, we define the domestic and foreign reduced-form future disposable incomes:

$$I(R, W_0, T) = (R - 1)A\gamma\delta W_0 + \left[1 + \frac{(1 - \gamma)RA}{R - \gamma}\right](\bar{Y}_x - T) \quad (6.22)$$

and

$$I^*(R) = (R - 1)A^*\gamma\delta^*W_0^*(R) + \left[1 + \frac{(1 - \gamma)RA^*}{R - \gamma}\right]\bar{Y}_x^*. \quad (6.23)$$

Equation (6.22) expresses disposable income (in terms of tradable goods) as a negative function of future taxes, T, and a positive function of the relative price of nontradable goods, p_n. The latter in turn depends negatively on R (through its effect on future wealth of those yet unborn) and positively on W_0 (through its effect on the demand for those alive). An analogous interpretation applies to the foreign disposable income, I^*, where in (6.23) we incorporate the functional dependence of W_0^* on R, and the assumption that $G = G^* = T_0^* = T^* = 0$ yields

$$(1 - \beta_n)(1 - \gamma\delta)W_0 + (1 - \beta_n^*)(1 - \gamma\delta^*)W_0^*(R) = \bar{Y}_x + \bar{Y}_x^*, \quad (6.24)$$

$$(1 - \beta_n)\left[\gamma\delta^*W_0 + \frac{(1 - \gamma)R}{(R - 1)(R - \gamma)}I(R, W_0, T)\right]$$

$$+ (1 - \beta_n^*)\left[\gamma\delta^*W_0^*(R) + \frac{(1 - \gamma)R}{(R - 1)(R - \gamma)}I^*(R)\right]$$

$$= \frac{1}{R - 1}(\bar{Y}_x + \bar{Y}_x^*). \quad (6.25)$$

Equations (6.24) and (6.25) are the reduced-form equilibrium conditions (6.10) and (6.11). These equations underline the diagrammatical analysis of the text.

We turn next to a more formal analysis of the comparative statics results reported in the text. For this purpose we return to the complete model outlined in equations (6.2) through (6.8), omitting equation (6.9) by Walras's law. We continue to assume that $G = G^* = T_0^* = T^* = 0$. Substituting (6.24) and equation (6.4) into equation (6.3) yields

$$W_0 = D\left\{\bar{Y}_x - T_0 + \frac{\gamma}{R - \gamma}\left[1 + A\frac{(1 - \gamma)R}{R - \gamma}\right](\bar{Y}_x - T)\right.$$

$$\left. + (1 + r_{-1})(B_{-1}^g - B_{-1})\right\}, \quad (6.26)$$

where

$$D = \left\{1 - \beta_n\left[\frac{(R-1)\gamma^2\delta}{(R-\gamma) - \beta_n(1-\gamma)R} + (1 - \gamma\delta)\right]\right\}^{-1}.$$

Likewise, with zero foreign government spending and taxes, equation (6.17) becomes

$$W_0^* = D^*\left\{\bar{Y}_x^* + \frac{\gamma}{R-\gamma}\left[1 + A^*\frac{(1-\gamma)R}{R-\gamma}\right]\bar{Y}_x^* + (1 + r_{-1})(B_{-1}^{*g} + B_{-1})\right\},$$

(6.27)

where

$$D^* = \left\{1 - \beta_n^*\left[\frac{(R-1)\gamma^2\delta^*}{(R-\gamma) - \beta_n^*(1-\gamma)R} + (1 - \gamma\delta^*)\right]\right\}^{-1}$$

and feasibility requires that $D \geqslant 0$ and $D^* \geqslant 0$. Finally, using equation (6.8), we get

$$(1 - \beta_n)(1 - \gamma\delta)W_0 + (1 - \beta_n^*)(1 - \gamma\delta^*)W_0^* = \bar{Y}_x + \bar{Y}_x^*. \tag{6.28}$$

The system of equations (6.26) through (6.28) solves for the equilibrium values of W_0, W_0^*, and R. Differentiating this system, and noting that from the government budget constraint $dT_0 = -[1/(R-1)]dT$, we have

$$\frac{dW_0}{dT} = -(1 - \gamma)\frac{J_1J_2}{\Delta}(1 - \beta_n^*)(1 - \gamma\delta^*) > 0, \tag{6.29}$$

$$\frac{dW_0^*}{dT} = (1 - \gamma)\frac{J_1J_2}{\Delta}(1 - \beta_n)(1 - \gamma\delta) < 0, \tag{6.30}$$

$$\frac{dR}{dT} = (1 - \gamma)\frac{J_2}{\Delta}(1 - \beta_n)(1 - \gamma\delta) > 0, \tag{6.31}$$

where

$$\Delta = \left\{(1 - \beta_n^*)^2(1 - \gamma\delta^*)\frac{\gamma[1 - \beta_n^*(1-\gamma)]\bar{Y}_x^*D^{*2}}{[(R-\gamma) - \beta_n^*(1-\gamma)R]^2}\right.$$

$$\left. + (1 - \beta_n)^2(1 - \gamma\delta)\frac{\gamma[1 - \beta_n(1-\gamma)]\bar{Y}_xD^2}{[(R-\gamma) - \beta_n(1-\gamma)R]^2}\right\} < 0,$$

$$J_1 = \frac{(1 - \beta_n^*)\gamma[1 - \beta_n^*(1-\gamma)]\bar{Y}_x^*D^{*2}}{[(R-\gamma) - \beta_n^*(1-\gamma)R]^2} > 0,$$

$$J_2 = \frac{(1 - \beta_n)RD}{[(R - 1)(R - \gamma) - \beta_n(1 - \gamma)R]} > 0.$$

Using (6.29)–(6.31) with equation (6.12) and (6.13) yields

$$\frac{dp_{n0}}{dT} = -(1 - \gamma)\frac{J_1 J_2}{\Delta \overline{Y}_n}\beta_n(1 - \gamma\delta)(1 - \beta_n^*)(1 - \gamma\delta^*) > 0, \tag{6.32}$$

$$\frac{dp_{n0}^*}{dT} = (1 - \gamma)\frac{J_1 J_2}{\Delta \overline{Y}_n^*}\beta_n^*(1 - \gamma\delta^*)(1 - \beta_n)(1 - \gamma\delta) < 0. \tag{6.33}$$

The results reported in (6.29) through (6.33) justify the diagrammatic analysis of the text. They show that a current budget deficit (necessitating a future rise in taxes so that $dT > 0$) raises domestic wealth, lowers foreign wealth, raises the world rate of interest, lowers the domestic current real exchange rate (the reciprocal of p_{n0}), and raises the foreign current real exchange rate. All these real effects vanish if the value of γ approaches unity. In that case the pure wealth effects of budget deficits do not exist.

A similar computation reveals that the effects of the budget deficit on the future value of the real exchange rates are ambiguous. This ambiguity reflects the conflicting forces exercised by the wealth and substitution effects induced by the change in the rate of interest that in the home country supplements the direct wealth effects of the tax policy. It can be shown, however, that the budget deficit decelerates the rate of increase of the foreign real exchange rate between the present and the future period.

7

Deficits with Distortionary Taxation

The international effects of budget deficits arise in part from tax and transfer policies; the specific consequences of these policies and the characteristics of the international transmission mechanism depend critically on the precise composition of taxes. Specifically, the international effects of a budget deficit of a given size differ sharply according to the types of taxes used to generate the deficit. On the one hand, a budget deficit in the home country arising from a cut in consumption taxes raises the world rate of interest and thereby crowds out home and foreign investment. It also worsens the trade balance of the home economy. On the other hand, a budget deficit in the home country that arises from a cut in income taxes lowers the world rate of interest and crowds out home investment but crowds in investment from abroad. In that case the domestic economy's trade balance improves. The great sensitivity of the consequences of a budget deficit to the specific tax policy generating the deficit underscores the desirability of using more detailed information than that provided by the statistic measuring the aggregate budget deficit.

To focus on issues of public finance, we assume that the path of government spending is given, and we examine the implications of alternative time profiles of taxes and of public-debt issue.[1] To conduct a meaningful analysis of budget deficits, we depart from the pure Ricardian model (in which the timing of taxes does not matter) by allowing for distortionary taxes and examine the effects of budget deficits arising from tax policies under alternative tax systems. We consider deficit policies involving taxes of different types: consumption taxes, taxes on income from domestic investment, taxes on income from foreign lending, and taxes on labor income.

Throughout, we assume that capital markets in the world economy are fully integrated and, therefore, that individuals and governments of different countries face the same world rate of interest. This feature provides the key channel through which the effects of policies undertaken in one country are transmitted to the rest of the world.

7.1 The Analytical Framework

In developing the analytical framework, we start again with a formulation of the budget constraint that focuses attention on the key economic variables and tax-policy parameters that play a central role in the subsequent analysis. The home country's private sector (full-income) budget constraint applicable to period ($t = 0, 1, \ldots, T - 1$) is

$$(1 + \tau_{Ct})C_t + (1 - \tau_{yt})w_t(1 - \ell_t)$$

$$= (1 - \tau_{yt})\left[w_t + r_{kt}(K_{t-1} + I_{t-1}) - I_t\left(1 + \frac{g}{2}\frac{I_t}{K_t}\right)\right]$$

$$+ (1 - \tau_{bt})[B_t^P - (1 - r_{t-1})B_{t-1}^P], \tag{7.1}$$

where τ_{Ct}, τ_{yt}, and τ_{bt} denote the tax rate on consumption, the cash-flow tax on income[2] and the cash-flow tax on international borrowing, respectively. The levels of consumption, labor supply, capital stock, investment, and the private-sector international borrowing are denoted, respectively, by C_t, ℓ_t, K_t, I_t, and B_t^P. The wage rate, the capital-rental rate, and the interest rate are denoted, respectively, by w_t, r_{kt}, and r_t. Note that due to costs of adjustment of investment, the capital-rental rate, r_{kt}, is not necessarily equal to the interest rate, r_t. For convenience, we normalize the endowment of leisure to unity and assume that capital does not depreciate ($K_t = K_{t-1} + I_{t-1}$) and that costs of adjustment in capital formation are of the form $(\frac{1}{2})gI_t^2/K_t$.[3] We note that in the final period (period T) the private sector settles its debt commitments, and no new investment or new borrowing occurs. Accordingly, $I_T = B_T^P = 0$. We assume that a unit of capital in the final period (after production is completed) has a residual value for consumption denoted by a.

As was already elaborated upon in chapter 2, the consumption tax is equivalent to a destination-based VAT. A cash-flow income tax is essentially a tax on GDP less gross investment. As pointed out in chapter 2, a source-based VAT is equivalent to a tax on GDP less gross investment. Thus, the distinction between the consumption tax and the cash-flow income tax analyzed in this chapter is essentially a distinction between a destination-based VAT and a source-based VAT.

To simplify the exposition, we assume a linear production function with fixed coefficients. Thus, the competitive equilibrium conditions imply that the wage rate and the capital-rental rate, w and r_k, are constant. To simplify further, we also assume that the historical debt commitment of the private sector, B^p_{-1}, is zero.

The formulation of the periodic budget constraint illustrates the equivalence relation existing among the taxes on consumption, income, and international borrowing. Indeed, the real effects of any given combination of the three taxes can be duplicated by a policy consisting of any two of them. For example, consider an initial situation with a positive consumption tax rate, $\bar{\tau}_C$, and zero income and international borrowing tax rates. If the consumption tax is eliminated and the income and international borrowing taxes are both set equal to $\bar{\tau}_C/(1 + \bar{\tau}_C)$, then the effective tax rates associated with this new combination of taxes are zero income and international borrowing taxes and a positive ($\bar{\tau}_C$) consumption tax. It follows that the real equilibrium associated with the new tax pattern ($\tau_C = 0, \tau_y = \tau_b = \bar{\tau}_C/[1 + \bar{\tau}_C]$) is identical to the one associated with the initial tax pattern ($\tau_C = \bar{\tau}_C, \tau_y = \tau_b = 0$). For a more elaborate analysis of tax equivalences see chapter 4.

The periodic (full-income) budget constraints specified in equation (7.1) can be consolidated to yield the lifetime present-value budget constraint. To facilitate the diagrammatic analysis of subsequent sections, we illustrate the lifetime present-value budget constraint for a two-period case ($t = 0, 1$). Accordingly,

$$C_0 + \alpha_C C_1 + \left(\frac{1 - \tau_{y0}}{1 + r_{C0}}\right)[w(1 - \ell_0) + \alpha_L w(1 - \ell_1)]$$

$$= \left(\frac{1 - \tau_{y0}}{1 + \tau_{C0}}\right)w + \left(\frac{1 - \tau_{y1}}{1 + \tau_{C1}}\right)\alpha_C w + \left(\frac{1 - \tau_{y0}}{1 + \tau_{C0}}\right)$$

$$\cdot \left[r_k K_0 + \alpha_I(a + r_k)K_1 - I_0\left(1 + \frac{g}{2}\frac{I_0}{K_0}\right)\right], \tag{7.2}$$

where

$$\alpha_C = \frac{(1 + \tau_{C1})}{(1 + \tau_{C0})}\frac{(1 - \tau_{b0})}{(1 - \tau_{b1})}\frac{1}{(1 + r_0)},$$

and

$$\alpha_L = \alpha_I$$

$$= \frac{(1 - \tau_{y1})}{(1 - \tau_{y0})}\frac{(1 - \tau_{b0})}{(1 - \tau_{b1})}\frac{1}{(1 + r_0)}.$$

As indicated, the discount factors α_C, α_L, and α_I are the effective (tax-adjusted) discount factors governing intertemporal consumption, leisure, and investment decisions, respectively. The intratemporal choice between labor supply (leisure) and consumption of ordinary goods is governed by the prevailing effective intratemporal tax ratio $(1 - \tau_y)/(1 + \tau_C)$. We note that in this cash flow formulation the effective discount factor governing intertemporal consumption decisions, α_C, is independent of the income tax, whereas the effective discount factors governing investment and leisure decisions, α_I and α_L, are independent of the consumption tax. In addition, the effective discount factors depend on the time path of the various taxes rather than on their levels. Specifically, if the various tax rates do not vary over time, then their time paths are "flat," and the effective discount factors α_C, α_L, and α_I are equal to the undistorted tax-free factor, $\alpha = 1/(1 + r_0)$. In that case the intertemporal allocations are undistorted, whereas the intratemporal allocations are distorted if the intratemporal tax ratio differs from unity.

Having discussed the formulation of the private-sector budget constraint, we turn next to the specification of the multiperiod utility function. To facilitate the discussion of the simulations reported in subsequent sections, we need to specify its form in some detail. We thus suppose that the homothetic intraperiod utility function between consumption of ordinary goods and leisure is of the constant elasticity of substitution (CES) form:

$$u_t = [\beta C_t^{(\sigma-1)/\sigma} + (1 - \beta)(1 - \ell_t)^{(\sigma-1)/\sigma}]^{\sigma/\sigma-1}, \tag{7.3}$$

whereas the interperiod utility function is

$$U_0 = \sum_{t=0}^{T} \delta^t \log(u_t), \tag{7.4}$$

where σ is the temporal elasticity of substitution between leisure and consumption of ordinary goods, β is the distributive parameter of consumption, and δ is the subjective discount factor. We have $0 < \sigma \neq 1, 0 < \beta < 1$, and $\delta < 1$.

Maximizing the utility function specified in equation (7.3) and (7.4) subject to the lifetime present-value budget constraint yields the utility-based real spending, u, its associated price index, P, and the periodic demand functions for the consumption of ordinary goods, C, and leisure, $1 - \ell$, as follows:

$$u_t = \left(\sum_{s=0}^{T} \delta^s\right)^{-1} \frac{W_0 \delta^t}{P_t \alpha_t}, \tag{7.5}$$

$$P_t = \left\{ \beta^\sigma \left(\frac{1 + \tau_{Ct}}{1 - \tau_{bt}} \right)^{1-\sigma} + (1 - \beta)^\sigma \left[\frac{(1 - \tau_{yt})}{(1 - \tau_{bt})} w \right]^{1-\sigma} \right\}^{1/(1-\sigma)}, \tag{7.6}$$

$$C_t = \frac{\beta^\sigma \left[\frac{(1 + \tau_{Ct})}{(1 - \tau_{bt})} \right]^{-\sigma} P_t u_t}{\beta^\sigma \left(\frac{1 + \tau_{Ct}}{1 - \tau_{bt}} \right)^{1-\sigma} + (1 - \beta)^\sigma \left[\frac{(1 - \tau_{yt})}{(1 - \tau_{bt})} w \right]^{1-\sigma}}, \tag{7.7}$$

$$1 - \ell_t = \frac{(1 - \beta)^\sigma \left[\frac{(1 - \tau_{yt})}{(1 - \tau_{bt})} w \right]^{-\sigma} P_t u_t}{\beta^\sigma \left(\frac{1 + \tau_{Ct}}{1 - \tau_{bt}} \right)^{1-\sigma} + (1 - \beta)^\sigma \left[\frac{(1 - \tau_{yt})}{(1 - \tau_{bt})} w \right]^{1-\sigma}}, \tag{7.8}$$

where α_t is period $= t$ persent-value factor, that is,

$$\alpha_t = [(1 + r_0)(1 + r_1)\dots(1 + r_{t-1})]^{-1},$$

and where wealth is

$$W_0 = \sum_{t=0}^{T} \alpha_t \frac{(1 - \tau_{yt})}{(1 - \tau_{bt})} \left[w + r_k K_t - I_t \left(1 + \frac{g}{2} \frac{I_t}{K_t} \right) \right] + \alpha_T \frac{(1 - \tau_{yT})}{(1 - \tau_{bT})} a K_T.$$

To complete the description of the private-sector behavior, we maximize the representative individual wealth, W_0, with respect to investment, I_t. This yields

$$-\frac{1 - \tau_{yt}}{1 - \tau_{bt}} \alpha_t \left(1 + g \frac{I_t}{K_t} \right) + \sum_{s=t+1}^{T-1} \frac{(1 - \tau_{ys})}{(1 - \tau_{bs})} \alpha_s \left[r_k + \frac{g}{2} \left(\frac{I_s}{K_s} \right)^2 \right]$$

$$+ \frac{1 - \tau_{yT}}{1 - \tau_{bT}} (r_k + a)\alpha_T = 0. \tag{7.9}$$

Equation (7.9) represents the implicit investment rule. The negative term is equal to the marginal cost of investment in period t, whereas the positive terms are equal to the marginal benefits consisting of the rise in output resulting from the increased capital stock (the terms with r_k and a) and the fall in the future cost of investment [the terms associated with $(g/2)(I/K)^2$]; all terms are expressed as present values adjusted for taxes. For the two-period case the investment function implied by equation (7.9) is

$$I_0 = \frac{1}{g}[\alpha_I(a + r_k) - 1]K_0. \tag{7.10}$$

Equation (7.10) together with the assumption that $(a + r_k)$ exceeds unity (an assumption necessary for a positive level of investment in the two-period case) implies that the level of investment rises with the initial capital stock, K_0, with the effective (tax-adjusted) discount factor, α_I, with the rental rate, r_k, and with the consumption coefficient, a, attached to the final-period capital. On the other hand, investment falls with an increase in the cost-of-adjustment parameter, g.

7.2   Diagrammatic Analysis

In what follows we carry out the analysis by means of a simple diagrammatic apparatus. To simplify, we assume in this section that labor supply is inelastic. The initial equilibrium is portrayed in figure 7.1, in which the upward-sloping schedule, S^w, describes the ratio, z^w, of current to future world GDP net of investment as an increasing function of the rate of interest. Accordingly, the world relative supply (evaluated at $r = r_0$) is

$$z^w = \frac{Y_0 - I_0\left[1 + \frac{1}{2}g(I_0/K_0)\right] + Y_0^* - I_0^*\left[1 + \frac{1}{2}g^*(I_0^*/K_0^*)\right]}{Y_1 + Y_1^*}. \qquad (7.11)$$

where Y denotes output.

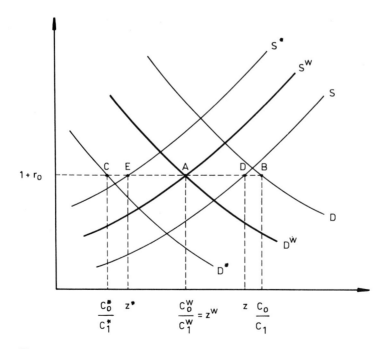

Figure 7.1
Relative demands, relative supplies, and the world equilibrium

The positive dependence of z on the rate of interest reflects the fact that a rise in the rate of interest lowers investment. The world relative supply schedule, S^w, is a weighted average of the home-country relative supply schedule, S, and the foreign-country relative supply schedule, S^*, where

$$S = \frac{Y_0 - I_0\left[1 + \frac{1}{2}g(I_0/K_0)\right]}{Y_1},$$

and

$$S^* = \frac{Y_0^* - I_0^*\left[1 + \frac{1}{2}g^*(I_0^*/K_0^*)\right]}{Y_1^*}.$$

Accordingly,

$$S^w = \mu_s S + (1 - \mu_s)S^*, \tag{7.12}$$

where the home-country weight is

$$\mu_s = \frac{Y_1}{Y_1 + Y_1^*}. \tag{7.13}$$

The downward-sloping schedules in figure 7.1 plot the desired ratio of current to future consumption as a decreasing function of the rate of interest. The home and foreign relative demands are denoted by D and D^*, respectively, and their values at the point in which $C_0/C_1 = C_0^*/C_1^* = 1$ are one plus the subjective rate of time preference, $1/\delta$ and $1/\delta^*$.

Analogously to the construction of the world relative supply, the world relative demand, $D^w = C_0^w/C_1^w = (C_0 + C_0^*)/(C_1 + C_1^*)$, is a weighted average of the two countries' relative demands, $D = C_0/C_1$ and $D^* = C_0^*/C_1^*$. Accordingly,

$$D^w = \mu_d D + (1 - \mu_d)D^*, \tag{7.14}$$

where the home-country weight is

$$\mu_d = \frac{C_1}{C_1 + C_1^*}. \tag{7.15}$$

The initial equilibrium is exhibited by point A in figure 7.1. As shown, the world rate of interest is r_0, and the world consumption ratio (indicating the reciprocal of the growth rate of world consumption) is C_0^w/C_1^w. The home and foreign consumption ratios corresponding to this equilibrium are C_0/C_1

and C_0^*/C_1^*, as indicated by points B and C, respectively. We also note that the home and foreign relative supplies associated with this equilibrium are z and z^*, as indicated by points D and E, respectively. As is evident, these levels of relative supplies are associated with the equilibrium levels of home and foreign investment. Finally, because point B lies to the right of point D, whereas point C lies to the left of point E, the home economy runs an initial-period trade-balance deficit, whereas the foreign economy runs an initial-period trade-balance surplus.

7.3   Budget Deficit and the World Rate of Interest

We consider next the effects of a budget deficit in the home country arising from a current tax cut. Of course, the intertemporal government budget constraint implies that, as long as government spending remains intact, the current tax cut must be followed by a future rise in taxes. The main conclusion of the analysis is that the effect of budget deficits depends critically on whether it arises from changes in the timing of consumption or income taxes.

Consider first a budget deficit in the home country arising from a current-period consumption tax cut (followed by a corresponding rise in future consumption taxes). As is evident from the definitions of the effective discount factors in equation (7.2), such a tax shift raises the effective discount factor governing consumption decisions, α_c, while leaving the discount factor governing investment decisions intact. These changes induce a substitution of demand from future to current consumption and induce rightward shifts of the home (and the world) relative demand schedules in figure 7.1 while leaving the relative supply schedules intact.

The budget deficit raises the world rate of interest and crowds out home and foreign investment. It also lowers the growth rate of home consumption while raising the growth rate of foreign consumption.

As is evident from the definitions of the effective discount factors in equation (7.2), a budget deficit in the home country arising from a cut in current income tax rates (and followed by a corresponding rise in future income tax rates) lowers the effective discount factor governing investment decisions, α_I, and discourages home investment while leaving α_c intact. In terms of figure 7.1 these tax changes induce a rightward shift of the home (and the world) relative supply schedule while leaving the relative demand schedules intact. As a result, the world rate of interest falls, foreign investment rises, and the home investment is crowded out. At the same time the lower world rate of interest lowers the growth rate of both home and foreign consumption.

7.4   Dynamic Simulations of Budget Deficits

The simulations that allow for a variable labor supply in a multiperiod model illustrate the key relations implied by the theoretical model: they underscore the critical importance of the underlying tax system in determining the macroeconomic effects of budget deficits. They also provide further insights into the dynamic consequences of budget deficits.

Figures 7.2 and 7.3 contain selected simulations of the dynamic effects of current-period budget deficits under a consumption tax (that is a destination-based VAT) system and under a cash-flow income tax (that is a source-based VAT) system, respectively. We assume that the current-period deficit arises from a 10 percent reduction in tax rates, which is made up for by a permanent rise in tax rates in all future periods. By and large, the directions of changes in the various variables in the two figures are the opposite of each other. This underscores the key proposition of the theoretical analysis. In addition, the simulations show that the effects of the budget deficit on the qualitative characteristics of the time path of employment and output also depend critically on the underlying tax system. Specifically, under a consumption tax system, a home budget deficit exerts recessionary effects on the contemporaneous levels of home employment and output and expansionary effects on the corresponding levels abroad. These employment and output effects are reversed in all future periods. In contrast, under an income tax system, the same budget deficit induces a contemporaneous expansion at home and a recession abroad. These changes are reversed in subsequent periods. In general, the international transmission of the effects of budget deficits is shown to be negative in both the short and the medium run.

We also note that the current-period budget deficit exerts opposite effects on the levels of domestic and foreign consumption. Under a consumption tax system the deficit raises current-period home consumption and lowers the corresponding level of foreign consumption. These changes are reversed in subsequent periods. In contrast, under an income tax system home consumption falls in the current period while foreign consumption rises, and, as before, these changes are reversed in subsequent periods. Again, in terms of the correlations between home and foreign consumption, the simulations demonstrate the negative transmission of the effects of home budget deficits.

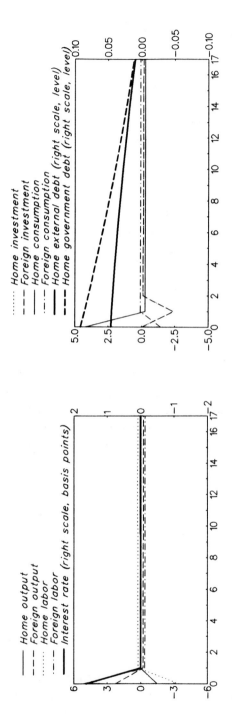

Figure 7.2
Budget deficit under the consumption tax system: 10 percent decrease in consumption tax in year 0, $\delta = \delta^*$, $r_k = r_k^*$

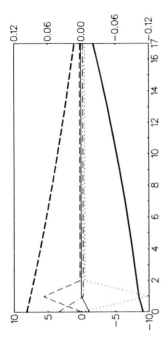

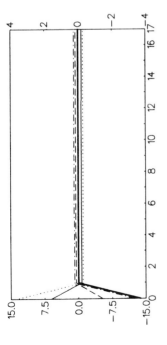

Figure 7.3
Budget deficit under the income tax system: 10 percent decrease in consumption tax in year 0, $\delta = \delta^*$, $r_k = r_k^*$

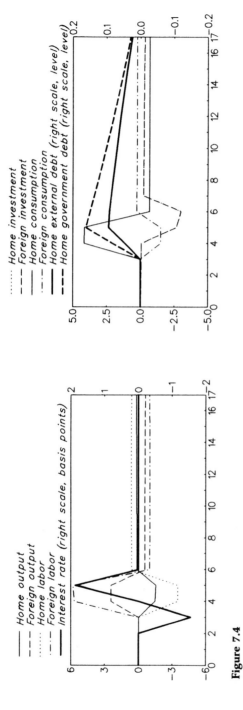

Figure 7.4
Budget deficit system: 10 percent decrease in consumption tax in years 4 and 5, $\delta = \delta^*$, $r_k = r_k^*$

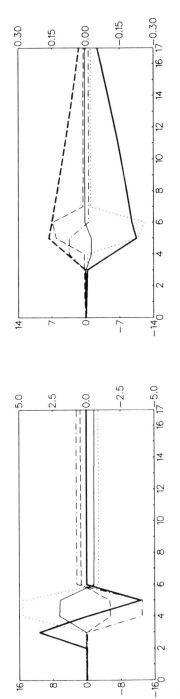

Figure 7.5
Budget deficit under the income tax system: 10 percent decrease in income tax in years 4 and 5, $\delta = \delta^*$, $r_k = r_k^*$

The effects of the budget deficits on the time path of consumption and leisure influence the levels of home and foreign welfare. Using the utility function specified in equations (7.3) and (7.4), our simulations show that the current period budget deficit, arising from a 10 percent reduction in consumption tax rate, raises the level of home welfare (by about 2 percent) and lowers the level of foreign welfare (by about 1.5 percent). In contrast, if the current-period budget deficit arises from a 10 percent reduction in the income tax rate, then the level of home welfare falls (by about 3.5 percent). These opposite changes in the levels of home and foreign welfare reflect the negative transmission of the effects of budget deficits.

The effects of an expected future-period budget deficit are shown in figures 7.4 and 7.5. These simulations show the consequences of an expected 10 percent tax cut in period 4 and 5 that is then made up for by a permanent rise in tax rates in all subsequent periods. As before, they reveal the central role played by the tax system. They also reveal the general feature of a negative transmission. However, because the various changes in tax rates occur only in the more distant future, our simulations show that their effects on the levels of home and foreign utility (viewed from the standpoint of the current period) are very small.

8

Simulations of International VAT Harmonization

This chapter presents a simulation analysis of the dynamic effects of international VAT harmonization.[1] Such policies form an important ingredient of the wide-ranging measures associated with the move toward the single European market of 1992. In the fiscal area the European Commission has drawn up various proposals on the approximation of the rates and the harmonization of the structures of VAT.

The process of harmonization of the VAT systems started with the First Council Directive of April 1967 and has proceeded thereafter through consecutive Directives. The process involved the adoption of VAT in various member countries and the continuous convergence of rates and structures among members of the community. Much of the discussions surrounding the practical implementation of the convergence of the VAT rates concerned the width of bands within which various VAT rates should be placed, the products to which a reduced rate would be applicable, and the problem of zero-rated products.[2] For 1992 the Commission envisages a standard VAT rate ranging between 14 percent and 20 percent, and a reduced rate (applied to selected categories, such as foodstuffs) ranging between 4 percent and 9 percent. The Commission proposes to abolish the higher rate that presently exists in some member countries on certain categories of goods. In subsequent discussions an alternative proposal was considered according to which the standard rate band would be replaced by a minimum rate applicable from January 1, 1993. Each member state would choose a rate at least equal to the minimum rate, with due regard to the budgetary implications and to the "competitive pressures" arising from the rates chosen by other neighboring states and main trading partners. Table 8.1 (reproducing table 3.2 in chapter 3) provides a summary of VAT in the European Community. It illustrates the disparities among the various member-country VAT rates.[3]

Table 8.1
Value-added taxes in the European Community

Country	Year of introduction	Statutory rates[a]			Scope of zero rate	VAT as percent of tax revenue[b]	VAT as percent of GDP[b]
		Standard rate	Increased rate	Reduced rate			
Belgium	1971	19	25, 33	1, 6, 17	Newspapers	16.3	7.2
Denmark	1967	22	—	—	Newspapers, large ships, aircraft	26.9	
France[c]	1968	18.6	25	5.5	—	20.9	8.7
Germany, Fed. Rep. of	1968	14	—	7	—	13.1	3.8
Greece[d]	1987	16	36	3, 6	—	20.9	7.8
Ireland	1972	23	—	0, 5, 10	Wide range of items	18.9	8.0
Italy	1973	19	38	4, 9	Newspapers, some minor items	13.1	4.7
Luxembourg	1970	12	—	3, 6	—	13.3	6.0
Netherlands	1969	18.5	—	6	—	15.2	7.9
Portugal[e]	1986	17	30	8	Basic foods, newspapers, medicines, agricultural inputs	18.8	7.7
Spain	1986	12	33	6	—	16.0	5.3
United Kingdom	1973	17.5	—	0	Wide range of items	16.3	6.0

Sources: "EC: The Evolution of VAT Rates Applicable in Member States of the Community," *Intertax*, (1987/3); International Bureau of Fiscal Documentation, *Tax News Service*, various issues; IMF, *Government Finance Statistics Yearbook* (1989), and OECD, *Revenue Statistics of OECD Member Countries, 1966–1988* (Paris, 1989).

a. As of July 1990.

b. Data for 1987.

c. France applies VAT rates of 2.1 percent to daily newspapers and some medicines, and 13 percent to sales and transfers of building land. Different VAT rates apply in Corsica.

d. Different rates apply in Dodecanese.

e. Different rates apply in the Azores and Madeira.

One of the central issues that needs to be addressed is the budgetary consequences of the harmonization in the VAT systems. As table 8.1 indicates, the VAT constitutes a significant revenue source in the European Community. As a result, a few member states (notably Denmark and Ireland) would suffer considerable tax revenue losses, whereas others (notably Spain, Luxembourg, and Portugal) would see their tax revenue go up considerably. In the subsequent section we present dynamic simulations of the consequences of international harmonization of VAT.

8.1   Simulations of VAT Harmonization with Current-Account Imbalances

In this section we analyze the effects of revenue-neutral VAT harmonization by means of dynamic simulations. We use a two-country model of the world economy and presume that prior to the VAT harmonization the two countries use very different tax systems. The home-country tax revenue stems from a high income tax, whereas the foreign-country revenue stems from a high VAT. The harmonization of VAT entails a rise in the home-country VAT rate and an equivalent reduction in the foreign VAT rate. Our analysis allows for current-account imbalances.

To avoid the budgetary imbalances consequent on the changes in the VAT rates, we ensure revenue neutrality, *period by period*, by assuming that the induced budgetary imbalances are corrected through changes in income tax rates. Accordingly, in the home country the rise in the VAT is accompanied by a reduction in income tax rates, whereas in the foreign country the fall in the VAT rate is accompanied by a corresponding rise in income tax rates. The narrowing of the international disparities among VATs captures the Commission's proposal of reducing the disparities of VAT rates among member countries and categories of goods. The maintenance of budgetary balance through appropriate changes in income tax rates reflects the supposition that due to considerations involving monetary policy and debt management, member countries do not wish to change drastically their budgetary stance.

In performing the simulations we first computed a baseline equilibrium. This equilibrium was then perturbed by the assumed VAT harmonization. The various figures presented show the effects of the tax restructuring, measured as percentage deviations from the baseline levels. The Appendix outlines the formal simulation model.

As indicated by previous theoretical analysis, one of the key factors governing the effects of revenue-neutral tax conversions is the time pattern of the current-account position.[4] Because the current-account positions can be expressed in terms of the saving-investment gap, they reflect inter-country differences either in saving propensities, induced, for example, by differences between the subjective discount factors, δ and δ^*, or in invest-ment patterns induced, for example, by differences between the productivi-ties of capital, r_k and r_k^*. To highlight the key role played by current-account positions, we plot in figures 8.1–8.4 the simulation results for cases dis-tinguished according to the time pattern of current-account imbalances. In these figures we assume that the income tax used in both countries is of the cash-flow variety.[5]

We assume that the home country raises permanently its VAT by 6 percent and restores its tax revenue by lowering its cash-flow income tax rates; the foreign country (whose initial VAT rate is assumed to be high) lowers permanently its VAT by 6 percent and restores its tax revenue by raising its cash-flow income tax rates. The figures show the paths of domestic and foreign output, labor supply, savings, investment, and consumption as well as the paths of the world rate of interest and the home country's external debt consequent on the VAT harmonization. All paths are expressed as percentage deviations from baseline (except for the rate of interest, whose deviation is expressed in basis points). The simulations reveal that the international VAT harmonization triggers a dynamic response in all the key macroeconomic variables. The specific nature of the dynamic response reflects international differences in the parameters governing saving and investment patterns.

The key features of the simulation analysis of tax harmonization under-lying figures 8.1–8.4 are summarized in table 8.2, which also reports the implied welfare implications of the VAT harmonization. To capture the es-sence of the dynamic evolution of the various variables, we report in table 8.2 the directions of change for both the short run (SR) and the medium run (MR).

The results in table 8.2 demonstrate the key role played by the current-account position. Specifically, if in the early stage the home country runs a current-account deficit due to low saving or high investment (e.g., if $\delta < \delta^*$, or $r_k > r_k^*$), then the paths of domestic and foreign income tax rates rise over time so as to maintain constant tax revenue. As a result, the world rate of interest falls.[6] In that case the rates of growth of domestic and foreign consumption (g_c and g_c^*, respectively) fall, in both the short and the medium runs.

If, on the other hand, the configuration of saving and investment pro-pensities is such that the home country runs a current-account surplus in the early stage, then the dynamic effects of the VAT harmonization on these variables are reversed. Specifically, if in the home country saving is high or investment is low (e.g., if $\delta > \delta^*$, or $r_k < r_k^*$), then the paths of domestic and foreign income tax rates fall while the world rate of interest rises. In that case the rates of growth of domestic and foreign consumption rise. Thus, under the present cash-flow income tax system the directions of changes in the world rate of interest and in the growth rates of consumption consequent on international VAT harmonization depend exclusively on the paths of the saving-investment gap.

The lower panel of table 8.2 summarizes the corresponding short- and medium-run changes in other key economic variables. As can be seen in the cases considered, the international VAT harmonization crowds out domestic investment and crowds in foreign investment independent of the current-account positions. These investment responses reflect the induced changes in the domestic and foreign tax incentives and in the world rate of interest. These changes yield two conflicting effects: the effect of the change in the world rate of interest and the opposite effect of the change in the tax wedges induced by the alteration of the time paths of income tax rates.

The changes in the tax structure also alter the intraperiod tax incentives governing labor supply and consumption demand. These tax incentives are subject to conflicting forces, because the changes in the consumption-tax rates and the associated changes in the income tax rates induce opposite effects on both labor supply and consumption demand. In addition to these conventional substitution mechanisms the simulation results also reflect wealth effects on labor supply and consumption demand induced by changes in the intertemporal terms of trade (the world rate of interest) and by changes in the excess burden associated with the distorted tax system. Finally, the time paths of labor supply and consumption demand are altered by the intertemporal substitution induced by changes in incentives governing labor supply and consumption demand. The changes in incentives arise from the change in the world rate of interest and, in the case of labor supplies, from the changes in the time paths of income taxes.

The welfare effects of term-of-trade changes depend on the magnitude of the change in the terms of trade and on the gap between purchases and sales of the good whose relative price has changed. In our intertemporal context the terms of trade correspond to the world rate of interest, and the gap between purchases and sales corresponds to the current-account position. As illustrated by table 8.2, in all cases the change in the terms of trade operates in favor of the country that raises its VAT. When the country runs a current-account deficit (i.e., when it borrows in the world economy), its intertemporal terms of trade improve, because the rate of interest falls.

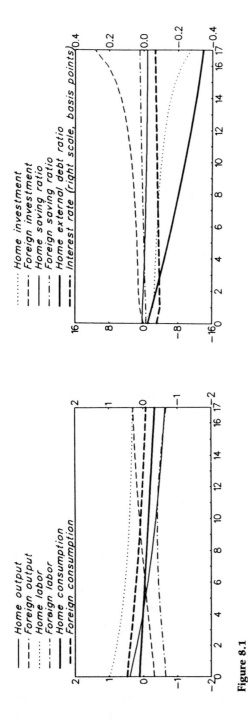

Figure 8.1
VAT harmonization: 6 percent permanent increase in home country VAT and 6 percent permanent reduction in foreign country VAT (percentage deviations), $\delta < \delta^*$

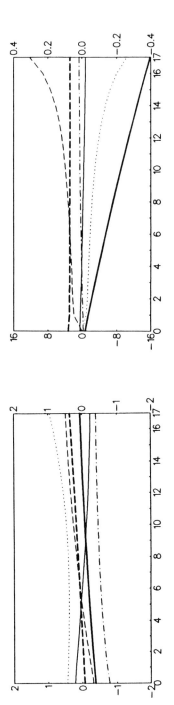

Figure 8.2
VAT harmonization: 6 percent permanent increase in home country VAT and 6 percent permanent reduction in foreign country VAT (percentage deviations). $\delta > \delta^*$

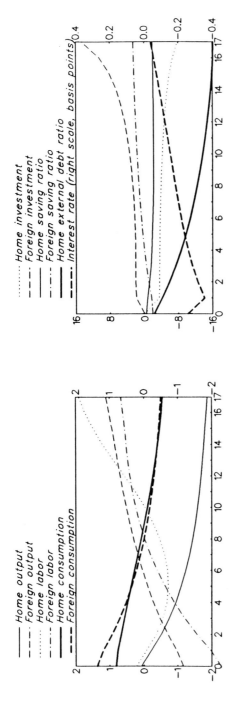

Figure 8.3
VAT harmonization: 6 percent permanent increase in home country VAT and 6 percent permanent reduction in foreign country VAT (percentage deviations), $r_k > r_k^*$

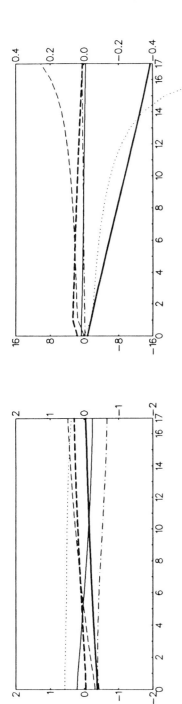

Figure 8.4
VAT harmonization: 6 percent permanent increase in home country VAT and 6 percent permanent reduction on foreign country VAT (percentage deviations), $r_k < r_k^*$

Table 8.2
Effects of VAT harmonization under alternative current-account positions (deviations from baseline)

	Home-country current-account deficit				Home-country current-account surplus			
	$\delta < \delta^*$ $r_k = r_k^*$		$\delta = \delta^*$ $r_k > r_k^*$		$\delta > \delta^*$ $r_k = r_k^*$		$\delta = \delta^*$ $r_k < r_k^*$	
Variable	SR	MR	SR	MR	SR	MR	SR	MR
Path of τ_y	Rising		Rising		Falling		Falling	
Path of τ_y^*	Rising		Rising		Falling		Falling	
r	−	−	−	−	+	+	+	+
g_c	−	−	−	−	+	+	+	+
g_c^*	−	−	−	−	+	+	+	+
I	−	−	−	−	−	−	−	−
I^*	+	+	+	+	+	+	+	+
L	+	+	−	+	+	+	+	+
L^*	−	−	−	−	−	−	−	−
Y	+	−	−	−	+	−	+	+
Y^*	−	+	−	+	−	+	−	+
C	+	−	+	−	−	+	−	−
C^*	+	−	+	−	−	+	+	+
S	+	−	−	−	+	−	+	−
S^*	−	+	−	+	−	+	−	+
B	−	−	−	−	−	−	−	−
U	0.2	−8.2	−0.1	−6.7	0.3	−7.6	0.3	−8.5
U^*	−0.3	8.4	−0.3	10.9	−0.3	9.2	−0.3	7.8

Note: The VAT harmonization obtains through a permanent narrowing of the gap in the consumption tax between the two countries (i.e., a 6 percent reduction in the home country together with a 6 percent rise in the foreign country). Budget balance obtains through appropriate adjustments in the periodic income tax rates, τ_y and τ_y^*. SR and MR denote, respectively, the short run and the medium run. The tax system is a cash-flow system. In general, the short run pertains to the first new periods, whereas the medium run pertains to the remaining periods in the simulation. For the utility index, SR pertains to the discounted sum of utilities over the entire periods except for the final one, whereas MR pertains to the final-period utility (reflecting the entire future beyond the simulation period). The other symbols are defined as follows: δ = subjective discount rate, r_k = marginal product of capital, r = rate of interest, g_c = growth rate of consumption, I = net investment, L = labor supply, Y = income, C = consumption, S = savings, B = international borrowing, U = utility, (asterisks denote the foreign-country variable). The welfare measure is the percentage factor by which post-harmonization path of consumption must be raised to bring utility up to the preharmonization level.

Likewise, if the country's current-account position is in surplus, its inter-temporal terms of trade also improve, because the rate of interest rises. As illustrated by the table, this improvement in the home-country welfare induced by the changes in the world rate of interest can be mitigated (or even offset) by the excess-burden effects of the VAT harmonization. Similar considerations apply to the welfare consequences of the reduction in VAT in the foreign economy.

A comparison between the effects of the international VAT harmoniza-tion on the domestic and the foreign economies reveals that in the two countries the levels of foreign employment, investment, output, and some other key macroeconomic indicators change in opposite directions. In fact, in most cases the utility index indicates that home and foreign welfare move in opposite directions. These phenomena suggest the possibility that inter-national VAT harmonization may induce international conflicts of interest. A resolution of such conflicts may necessitate international fiscal transfers from countries benefiting from the VAT harmonization to countries that lose. The potential difficulties arising from international conflicts of interest may be augmented by internal conflicts of interest associated with re-distributions of income between labor and capital in the short and medium runs.[7]

8.2   Simulations of VAT Harmonization with Current-Account Balances

The foregoing analysis was confined to the case in which the income taxes used to restore budgetary balance following the international VAT harmonization are of the cash-flow variety. Under such circumstances the current-account positions play the key role in determining the direction of changes in the world rate of interest and the growth rates of home and foreign consumption. As indicated by the simulations in figures 8.1–8.4 and in the summary results in the lower panel of table 8.2, the dynamic effects of the international VAT harmonization on the paths of the other key macroeconomic variables do not depend only on the current-account posi-tions. In fact, for the cases shown in these simulations home investment, foreign employment, foreign savings (in the short run), and the level of the home country's external debt are reduced independent of the current-account positions, whereas foreign investment and foreign savings (in the medium run) always rise.

To gain further insights into the effects of VAT harmonization under alternative income tax systems in cases where the current-account position does not play a role, we focus in this section on an analysis of VAT harmonization in circumstances where the saving and investment propensities do not differ internationally. Accordingly, we assume in what follows that $\delta = \delta^*$ and $r_k = r_k^*$, and we consider in addition to the cash-flow income tax system other tax systems: labor-income tax, capital-income tax, capital-income tax combined with saving incentives, and capital-income tax combined with investment incentives. These tax and incentive schemes are formulated in the Appendix. The results of the simulations are shown in figures 8.5−8.9 and are summarized in table 8.3.

The multiplicity of mechanisms and channels operating on the various tax incentives result in a variety of configurations of the response of the other key economic variables, as illustrated for the cases shown in table 8.3. Of special interest are the welfare effects indicated by the utility index in the simulations. As always, the welfare consequences of tax policies can be decomposed into two components: (1) those arising from changes in excess burden and (2) those arising from terms-of-trade effects. The changes in the degree of excess burden induced by VAT harmonization depend on the elasticity of the tax base as well as on the magnitude of the existing distortion. In the cases illustrated by the simulations, we have chosen parameters that result in relatively low investment and labor-supply elasticities and a relatively high consumption elasticity.[8] This choice suggests that in this cash-flow income tax system the excess burden associated with a consumption tax is relatively high in comparison with the corresponding excess burden associated with an income tax.

The assumption that the saving and investment propensities do not differ internationally implies that the initial current-account positions are balanced. As a result, the international VAT harmonization does not alter the world rate of interest. The dynamics of adjustment in this case arise only from the effects of the tax wedges on the various incentives. These are the circumstances underlying figures 8.5−8.9 and table 8.3.

We note first that with a labor-income tax system the VAT harmonization does not induce any change in the time path of domestic and foreign investment. Second, whenever the income tax system contains an investment-incentive component, it dominates in its effect on the paths of investment. Indeed, under the cash-flow income tax system (which obviously contains an investment-incentive component), and under a system of capital-income tax combined with investment incentives, the path of domestic investment consequent on the reduced income tax is lowered for both the short and the medium runs. The opposite occurs in the foreign country.

This pattern is reversed under income tax systems that do not contain incentives to investment.

Third, and analogously to the foregoing reasoning, whenever the income tax system contains a saving-incentive component (which alleviates the double taxation of savings), its effect dominates the changes in consumption. Thus, under the cash-flow income tax system and under a system of capital-income tax combined with saving incentives, the path of home consumption consequent on the VAT harmonization is lowered for both the short and the medium runs. The opposite occurs in the foreign country. This pattern is reversed under the labor-tax system.

Fourth, whenever the income tax system contains a tax on labor income, changes in that tax dominate the effect of the VAT harmonization on employment. Thus, under the cash-flow income tax system and under the system of labor-income tax, the path of home employment consequent on the reduced income tax is raised for both the short and the medium runs. The opposite occurs in the foreign country in which income taxes rise. Finally, by inspecting the figures, we can infer the effects of the VAT harmonization under alternative tax systems on the growth rates of home and foreign output and on the path of external debt.

The previous discussion of the simulations underlying figures 8.1–8.4 and table 8.3 indicated the potential for international conflicts of interest with respect to the implementation of VAT harmonization under the cash-flow income tax system. An examination of figures 8.5–8.9 and table 8.3 suggests that the potential for such conflicts of interest is not unique to the cash-flow system. In fact, as is evident under all tax systems considered, the directions of changes in home and foreign employment, output, consumption, savings, and investment consequent on the international VAT harmonization are the opposite of each other in both the short and the medium runs. The same phenomenon emerges from an examination of the utility indices of economic welfare: home and foreign SR welfare changes (expressed by the factor by which post-harmonization consumption path must be raised to bring utility up to the preharmonization level) move in opposite directions, and in general the same holds for the MR utility indices (reflecting the entire future beyond the simulation period). Furthermore, the cases considered the VAT harmonization results in a redistribution of welfare between generations. This is evident from the opposite directions of changes in the SR and MR utility indices within each country. The various simulations show that the changes in the utility indices largely reflect a *redistribution* of world welfare, since the *sum* of the home and foreign utility indices does not change appreciably. This result underscores the notion that

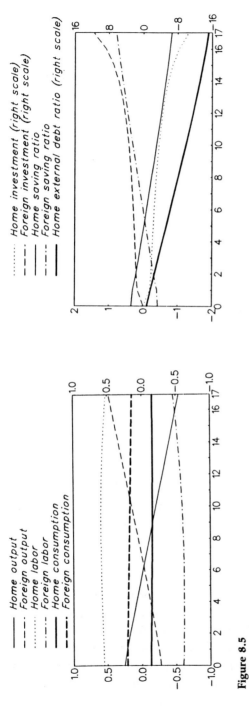

Figure 8.5
VAT harmonization: 6 percent permanent increase in home country VAT and 6 percent permanent reduction in foreign country VAT under the cash flow tax system (percentage deviations)

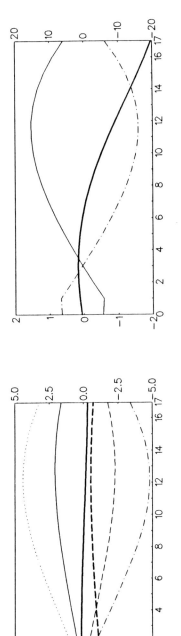

Figure 8.6
VAT harmonization: 6 percent permanent increase in home country VAT and 6 percent permanent reduction in foreign country VAT under labor income tax system (percentage deviations)

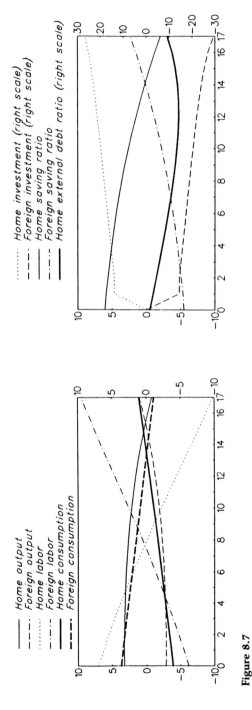

Figure 8.7
VAT harmonization: 6 percent permanent increase in home country VAT and 6 percent permanent reduction in foreign country VAT under capital income tax system (percentage deviations)

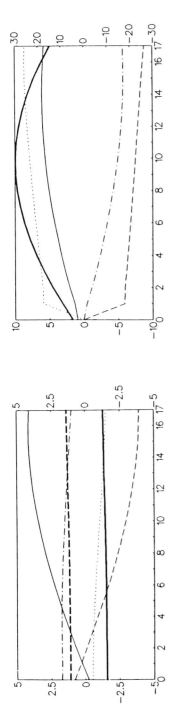

Figure 8.8
VAT harmonization: 6 percent permanent increase in home country VAT and 6 percent permanent reduction in foreign country VAT under capital income tax and saving incentives system (percentage deviations)

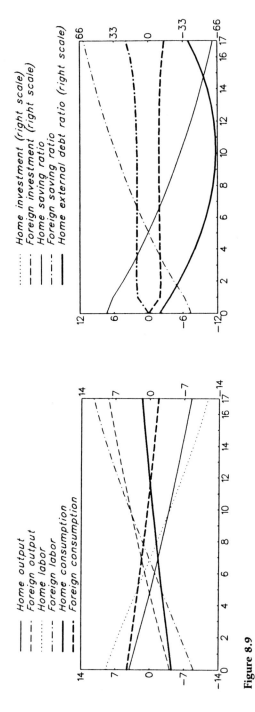

Figure 8.9
VAT harmonization: 6 percent permanent increase in home country VAT and 6 percent permanent reduction in foreign country VAT under capital income tax and investment incentives system (percentage deviations)

Table 8.3
Effects of VAT harmonization under alternative tax systems

Variable	Cash flow income tax		Labor income tax		Capital income tax		Capital income tax and saving incentives		Capital income tax and investment incentives	
	SR	MR	SR	MR	SR	MR	SR	MR	SR	MR
r	0	0	0	0	0	0	0	0	0	0
I	—	—	0	0	+	+	+	+	—	—
I^*	+	+	0	0	—	—	—	—	+	+
L	+	+	+	+	+	—	—	—	+	—
L^*	—	—	—	—	—	+	+	+	—	+
Y	+	—	+	+	+	—	—	+	+	—
Y^*	—	+	—	—	—	+	+	—	—	+
C	—	—	+	+	—	+	—	—	—	+
C^*	+	+	—	—	+	—	+	+	+	—
S	+	—	—	+	+	—	+	+	+	—
S^*	—	+	+	—	—	+	—	—	—	+
B	—	—	+	—	—	—	+	+	—	—
U	0.3	−7.8	0.0	−12.5	1.4	−7.0	1.2	−3.0	1.0	−7.8
U^*	−0.3	8.7	0.1	14.6	−1.0	7.3	−0.8	2.2	−0.8	8.4

Note: The VAT harmonization obtains through a permanent 6 percent rise in τ_C and a 6 percent fall in τ_C^*. Budgetary balance obtains through appropriate adjustments in the periodic rates of cash flow, labor income, and capital income taxes (with and without saving incentives). The technology and preference parameters of the two countries are assumed to be equal (so that the current account position is balanced). SR and MR are defined as short run and medium run, respectively. The welfare measure is defined by the percentage factor by which the post-harmonization path of consumption must be raised in order to bring utility up to the preharmonization level.

the resolution of international conflicts of interest in implementing the VAT harmonization may necessitate a compensation mechanism from gainers to losers.

8.3   Conclusion

One of the major developments in the world economy during the 1990s is likely to be the move toward the single market of Europe of 1992. The removal of barriers to trade and factor movements, the unification of markets, the developments of new monetary arrangements, and the increased harmonization of fiscal policies and tax structures are all key factors in a process that is likely to shape the global economic system for years to come.

One of the elements of the move toward tax harmonization in the European Community involves a convergence of the various VAT systems. In this chapter we analyzed the global effects of such an international VAT harmonization. To examine the quantitative implications of international VAT harmonization, we performed dynamic simulations. The analysis as well as the simulations demonstrated that the effects of VAT harmonization on the key macroeconomic variables (such as output, employment, investment, consumption, interest rates, the current account, and the value of external debt) are very significant. Furthermore, these effects (quantitatively and qualitatively) are not spread evenly across income groups, generations, and countries. As a result such a VAT harmonization may give rise to internal conflicts of interest within each country (arising from changes in the distribution of income among members of each generation as well as among generations) and among countries. The international differences in the incidence of the VAT harmonization arise from differences in the current-account positions (reflecting underlying differences in saving and investment propensities) as well as from differences in the tax structures. The resolution of the various conflicts of interest regarding the adoption of VAT harmonization may give rise to the development of a fiscal mechanism by which gainers compensate losers within countries as well as among countries.

8.4   Appendix

The Tax Model

We start with a formulation of the budget constraint. The home country's private-sector (full-income) budget constraint applicable to period t ($t = 0, 1, \ldots, T - 1$) is

$$(1 + \tau_{Ct})C_t + (1 - \tau_{wt})w(1 - \ell_t)$$

$$= (1 - \tau_{wt})w + (1 - \tau_{kt})(r_k - \theta)K_t - (1 - \tau_{It})I_t\left(1 + \frac{g}{2}\frac{I_t}{K_t}\right)$$

$$+ (B_t^p - B_{t-1}^p) - (1 - \tau_{kt})(1 + \tau_{st})r_{t-1}B_{t-1}^p, \tag{8.1}$$

where τ_{Ct}, τ_{wt}, and τ_{kt} denote the tax rates on consumption (a destination-based VAT), labor income, and capital income, respectively; the income taxes are residence-based. The terms τ_{It} and τ_{st} denote an investment incentive and a foreign-lending incentive, respectively. (These can be viewed as some variants of investment-tax credit and saving-tax credit, respectively.) The levels of consumption, labor supply, capital stock, investment, and the private-sector international borrowing are denoted, respectively, by C_t, ℓ_t, K_t, I_t, and B_t^P. The wage rate, the capital-rental rate, and the interest rate are denoted, respectively by w, r_k, and r_t; and θ denotes the rate of depreciation. For convenience, we normalize the endowment of leisure to unity and assume costs of adjustment in capital formation of the form $(\frac{1}{2})gI_t^2/K_t$. We note that in the final period (period T) the private sector settles its debt commitments, and no new investment or new borrowing occurs, so that $I_T = B_T^P = 0$.[9] To facilitate the simulation analysis in subsequent sections, we need to adopt a specific form of the multiperiod utility function. Accordingly, we assume that the intraperiod utility function between consumption of ordinary goods and leisure is

$$u_t = [\beta C_t^{(\sigma-1)/\sigma} + (1-\beta)(1-\ell_t)^{(\sigma-1)/\sigma}]^{\sigma/(\sigma-1)}, \tag{8.2}$$

and the interperiod utility function is

$$U_0 = \sum_{t=0}^{T} \delta^t \log(u_t) \tag{8.3}$$

where σ is the temporal elasticity of substitution between leisure and consumption of ordinary goods, β is the distributive parameter of consumption, and δ is the subjective discount factor. This formulation implies a unitary intertemporal elasticity of substitution.

The maximization of the utility functions subject to the lifetime present-value budget constraint yields

$$u_t = \left(\sum_{s=0}^{T} \delta^s\right)^{-1} \frac{W_0}{p_t} \frac{\delta^t}{\alpha_t} \tag{8.4}$$

$$p_t = [\beta^\sigma(1+\tau_{Ct})^{1-\sigma} + (1-\beta)^\sigma((1-\tau_{wt})w)^{1-\sigma}]^{1/(1-\sigma)} \tag{8.5}$$

$$C_t = \frac{\beta^\sigma(1+\tau_{Ct})^{-\sigma}p_t u_t}{\beta^\sigma(1+\tau_{Ct})^{1-\sigma} + (1-\beta)^\sigma((1-\tau_{wt})w)^{1-\sigma}} \tag{8.6}$$

$$1-\ell_t = \frac{(1-\beta)^\sigma((1-\tau_{wt})w)^{-\sigma}p_t u_t}{\beta^\sigma(1+\tau_{Ct})^{1-\sigma} + (1-\beta)^\sigma((1-\tau_{wt})w)^{1-\sigma}}, \tag{8.7}$$

where u denotes the utility-based real spending, p denotes the associated price index, C denotes consumption of ordinary goods, and $1-\ell$ denotes leisure. In these equations $t = 1, 2, \ldots, T$; a_t is the tax-adjusted present-value factor applicable to period t, that is, $\alpha_t = (1+(1-\tau_{k1})(1+\tau_{s1})r_0)^{-1}$ $(1+(1-\tau_{k2})(1+\tau_{s2})r_1)^{-1} \ldots (1+(1-\tau_{kt})(1+\tau_{st})r_{t-1})^{-1}$; and wealth,

W_0, is

$$W_0 = \sum_{t=0}^{T} \alpha_t \left[(1 - \tau_{wt})w + (1 - \tau_{kt})(r_k - \theta)K_t - (1 - \tau_{It})I_t \left(1 + \frac{g}{2}\frac{I_t}{K_t} \right) \right]$$

$$+ \alpha_T(1 - \tau_{kT})aK_T - [1 + (1 - \tau_{k0})(1 + \tau_{s0})r_{-1}]B^p_{-1}. \tag{8.8}$$

The investment equation, I_t, is obtained by a maximization of wealth, W_0, with respect to investment, I_t, which yields

$$-(1 - \tau_{It})\alpha_t \left(1 + g\frac{I_t}{K_t} \right) + \sum_{s=t+1}^{T-1} \alpha_s(1 - \theta)^{s-t-1} \left[(1 - \tau_{ks})(r_k - \theta) \right.$$

$$\left. + (1 - \tau_{Is})\frac{g}{2}\left(\frac{I_s}{K_s} \right)^2 \right] + \alpha_T(1 - \theta)^{T-t-1}(1 - \tau_{kT})(r_k + a - \theta) = 0.$$

$$\tag{8.9}$$

Equation (8.9) represents an implicit investment rule. The negative term is equal to the marginal cost of investment in period t, whereas the positive terms are equal to the marginal benefits consisting of the rise in output and the decline in costs of adjustment resulting from the increased capital stock (the terms associated with $(g/2)(I/K)^2$) and the residual value of period T's capital. To illustrate, in the two-period case the investment function implied by equation (8.9) is

$$I_0 = \frac{1}{g}[\alpha_1 \frac{(1 - \tau_{k1})}{(1 - \tau_{I0})}(a + r_k - \theta) - 1]K_0. \tag{8.10}$$

Equation (8.10) together with the assumption that $(a + r_k - \theta)$ exceeds unity (an assumption necessary for a positive level of investment in the two-period case) implies that the level of investment rises with the initial capital stock, K_0, with the effective (tax-adjusted) discount factor, $\alpha_1(1 - \tau_{k1})/(1 - \tau_{I0})$, with the rental rate net of depreciation, $r_k - \theta$, and with the consumption coefficient, a, attached to the final-period capital. On the other hand, investment falls with an increase in the cost-of-adjustment parameter, g. Substituting equation (8.10) into (8.8) yields the corresponding value of wealth:

$$W_0 = \sum_{t=0}^{1} \alpha_t(1 - \tau_{wt})w + q_0K_0 - [1 + (1 - \tau_{k0})(1 + \tau_{s0})r_{-1}]B^p_{-1}, \tag{8.11}$$

where q_0 denotes the tax-adjusted market value of a unit of the capital stock (Tobin's q):

$$q_0 = (1 - \tau_{k0})(r_k - \theta) + \alpha_1(1 - \tau_{k1})(m + 1 - \theta)(r_k + a - \theta)$$
$$- (1 - \tau_{I0})m(1 + gm/2), \tag{8.12}$$

where

$$m = (1/g)[\alpha_1(1 - \tau_{k1})(r_k + a - \theta)/(1 - \tau_{I0})] - (1/g).$$

The parameter values used in the baseline simulations are $\beta = \beta^* = 0.4$, $\delta = \delta^* = 0.97$, $\sigma = \sigma^* = 0.3$, $r_k = r_k^* = 0.3$, and $a = a^* = 0.2$. For intercountry differences in the parameter values of the discount factor we use $(\delta = 0.95, \delta^* = 0.97)$ or $(\delta = 0.97, \delta^* = 0.95)$; and for intercountry differences in the parameter values of the marginal product of capital we use $(r_k = 0.2, r_k^* = 0.3)$ or $(r_k = 0.3, r_k^* = 0.2)$.

IV

International Taxation and
Capital Flows

9

Capital Market Integration and the Cost of Public Funds

International capital market integration has become the subject of major theoretical and practical interest in recent times. Both economists and policymakers are becoming increasingly aware of the potential benefits accruing from such integration, because it allows more efficient allocations of investment and saving between the domestic and foreign markets.

The opening up of an economy to international capital movements affects, as expected, both the size and the structure of the fiscal branch of its government. Evidently, capital flows influence both the optimal structure of taxes, on domestic and foreign-source income, and the welfare cost of taxation. As a result, the optimal size of government (the optimal provision of public goods) and the magnitude of redistribution (transfer) policies are affected as well. In this broad context this chapter analyzes the effects of relaxing restrictions on the international flow of capital on the fiscal branch of government.

The optimal size of government, or, more precisely, the optimal provision of public goods, must be determined by an appropriate cost-benefit analysis. Such an analysis concludes that the marginal cost of public funds must be equated to the marginal utility of public goods. Accordingly, to assess the effects of liberalization in the international capital markets on the optimal quantity of public goods, we study here the effect of the liberalization on the cost of public funds. In addition to the deadweight losses from taxes, these costs arise also from changes in the internal terms of trade associated with nontradables and labor costs.

In calculating the cost of public funds one must take into account the optimal response of the structure of taxation (on incomes from all sources) to the liberalization policy, because the cost of public funds is ultimately derived from a process of tax optimization. Therefore, we analyze the effect of the liberalization on the structure of taxation. Evidently, entangled with the structure of taxation is also the issue of the optimal size of income redistribution. For this reason we also analyze the effect of international capital market liberalization on the optimal redistribution (transfer) policy of the government.

The economic rationale underlying the effect of liberalization on the cost of public funds is as follows. Suppose that the government can effectively tax income from capital invested abroad. As elaborated upon in chapter 5, a liberalization of the capital market improves welfare. Therefore, such a liberalization entails an income effect. And such an effect usually tends to increase the marginal utility of public goods. In addition, it may lower the marginal cost of public funds, because the government benefits directly from the liberalization as it taxes the increased amount of income from the capital invested abroad and can therefore lower the tax burden on domestic sources. Therefore, the income effect tends to increase the provision of public goods and the size of income redistribution. On the other hand, the liberalization may change the internal terms of trade (e.g., the real wage) and affect directly the cost of producing public goods. The effect of this change in the terms of trade on the cost of public funds and the size of government cannot be determined a priori and is examined both analytically and numerically.

9.1   The Analytical Framework

To highlight the issue of the effect of liberalization on the cost of public funds we employ here a simplified version of the workhorse model of the small open economy of chapter 5. This simple version has the following features. There is a single all-purpose good that can be used for private or public consumption or for investments. In the first period the economy possesses an initial endowment of this composite good. Individuals can decide how much of their initial endowments to consume and how much to save. Saving is allocated to either domestic investment or foreign investment. In the second period, output (produced by capital and labor) and income from foreign investment are allocated between private and public consumption. To simplify we assume that the government is active only in the second period and that the adjustment costs associated with the investment process are negligible. As before, the government employs taxes on labor, taxes on income from domestic investment, and taxes on income from investment abroad to finance optimally (that is, taking into account both efficiency and equity considerations) both public consumption and a (uniform, lump-sum) subsidy for redistribution purposes.

For simplicity, while still capturing real-world basic features, we also assume that government spending on public goods does not affect individual demand patterns for private goods or the supply of labor. That is, the taxes needed to finance these expenditures do affect individual demands and supplies, but the expenditures themselves do not. Formally, this feature is captured in the model by assuming that the utility function is weakly separable between private goods and services on the one hand and public goods and services on the other. That is, individual h's utility is

$$U^h(C_{0h}, C_{1h}, \ell_h, G) = u^h(C_{0h}, C_{1h}, \ell_h) + m^h(G), \tag{9.1}$$

where u^h and m^h are the private and public components of the utility function, respectively; C_{0h}, C_{1h}, and ℓ_h denote present consumption, future consumption, and future first-period labor supply, respectively; and G denotes (future) public consumption.

We denote saving in the form of domestic capital by K_h and saving in the form of capital invested abroad by L_h. Aggregate saving in the form of domestic capital is equal to the stock of capital in period one, since we assume for concreteness, without affecting the results, that the patterns of capital flows are such that the country is a capital exporter (i.e., $\Sigma_h L_h \geqslant 0$). Hence, the budget constraints of individual h are

$$C_{0h} + K_h + L_h = E_h, \tag{9.2}$$

$$C_{1h} = K_h[1 + r(1 - \tau_{rD})] + L_h[1 + r^*(1 - \tau_{rA})] + (1 - \tau_\ell)w\ell + S', \tag{9.3}$$

where

τ_{rD} = tax on capital income from domestic sources;

τ_{rA} = tax on capital income originating abroad;

τ_ℓ = tax on labor income;

S' = lump-sum subsidy;

r = domestic rate of interest;

r^* = foreign rate of interest (net of taxes levied abroad);

w = wage rate; and

E_h = initial (first-period) endowment.

Obviously, in the absence of quantity restrictions on capital flows, individuals must earn the same net return on both forms of investments, that is, $r(1 - \tau_{rD}) = r^*(1 - \tau_{rA})$. However, with restrictions on capital flows, the latter equality does not have to hold. In such a case inframarginal profits on investment abroad are generated, resulting from (net) interest differential. One possibility is for these profits to accrue to the individual investors.

Another possibility is for the government fully to tax away these profits. (This is the equivalent capital-export tax version of the capital-export quota.) We adopt here the second possibility, namely, that the government chooses the level of the tax on capital income originating abroad (τ_{rA}) so as to eliminate any inframarginal profits. Thus, whether or not there are restrictions on foreign investment, the government chooses τ_{rA} so as to maintain the equality $r(1 - \tau_{rD}) = r^*(1 - \tau_{rA})$. That is, the rate of tax on capital income originating abroad is equal to

$$\tau_{rA} = \frac{r^* - r(1 - \tau_{rD})}{r^*}.$$

Under this tax scheme the individual is indifferent between investing at home (K_h) or abroad (L_h), caring only about the level of total investment ($K_h + L_h$). Thus, at equilibrium the size of the aggregate domestic capital is determined by the demand for capital by domestic firms. The latter is determined by the standard equalization of the marginal product of capital to the domestic rate of interest, r.

We can consolidate the two budget constraints into a single (present-value) constraint:

$$C_{0h} + q_C C_{1h} = E_h + q_\ell \ell_h + S, \tag{9.4}$$

where

$$q_C = [1 + (1 - \tau_{rD})r]^{-1} \tag{9.5}$$

is the consumer (after-tax) price of future consumption,[1]

$$q_\ell = (1 - \tau_\ell)w[1 + (1 - \tau_{rD})r]^{-1} \tag{9.6}$$

is the consumer price of labor, and $S = q_C S'$ is the present value of the subsidy. Maximization of the utility function u^h, subject to the budget constraint (9.4), yields the consumption-demand functions

$$C_{ih} = c_{ih}(q_C, q_\ell; E_h + S), \qquad (i = 0, 1,) \tag{9.7}$$

and the labor-supply function

$$\ell_h = \ell_h(q_C, q_\ell; E_h + S), \tag{9.8}$$

and the utility obtained from these demand and supply functions, namely, the indirect utility function,

$$V_h = v_h(q_C, q_\ell; E_h + S). \tag{9.9}$$

Domestic output, Y, is produced in the second period by capital and labor, according to a constant-returns-to-scale production function

$$Y = F(K, \ell), \tag{9.10}$$

where $K = \Sigma_h K_h$ is the stock of domestic capital, and $\ell = \Sigma_h \ell_h$ is the aggregate supply of labor.

The economywide resource constraints require that

$$E = C_0 + L + K \tag{9.11}$$

and

$$Y + (1 + r^*)L + K = C_1 + G, \tag{9.12}$$

where $E = \Sigma_h E_h$ is aggregate present endowment, $L = \Sigma_h L_h$ is aggregate investment abroad, $C_0 = \Sigma_h C_{0h}$ is aggregate consumption in period zero, and $C_1 = \Sigma_h C_{1h}$ is aggregate consumption in period one.

Substituting (9.2), (9.7), (9.8), (9.10), and the present-period resource constraint (9.11) into the future-period resource constraint (9.12) yields the equilibrium condition

$$F[E - c_0(q_C, q_\ell; E_1 + S, \dots, E_n + S)$$
$$- L, \ell(q_C, q_\ell; E_1 + S, \dots, E_n + S)] + (1 + r^*)L$$
$$+ [E - c_0(q_C, q_\ell; E_1 + S, \dots, E_n + S) - L]$$
$$- c_1(q_C, q_\ell; E_1 + S, \dots, E_n + S) - G = 0. \tag{9.13}$$

Observe that aggregate consumptions, c_0 and c_1, and the aggregate labor supply, ℓ, depend not only on aggregate income but also on the distribution of income.

9.2 International Capital Flows: Alternative Regimes

We consider now two alternative regimes. In the first the government sets quantity restrictions on capital exports; in the second there are no restrictions on capital exports, and L is determined by market clearance.

The optimal tax/transfer policy and provisions of public goods are obtained as a solution to the program of maximizing the indirect social welfare function

$$W(q_C, q_\ell; E_1 + S, \dots, E_n + S) = \Sigma_h \gamma_h v^h(q_C, q_\ell; E_h + S) + \Sigma_h \gamma_h m^h(G), \tag{9.14}$$

subject to the resource constraint (9.13). The coefficient γ_h may be viewed as the social weight of the individual h.[2] This specification, which is common in the public finance literature, enables the government to operate directly, not on private-sector demand and supply quantities, but rather on prices (through taxes) that affect these quantities. The government tax policy thus focuses on q_C, q_ℓ, and S as control variables. In the first regime we treat L as a parameter. In the second regime L is a control (endogenous) variable. Notice, however, that this does not mean that the government directly determines the level of investment abroad; rather, the government, through its tax policy, affects total savings $(K + L)$ and domestic investment, K, and L is determined as a residual (the difference between total savings and domestic investment).

Notice that, by Walras's law, the government budget constraint is satisfied. Also, the wage rate, w, and the domestic rate of interest, r, are determined by the standard marginal productivity conditions: $F_K = r$ and $F_\ell = w$. Given q_C and q_ℓ, we can solve for the tax rates, τ_{rD} and τ_ℓ, by using (9.5) and (9.6).

9.3 Efficient Capital Flows

Obviously, because distortionary taxes are part of the optimal program, resource allocation is not Pareto efficient: the intertemporal allocation of consumption, the leisure-consumption choice, and the private-public consumption trade-offs are all distorted. Nevertheless, as shown in chapter 5, the fully optimal program (namely, the second regime, where no restrictions on L exist) requires an efficient allocation of capital between investment at home and abroad, so that $F_K = r^*$. That is, the marginal product of domestic capital must equal the foreign rate of return on capital (net of foreign taxes).

To see this formally, observe that the endogenous variable L does not appear in the objective function (9.14), so that the first-order conditions for optimality require that the derivative of the resource constraint (9.13) with respect to L, that is, $- (1 + F_K) + (1 + r^*)$, be equal to zero. Hence, $F_K = r^*$. As was pointed out earlier, this is an open-economy variant of the aggregate efficiency theorem in optimal tax theory.

Notice again that this production efficiency result also implies that there should be no differential tax treatment of foreign and domestic sources of income. Namely, the *residence principle* applies:

$$\tau_{rD} = \tau_{rA} \tag{9.15}$$

It might be argued that our investment efficiency result (i.e., equating the return on capital at home to the return on capital abroad by means of free international capital flows) is not valid when the government is concerned about financing its debt, because the opening of an economy to international capital flows raises the domestic interest rate, r, to the world rate, r^*. In such a case a government burdened by an ongoing deficit incurs a higher interest cost of financing this deficit. In fact, the government loses its monopsony power in the domestic capital market. It can then be argued that the government may not wish to allow residents to invest abroad. Nevertheless, the investment efficiency result is still valid. The economic reasoning is that the government can offset the cost of losing its monopsony power by an appropriate welfare-enhancing tax policy, and indeed this is called for to ensure efficiency.

However, in the presence of restrictions on capital exports the production efficiency result does not hold: the return to capital at home may be lower than the net (after foreign taxes) return on investment abroad. Nevertheless, a small relaxation of this restriction still improves welfare.

9.4   The Cost of Public Funds in an Open Economy

We now turn to examine the first regime, where restrictions on L exist. In the presence of distortionary taxes the social cost of an additional dollar raised by taxes (namely, the marginal cost of public funds) may exceed one dollar, owing to the existence of excess burden (deadweight loss) of taxation. The optimal provision of public goods is determined by equating the marginal benefit with the marginal cost of public funds. In this section we directly examine the effect of relaxing the restrictions on L on the optimal level of G. Because we have assumed that the marginal benefit from G is diminishing (a concave m), it follows that the optimal G increases if and only if the marginal cost of public funds declines. In this way we indirectly analyze also the effect of the liberalization in the international capital markets on the marginal cost of public funds.

Formally, we treat L as a parameter and examine the effect of changing L on the optimal quantity of the public good. Specifically, the optimal level of the public good is a function of L, denoted by $\overline{G}(L)$. We then look for the sign of $d\overline{G}/dL$ in the region where $F_K = r < r^*$, so that increasing L enhances production efficiency and, thus, social welfare.

For given levels of G and L let us maximize the private component of W in (9.14) (namely, $\Sigma_h \gamma_h v_h[q_C, q_\ell; E_h + S]$), subject to the resource constraint (9.13). We denote the value of the maximand by $N(L, G)$. Then, for a given

L, the optimal G is determined by solving

$$\max_{G}\{N(L, G) + M(G)\}, \qquad (9.16)$$

where $M(G) = \Sigma_h \gamma_h m^h(G)$.
  The first-order condition is

$$N_2 + M' = 0, \qquad (9.17)$$

and the second-order condition is

$$N_{22} + M'' \leqslant 0. \qquad (9.18)$$

Totally differentiating (9.17) with respect to L yields

$$\frac{d\bar{G}}{dL} = \frac{N_{12}}{-(N_{22} + M'')}. \qquad (9.19)$$

By (9.18) the denominator in (9.19) is positive. Hence,

$$\text{Sign}\left(\frac{d\bar{G}}{dL}\right) = \text{Sign}(N_{12}). \qquad (9.20)$$

  To concentrate on efficiency in the next subsection, we abstract from redistribution considerations.

Efficiency Considerations

We suppose therefore that all individuals are alike so that we may consider a single representative individual and drop the index h. Alleviating the constraint on foreign lending affects the optimal size of government through two channels. First, increasing L generates an additional source of revenues for the government, thereby allowing lower distortionary taxes on existing sources. This tends to lower the marginal cost of public funds (and raise the size of government). Second, increasing L may adversely affect the internal terms of trade (associated with nontradable factors or goods) for government expenditures. This effect can raise the marginal cost of public funds (and lower the size of government). To highlight these two effects, we consider first the pure income effect.

Constant Internal Terms of Trade
We assume a linear production function, yielding constant real factor prices: $\bar{r}(\leqslant r^*)$ and $\bar{w}$, for capital and labor, respectively. In this case we can unambiguously show that $N_{12} > 0$ and, consequently, that $d\bar{G}/dL > 0$.

The function $N(L, G)$ is defined in this case by

$$N(L, G) = \max_{\{q_C, q_\ell, S\}} v(q_C, q_\ell; E + S), \tag{9.21}$$

subject to

$$\bar{r}[E - c_0(q_C, q_\ell; E + S) - L] + \bar{w}\ell(q_C, q_\ell; E + S)$$

$$+ [E - c_0(q_C, q_\ell; E + S) - L] + (1 + r^*)L$$

$$- c_1(q_C, q_\ell; E + S) - G = 0.$$

Hence, by the envelope theorem, we obtain

$$N_2(L, G) = -\lambda(L, G) \leqslant 0, \tag{9.22}$$

where $\lambda(L, G) \geqslant 0$ is the Lagrange multiplier associated with the constraint in (9.21). From (9.22) it follows that

$$N_{21}(L, G) = -\lambda_1(L, G). \tag{9.23}$$

Similarly, equation (9.21) (using the envelope theorem) yields

$$N_1(L, G) = \lambda(L, G)(r^* - \bar{r}) \geqslant 0. \tag{9.24}$$

Therefore,

$$N_{11}(L, G) = \lambda_1(L, G)(r^* - \bar{r}). \tag{9.25}$$

One can show (see the Appendix) that $N(.,.)$ is concave. Hence, $N_{11} < 0$, and it follows from (9.25) that $\lambda_1 < 0$. Thus, (9.23) implies that $N_{21} > 0$. Therefore, $d\bar{G}/dL > 0$. That is, the relaxation of international capital controls, in the absence of adjustment in the internal terms of trade, lowers the marginal cost of public funds and increases the optimal size of government.

Variable Internal Terms of Trade
To analyze the effect of variable internal terms of trade on government's expenditures in a simple manner, we assume that labor, the nontradable factor of production, exhibits diminishing marginal productivity and that government's expenditures are used entirely to hire labor. Specifically, we continue to assume constant internal intertemporal terms of trade, that is, that r is constant (at the level $\bar{r}$). However, in period one, consumption can be provided (in addition to saving in period zero) by a concave production function, $f(\ell)$, using labor alone. The rent (pure profit) generated by such a technology is assumed to be fully taxed by the government. The government hires ℓ_G units of labor in period one at the prevailing wage, $w = f'$.

The government does not purchase any quantity of the consumption good. We thus replace G with ℓ_G.

In this case the function $N(L, \ell_G)$ is defined by

$$N(L, \ell_G) = \max_{(q_C, q_\ell, S)} v(q_C, q_\ell; E + S) \tag{9.26}$$

subject to

$$\bar{r}[E - c_0(q_C, q_\ell; E + S) - L] + f[\ell(q_C, q_\ell; E + S) - \ell_G]$$

$$+ E - c_0(q_C, q_\ell; E + S) - L$$

$$+ (1 + r^*)L - c_1(q_C, q_\ell; E + S) = 0.$$

Following the same procedure as in the preceding section, we conclude that

$$N_{21}(L, \ell_G) = -\lambda_1(L, \ell_G)w - \lambda(L, \ell_G)\frac{dw}{dL}. \tag{9.27}$$

The first term in the expression for N_{21} is similar to (9.23). As before, it is straightforward to show that $\lambda_1 < 0$, so that this term contributes toward making N_{21} positive; that is, toward increasing the size of government in response to alleviating controls on foreign lending [see equation (9.19)]. However, the second term may work in the opposite direction: the pure income effect of raising L tends to increase the consumption of leisure, thereby increasing the cost of labor that the government hires. Thus, the optimal ℓ_G (namely, the real magnitude of government's consumption) may at the end decline in response to a liberalization of the international capital market. Note, however, that if capital and labor are substitutes in production, capital exports per se tend to lower the wage rate and thus lower the cost of public funds.

Redistribution Considerations

Now, we reintroduce the redistribution motive. To simplify the exposition we suppose that the economy consists of two individuals (or two classes of individuals), denoted by A and B. We further simplify the analysis by assuming a fixed labor supply (and dropping labor altogether from the model). Thus, we are left only with intertemporal decisions and tax-induced intertemporal distortions. Further, we employ a log-linear utility function to keep the analysis tractable.

To emphasize the equity issues, we consider the extreme case of a max-min social welfare criterion; that is, we assume for the social welfare function in (9.14) that $\gamma_B = 0$ and $\gamma_A = 1$ (where $E_A < E_B$). The function N, the maximized value of the private component in the social welfare function W, is defined in this case by

$$N(L, G) = \max_{\{\tau_{rD}, S\}} \{\alpha \log[\alpha(I_A + S)]$$

$$+ (1 - \alpha) \log[(1 - \alpha)(E_A + S)(1 + \bar{r}(1 - \tau_{rD}))]\} \qquad (9.28)$$

subject to

$$(1 + \bar{r})[(E_A + E_B)(1 - \alpha) - 2\alpha S]$$

$$- (1 - \alpha)[1 + \bar{r}(1 - \tau_{rD})](E_A + E_B + 2S)$$

$$+ (r^* - \bar{r})L - G = 0,$$

where the log-linear individual utility function is given by

$$u(C_0, C_1) = \alpha \log C_0 + (1 - \alpha) \log C_1. \qquad (9.29)$$

Employing the constraint to eliminate S, we can reduce (9.28) to

$$N(L, G) = \max_{\tau_{rD}} \{\log[2E_A(1 + \bar{r}) + \tau_{rD}(1 - \alpha)\bar{r}(E_B - E_A)$$

$$+ (r^* - \bar{r})L - G] - \log[1 + \bar{r}(1 - (1 - \alpha)\tau_{rD})]$$

$$+ (1 - \alpha) \log[1 + \bar{r}(1 - \tau_{rD})] + \text{constant}\}$$

$$= \max_{\tau_{rD}} H(\tau_{rD}, L, G). \qquad (9.30)$$

The first-order condition for τ_{rD} is

$$H_1(\tau_{rD}, L, G) = 0, \qquad (9.31)$$

whereas the second-order condition is

$$H_{11}(\tau_{rD}, L, G) \leqq 0. \qquad (9.32)$$

By the envelope theorem,

$$N_1(L, G) = H_2(\tau_{rD}, L, G);$$

hence,

$$N_{12} = H_{21} \frac{\partial \tau_{rD}}{\partial G} + H_{23}. \qquad (9.33)$$

Total differentiation of (9.31) with respect to G yields

$$\frac{\partial \tau_{rD}}{\partial G} = -\frac{H_{13}}{H_{11}}. \tag{9.34}$$

Hence, from (9.33) and (9.34) we obtain the following expression for N_{12}:

$$N_{12} = \frac{H_{12}H_{13} - H_{23}H_{11}}{-H_{11}}. \tag{9.35}$$

Because $H_{11} \leqslant 0$ (by (9.31)), it follows that

$$\text{Sign}(N_{12}) = \text{Sign}(H_{12}H_{13} - H_{23}H_{11}). \tag{9.36}$$

Using the definition of H [namely, equation (9.30)] to find the partial derivatives H_{ij}, and substituting these derivatives into (9.36), we conclude that

$$\text{Sign}(H_{12}H_{13} - H_{23}H_{11}) = \text{Sign}\left\{\frac{1}{[1 + \bar{r}(1 - \tau_{rD})]^2}\right.$$

$$\left. - \frac{(1 - \alpha)}{[1 + \bar{r}(1 - (1 - \alpha)\tau_{rD})]^2}\right\} \tag{9.37}$$

(see the Appendix).

Because $0 < 1 - \alpha < 1$, it follows that (9.37) is positive and hence that $d\bar{G}/dL > 0$.

We conclude that the liberalization lowers the costs of public funds and increases the provision of the public good.

Tax Structure and Income Redistribution in an Open Economy

We now examine the effects of relaxing the controls on international capital flows on the structure of taxation and size of redistribution. We continue to adopt the simplified framework of the previons subsection. We assume further that the public component in the utility function $m^4(G)$ is equal to $\delta \log G$. In this case the optimal policy is the solution to the following problem:

$$\max_{\{\tau_{rD}, G\}} \{H(\tau_{rD}, L, G) + \delta \log G\}, \tag{9.38}$$

where $H(\cdot)$ is defined in (9.30).

As before, L is a parameter, and we consider the relations between this parameter and the optimal values of τ_{rD} and G (denoted by $\bar{\tau}_{rD}(L)$ and $\bar{G}(L)$, respectively). In doing so, we also find the effect of changing L on τ_{rD} and S, as will be shown later.

The first-order conditions are

$$H_1(\tau_{rD}, L, G) = 0 \tag{9.39}$$

and

$$H_3(\tau_{rD}, L, G) + \frac{\delta}{G} = 0. \tag{9.40}$$

Total differentiation of (9.39)–(9.40) with respect to L yields

$$\frac{d\bar{\tau}_{rD}}{dL} = \frac{1}{\Delta}\left(-H_{12}H_{33} + H_{13}H_{23} + \frac{H_{12}\delta}{G^2}\right), \tag{9.41}$$

where Δ is positive by the second-order conditions for the solution to (9.38). In the Appendix we show that

$$-H_{12}H_{33} + H_{13}H_{23} = 0 \tag{9.42}$$

and

$$H_{12} < 0. \tag{9.43}$$

Hence, $d\bar{\tau}_{rD}/dL < 0$.

Thus, relaxing the controls on investments abroad reduces the optimal rate of tax on income from domestic investment. This conclusion is supported by economic intuition in view of the fact that relaxing the controls improves welfare. Because $\tau_{rA} = [r^* - (1 - \tau_{RD})\bar{r}]/r^*$, it follows that τ_{rA} should be lowered too. That is, the optimal response to relaxing the restrictions on investments abrod is to lower the tax on income form such investments.

To find $d\bar{S}/dL$ (the response of the optimal subsidy, denoted by $\bar{S}$, to a change in L), recall that the constraint in (9.28) was employed to solve for S in terms of τ_{rD}, L, and G:

$$S = \frac{\bar{r}\tau_{rD}(1 - \alpha)(E_A + E_B) + (r^* - \bar{r})L - G}{2\{1 + \bar{r}[1 - (1 - \alpha)\tau_{rD}]\}}. \tag{9.44}$$

We have already concluded that an increase in L raises G and lowers τ_{rD}. These changes have conflicting effects on S, as can be seen from (9.44). We employed numerical calculations to demonstrate the effect of raising L on the optimal S. These calculations suggest that raising L increases the size of the demogrant S. Again, this result is intuitive in view of the fact that relaxing the restrictions on international capital outflows improves the efficiency of total redistribution of income. (Note that if the government

Table 9.1
The effect of capital controls on the optimal supply of public good, tax rates, and
demogrant

L	G	τ_{rD}	τ_{rA}	S
0	0.191	1.399[a]	1.266[a]	0.381
0.25	0.193	1.391[a]	1.261[a]	0.402

Note: Parameter values: $\alpha = 0.6$, $\delta = 0.05$, $\bar{r} = 0.50$, $r^* = 0.75$, $E_A = 1.0$, $E_B = 3.0$, $\gamma_A = 1$, $\gamma_B = 0$.
a. Note that physical investment and foreign lending are the only forms of transferring resources from the present to the future. Hence, τ_{rD} and τ_{rA} may well exceed one, as long as $1 + (1 - \tau_{rD})$ and $1 + (1 - \tau_{rA})r^*$ are still positive.

does not tax away the inframarginal profits arising from the quota, then, due to the government's budget constraint, S must decline when G rises and τ_{rD} falls.)

The results of the numerical calculations are given in table 9.1.

9.6 Conclusion

In this chapter we analyzed the policy implications of the integration of the international capital markets. We paid special attention to the effects on the marginal cost of public funds, a crucial factor in the determination of the optimal size of government and the magnitude of income redistribution. Inherent in the determination of the cost of public funds is the design of the structure of taxation (on labor income, domestic-source capital income, and foreign-source capital income).

We reiterate that it is not efficient to impose restrictions on capital exports and that every incremental move toward a more liberalized policy concerning the international flows of capital is welfare improving. The liberalization lowers or raises the cost of public funds depending on the intensity of the welfare improvment and the behavior of the internal terms of trade.

9.7 Appendix

The function $N(L, G)$

In this section we prove that $N(L, G)$ is concave. Recall that $N(L, G)$ is defined by (9.21). Because there is only one individual and a lump-sum tax/subsidy is allowed, it follows that the government can choose any bundle (C_0, C_1, ℓ) that is feasible [i.e., that satisfies the resource constraint in (9.21)]. Thus, N may equivalently be defined by

$$N(L, G) = \underset{\{C_0, C_1, \ell\}}{\text{Max}} \ u(C_0, C_1, \ell) \tag{9.45}$$

subject to

$$\bar{r}(E - C_0 - L) + \bar{w}l + E - C_0 + r^*L - C_1 - G \geqslant 0.$$

We have to show that

$$N[aL' + (1 - a)L'', aG' + (1 - a)G''] \geqslant aN(L', G') + (1 - a)N(L'', G'')$$

for all (L', G'), (L'', G''), and $0 \leqslant a \leqslant 1$.

Suppose that the bundle (C_0', C_1', ℓ') is a solution to (9.45) for $(L, G) = (L', G')$ and that the bundle (C_0'', C_1'', ℓ'') is a solution to (9.45) for $(L, G) = (L'', G'')$; namely, $N(L', G') = u(C_0', C_1', \ell')$ and $N(L'', G'') = u(C_0'', C_1'', \ell'')$.

By being solutions to (9.45), the bundles (C_0', C_1', ℓ') and (C_0'', C_1'', ℓ'') satisfy the constraint in (9.45), namely,

$$\bar{r}(E - C_0' - L') + \bar{w}\ell' + E - C_0' + r^*L' - C_1' - G' \geqslant 0 \tag{9.46}$$

and

$$\bar{r}(E - C_0'' - L'') + \bar{w}\ell'' + E - C_0'' + r^*L'' - C_1'' - G'' \geqslant 0. \tag{9.47}$$

Hence, on multiplying (9.46) by the factor a and (9.47) by the factor $(1 - a)$ and adding them together, we have

$$\bar{r}\{E - [aC_0' + (1 - a)C_0''] - [aL' + (1 - a)L'']\}$$
$$+ \bar{w}[a\ell' + (1 - a)\ell''] + E - [aC_0' + (1 - a)C_0'']$$
$$+ r^*[aL' + (1 - a)L''] - [aC_1' + (1 - a)C_1'']$$
$$- [aG' + (1 - a)G''] \geqslant 0. \tag{9.48}$$

Thus, the bundle $[aC_0' + (1 - a)C_0'', aC_1' + (1 - a)C_1'', a\ell' + (1 - a)\ell'']$ is feasible for $(L, G) = [aL' + (1 - a)L'', aG' + (1 - a)G'']$. Therefore,

$$N[aL' + (1 - a)L'', aG' + (1 - a)G'']$$
$$\geqslant u[aC_0' + (1 - a)C_0'', aC_1' + (1 - a)C_1'', a\ell' + (1 - a)\ell'']$$
$$\geqslant au(C_0', C_1', \ell') + (1 - a)u(C_0'', C_1'', \ell'')$$
$$= aN(L', G') + (1 - a)N(L'', G''),$$

where the first inequality in (9.49) follows from the definition of $N(.,.)$ as the value of the maximand in (9.45), and the second inequality follows from the concavity of u. This completes the proof of the concavity of N.

Derivation of (9.37), (9.42)–(9.43)

In this subsection we verify the expressions of (9.37) and prove (9.42)–(9.43). The function H [see (9.30)] is given by

$$H(\tau_{rD}, L, G) = \log[2E_A(1 + \bar{r}) + \tau_{rD}(1 - \alpha)\bar{r}(E_B - E_A)$$
$$+ (r^* - \bar{r})L - G] - \log[1 + \bar{r}(1 - (1 - \alpha)\tau_{rD})]$$
$$+ (1 - \alpha)\log[1 + \bar{r}(1 - \tau_{rD})] + \text{constant}. \qquad (9.50)$$

The first-order derivatives are

$$H_1 = [2E_A(1 + \bar{r}) + \tau_{rD}(1 - \alpha)\bar{r}(E_B - E_A)$$
$$+ (r^* - \bar{r})L - G](1 - \alpha)\bar{r}(E_B - E_A)$$
$$+ \{1 + \bar{r}[1 - (1 - \alpha)\tau_{rD}]\}^{-1}\bar{r}(1 - \alpha)$$
$$- \bar{r}(1 - \alpha)[1 + \bar{r}(1 - \tau_{rD})]^{-1}, \qquad (9.51)$$

$$H_2 = [2E_A(1 + \bar{r}) + \tau_{rD}(1 - \alpha)\bar{r}(E_B - E_A)$$
$$+ (r^* - \bar{r})L - G]^{-1}(r^* - \bar{r}), \qquad (9.52)$$

and

$$H_3 = \frac{-H_2}{r^* - \bar{r}}. \qquad (9.53)$$

The second-order derivatives are

$$H_{11} = -(1 - \alpha)^2\bar{r}^2(E_B - E_A)^2[2E_A(1 + \bar{r}) + \tau_{rD}(1 - \alpha)\bar{r}(E_B - E_A)$$
$$+ (r^* - \bar{r})L - G]^{-2} + \bar{r}^2(1 - \alpha)^2\{1 + \bar{r}[1 - (1 - \alpha)\tau_{rD}]\}^2$$
$$- \bar{r}^2(1 - \alpha)[1 + \bar{r}(1 - \tau_{rD})]^{-2}, \qquad (9.54)$$

$$H_{12} = -(r^* - \bar{r})[2E_A(1 + \bar{r}) + \tau_{rD}(1 - \alpha)\bar{r}(E_B - E_A)$$
$$+ (r^* - \bar{r})L - G]^{-2}(1 - \alpha)\bar{r}(E_B - E_A), \qquad (9.55)$$

$$H_{13} = \frac{-H_{12}}{r^* - \bar{r}}, \qquad (9.56)$$

$$H_{22} = \frac{H_{12}(r^* - \bar{r})}{(1 - \alpha)\bar{r}(E_B - E_A)},$$ (9.57)

$$H_{23} = \frac{-H_{12}}{(1 - \alpha)\bar{r}(E_B - E_A)},$$ (9.58)

and

$$H_{33} = \frac{H_{12}}{(r^* - \bar{r})(1 - \alpha)\bar{r}(E_B - E_A)}.$$ (9.59)

Hence,

$$H_{12}H_{13} - H_{11}H_{33}$$
$$= \left(\frac{1}{[1 + \bar{r}(1 - \tau_{rD})]^2} - \frac{1 - \alpha}{\{1 + \bar{r}[1 - (1 - \alpha)\tau_{rD}]\}^2} \right)(r^* - \bar{r})\bar{r}^2(1 - \alpha)$$
$$\cdot \frac{1}{[2E_A(1 + \bar{r}) + \tau_{rD}(1 - \alpha)\bar{r}(E_B - E_A) + (r^* - \bar{r})L - G]^2}.$$

This verifies (9.37)

Next we prove (9.42) and (9.43). Employing (9.55), (9.56), (9.58), and (9.59), we find that

$$- H_{12}H_{33} + H_{13}H_{23} = \frac{-(H_{12})^2}{(r^* - \bar{r})(1 - \alpha)\bar{r}(E_B - E_A)}$$
$$+ \frac{(H_{12})^2}{(r^* - \bar{r})(1 - \alpha)\bar{r}(E_B - E_A)} = 0,$$

which proves (9.42). From (9.55), we observe that $H_{12} < 0$, which proves (9.43).

10

International Taxation and Capital Flight

The fundamental result of the theory of second-best suggests that adding distortions to already existing ones may very well enhance efficiency and welfare. To put it differently, reducing the number of distortions in the economy may well lower consumers' well-being. Thus, even though there are in general gains from international trade, some restrictions on free trade may be called for in a distortion-ridden economy. Nevertheless, in chapter 5 we showed that opening up an economy to international capital movements enhances efficiency and welfare, even in the presence of distortionary taxes (taxes that affect margins of substitution between labor and leisure, between consumption and savings, etc.), provided these taxes are designed optimally. The setup employed in that analysis assumed that the government can tax residents on their income from abroad.

However, there is now substantial evidence that governments encounter severe enforcement difficulties in attempting to tax foreign-source income. Dooley (1987) estimated that in the 1980–1982 time period as much as $250 billion might have been classified as capital flight by U.S. residents. Tanzi (1987a) reported that tax experts were concerned that lowering the U.S. individual and corporate tax rates in the U.S. Tax Reform Act of 1986 would induce capital drain from other countries by providing a tax advantage to investments in the United States. These concerns were based on the important assumption that the governments of these countries could not effectively tax their residents on their U.S. income so as to wipe out the U.S. tax advantage. The issue of capital flight is even more relevant for developing countries. Cumby and Levich (1987) estimated that a significant portion of the external debt in developing countries is channeled into investments abroad through overinvoicing of imports and underinvoicing of exports. Dooley (1988) estimated that capital flight from a large number of developing countries amounted to about one-third of their external debt in the period 1977–1984.

The purpose of this chapter is to examine the efficiency (from a social viewpoint) of free international capital movements in the presence of the severe difficulties of taxing foreign-source income due to capital flight. Specifically, we investigate whether it is appropriate to impose controls on capital exports or imports.

The economic intuition behind the desirability of imposing restrictions on capital mobility in the presence of tax enforcement failure is as follows. If the government allows unlimited exports of capital, then capital will flow out of the country up to the point where the net return on domestic investment equals the net return on investment abroad. This means that the marginal productivity of domestic capital will exceed the world rate of interest, so that the domestic stock of capital will be too small. The mirror image of such an underinvestment in capital at home is an overinvestment in capital abroad. In this context therefore it is efficient from the societal standpoint to restrict the exports of capital. How severe should the restriction be? One may ask, for instance, whether the restriction on exports of capital should bring the domestic capital stock all the way back to a level that is even higher than the level that is necessary for equating the marginal productivity of domestic capital to the world rate of interest (i.e., whether restrictions on capital exports should induce an overinvestment in domestic capital). Furthermore, is it possible that capital exports should be altogether banned when foreign-source income cannot be effectively taxed?

We show that when the government cannot effectively tax foreign-source income, it should put severe restrictions on capital exports and bring the marginal product of domestic capital to a level that is even below the world rate of interest. The loss in the return to the private sector on total investments (at home and abroad) due to the reallocation of capital from abroad to home is more than offset by the extra tax revenues accruing to the government from the income from the capital shifted back home.

Furthermore, if, under financial autarky, the marginal product of capital is sufficiently close to the world rate of interest, then a total ban on capital exports is called for. The rationale for this result is straightforward. When the marginal product of capital is close to the world rate of interest, investing abroad results in very little gain for society as a whole because this gain is equal only to the difference between the marginal product of capital and the world rate of interest (although the private sector can still gain considerably from investing abroad because the net-of-tax marginal product of capital may be considerably below the world rate of interest). However, the government loses a significant amount of tax revenues from the outflow of capital. Therefore, in this case, it is not efficient to allow exports of capital. To demonstrate how tight this argument is, we present a general equilibrium analysis of the effects of capital flight on capital market policies.[1]

10.1   The Analytical Framework

To focus on the issue of international capital mobility in the presence of tax enforcement failure, we employ again a simplified version of the workhorse model from chapter 5. The simplified model describes a small open economy with one composite good, serving both for private and public consumption and for investment. In the first period the economy possesses an initial endowment of the good, and individuals can decide how much of it to consume and how much of it to save. Savings are allocated either to investment at home or to investment abroad. As the focus of the chapter is on capital flows and capital-income taxation, we treat explicitly only capital as a variable factor of production. We assume other factors to be in fixed supply, thereby giving rise to a diminishing marginal productivity of capital. To simplify we assume no costs of adjustment for investment. In the second period, output and income from foreign investment are allocated between private and public consumption. To finance optimally public consumption, the government employs taxes on profits and capital income. For simplicity we assume that the government is active only in the second period.

In practice, governments encounter severe enforcement difficulties in attempting to impose taxes on foreign-source income. Accordingly, we concentrate on the case where such income is effectively taxed only partially. Under such circumstances one should consider quantitative restrictions on capital exports in addition to the tax instruments. In practice such restrictions are commonplace, taking various forms: exchange controls; currency convertibility constraints; specific bans on holding foreign bank accounts, foreign stocks, other securities and real estate abroad; and the like. Such measures usually reinforce each other. Even though in practice they are not completely effective in totally curtailing capital flight, they nevertheless form a fairly binding constraint on capital exports, giving rise to significant rate-of-return differentials between home and abroad.

Elaborate information on investments of home residents abroad is not required—neither the magnitudes of the investments nor their yields—for the implementation of these measures. Such information, which has to be updated periodically, is necessary to enforce taxes on foreign-source income of home residents. In other words, the enforcement technology associated

with quantity restrictions is relatively inexpensive and is therefore implementable. Notice that the method of auctioning off quotas of capital export,
which in theory is equivalent to a tax on foreign-source capital income, faces
essentially the same enforcement difficulties concerning information gather-
ing as the direct tax on foreign-source income. In essence the quota auctions
require continuous follow-up on the volume of the capital exported and the
reinvestment of the principal and the yield of the capital. This may explain
why in reality the method of auctioning off quotas of capital exports is
almost nonexistent.

We consider a representative individual with a utility function

$$U(C_0, C_1, G),   \tag{10.1}$$

where C_0 and C_1 are first-period (present) private consumption and second-
period (future) private consumption, respectively, and G is second-period
public consumption. We denote saving in the form of domestic capital by
K and saving in the form of foreign capital by L. Note that L represents
gross capital exports, but because in our deterministic economy there is no
room for the coexistence of capital exports and capital imports, L represents
also *net* capital exports. Since the focus of our analysis is on the case in which
income from capital invested abroad cannot be fully taxed, we assume that
the pattern of capital flows is such that the country is a capital exporter (i.e.,
$L \geq 0$). Hence, the amount of resident savings channeled to domestic investment constitutes also the domestic stock of capital in the second period.[2]

The private-sector budget constraints in the first and second period
are given, respectively, by

$$C_0 + K + L = E   \tag{10.2}$$

and

$$C_1 = K[1 + r(1 - \tau_{RD})] + L(1 + r^*),   \tag{10.3}$$

where:

τ_{RD} = tax on capital income from domestic sources;

r = domestic rate of interest;

r^* = world rate of interest (net of taxes levied abroad); and

E = initial endowment.

Efficiency considerations require government to tax pure profits (representing incomes from fixed factors) up to 100 percent before moving on
to employing distortionary taxes on capital income. We assume that the

size of government is large enough that taxing away pure profits is not sufficient to finance all government spendings. For this reason we assume that the pure profits are fully taxed away; therefore, no profit term appears on the right-hand side of the equation.[3]

Obviously, in the absence of quantity restrictions on capital flows, the private sector must earn the same rate of return on domestic investment and on investment abroad; that is, $r(1 - \tau_{RD}) = r^*$, where for simplicity we assume that foreign-source income is not taxed at all. However, when quantity restrictions are imposed on investment abroad, we have:

$$r(1 - \tau_{RD}) \leqslant r^*. \tag{10.4}$$

As is common, we consolidate the periodic budget constraints in equations (10.2) and (10.3) into a single (present-value) budget constraint:

$$C_0 + \alpha_1 C_1 = E + L[(1 + r^*)\alpha_1 - 1] \equiv N, \tag{10.5}$$

where

$$\alpha_1 = [1 + (1 - \tau_{RD})r]^{-1} \tag{10.6}$$

is the tax-adjusted discount factor that is also the consumer (after-tax) price of second-period consumption in present values.

The second term on the right-hand side of equation (10.5), namely, $L[(1 + r^*)\alpha_1 - 1]$, plays a crucial role in the analysis. Rate-of-return arbitrage eliminates this term if there are no restrictions on capital exports. Otherwise, when capital exports are restricted, the condition in equation (10.4) applies, and this term becomes positive, representing inframarginal gains to private-sector savings that are channeled abroad.

The maximization of the utility function U subject to the budget constraint in equation (10.5) yields the consumption-demand functions:

$$C_i = c_i\{\alpha_1, E + L[(1 + r^*)\alpha_1 - 1], G\}, \qquad i = 1, 2. \tag{10.7}$$

The utility obtained from these demand functions (the indirect utility function) is

$$V = v\{a_1, E + L[(1 + r^*)\alpha_1 - 1], G\}. \tag{10.8}$$

Domestic output, Y, is produced in the second period by capital according to a production function,

$$Y = F(K), \tag{10.9}$$

that exhibits diminishing marginal products. In the absence of investment costs of adjustment, the firm's demand for capital is determined by the marginal productivity condition:

$$F_K(K) = r. \tag{10.10}$$

Equilibrium in the first period requires that the demand for domestic capital, K, equal the supply of domestic capital, $E - C_0 - L$. That is,

$$K = E - C_0 - L. \tag{10.11}$$

Similarly, equilibrium in the second period requires the equalization of the (private and public) demand for and the supply of consumption goods:[4]

$$C_1 + G = F(K) + K + (1 + r^*)L. \tag{10.12}$$

Substituting equation (10.11) into equation (10.12) yields the single (consolidated) equilibrium condition[5]

$$F(E - C_0 - L) + (E - C_0 - L) + (1 + r^*)L - C_1 - G = 0. \tag{10.13}$$

10.2 Efficient Restrictions on Capital Exports

As we mentioned in the opening paragraph, if the government can fully tax foreign-source capital income, it is optimal to equate the marginal product of the domestic capital to the world rate of interest (the aggregate production efficiency proposition). That is, $F_K = r^*$. (This is the efficiency condition (5.37) in chapter 5 for the case $g = \theta = 0$.) Because $r = F_K$, it follows from the rate-of-return equalization (net of tax) that it is optimal to tax foreign-source capital income at the same rate as domestic capital income—the *residence principle*. We refer to this case as the *optimal regime*.

However, in this chapter we deal with the case where foreign-source income cannot be taxed. In this *suboptimal regime* capital export controls are potentially desirable. We now analyze the desirability of such controls.

If the government allows unlimited exports of capital, then capital will flow out of the country up to the point where the net return on domestic investment equals the net return on investment abroad:

$$(1 - \tau_{RD})r = r^*. \tag{10.14}$$

This means that $F_K = r > r^*$, so that the domestic stock of capital is smaller than in the optimal regime (where $F_K = r^*$), given that the marginal productivity of capital is diminishing. The mirror image of the under-investment in capital at home is the overinvestment in capital abroad.

An interesting question that arises in this context is whether it is efficient, from the society standpoint, to restrict the exports of capital, and if so, how severe should the restriction be? One could ask, for instance, whether restrictions on exports of capital should bring the domestic capital stock all the way back to a level that is even higher than in the optimal regime (thus generating an overinvestment in domestic capital.) Another question is whether capital exports should be altogether banned when foreign source income cannot be effectively taxed. We address these issues next.

The policy tools available to the government are the tax rate, τ_{RD}, on capital income from the domestic source, and the level of capital exports, L. Equivalently, the government can choose the tax-adjusted discount factor, α_1, and the exports quota, L. The objective is to maximize the welfare of the representative individual. Formally, the policy problem of optimally financing an exogenously given level of G is

$$\max_{\{\alpha_1, L\}} v\{\alpha_1, E + L[(1 + r^*)\alpha_1 - 1], G\} \tag{10.15}$$

subject to

$$F(E - c_0\{\alpha_1, E + L[(1 + r^*)\alpha_1 - 1], G\} - L)$$
$$+ E - c_0\{\alpha_1, E + L[(1 + r^*)\alpha_1 - 1], G\} + r^*L$$
$$- c_1\{\alpha_1, E + L[(1 + r^*)\alpha_1 - 1], G\} - G \geqslant 0.$$

If we assume an interior solution, the first-order conditions characterizing the optimal policy are[6]

$$\beta - \lambda = \frac{\alpha_1 \beta \tau_{RD} r \bar{c}_{0\alpha}}{(K/\alpha_1)} \tag{10.16}$$

and

$$\beta(r^* - r) = \frac{(\beta - \lambda)[(1 + r^*)\alpha_1 - 1]}{\alpha_1}, \tag{10.17}$$

where

$$\lambda = v_N \alpha_1 + \beta r \tau_{RD}(-c_{0N})\alpha_1. \tag{10.18}$$

In the preceding equations we denote the Lagrange multiplier of the optimal policy problem by $\beta > 0$; the partial derivatives of v and c_0 with respect to income (namely, $N \equiv E + L[(1 + r^*)\alpha_1 - 1]$) by v_N and c_{0N}, respectively; and the Hicks-Slutsky compensated derivative of c_0 with respect to α_1 by $\bar{c}_{0\alpha}$.

As pointed out by Peter Diamond (1975), λ is the social marginal value of private income. It consists of two terms: a direct change in utility created by giving the consumer an additional dollar of income, $v_N \alpha_1$, and an indirect effect consisting of the social value of the change in tax payments caused by the resulting change in the consumer's domestic savings, namely, $\beta r \tau_{RD} \alpha_1 (-c_{0N})$. (Recall that the consumer's domestic savings is $E - C_0 - L$, by equation (10.2).) Because β is the social marginal value of income in the hands of the government (i.e., the marginal utility of public consumption, if the public consumption is optimally chosen),[7] it follows that the term on the left-hand side of (10.6) measures the difference between the marginal value of income in the hands of the government and in the hands of the consumer. In a two-good (private) economy, with the two goods necessarily being substitutes, we must have $\bar{c}_{0\alpha} > 0$, and it follows from (10.16) that the latter difference must be positive—that is, income in a tax-distorted economy has a higher marginal value in the hands of the government than in the hands of the consumer.[8]

Equation (10.7) shows that the laissez-faire policy (no restriction on capital exports) is not efficient, for in the laissez-faire case $r(1 - \tau_{RD}) = r^*$ and hence $(1 + r^*)\alpha_1 - 1 = 0$. Thus, it follows from (10.17) that $r = r^*$ and hence $\tau_{RD} = 0$, which is impossible in view of the government's revenue needs. Therefore, we conclude that it is efficient to impose some quota on capital exports, so that $r(1 - \tau_{RD}) < r^*$. Hence, $(1 + r^*)\alpha_1 - 1 > 0$. Recalling that $\beta - \lambda > 0$, we see that

$$r^* > r = F_K. \tag{10.19}$$

follows from equation (10.17). Thus, if the government cannot effectively tax the income from the capital invested abroad, it is efficient to overinvest in capital at home up to a point where the marginal product, F_K, falls below the world rate of interest, r^*. That is, the stock of domestic capital is driven to a level that is higher than at the optimal regime (where $F_K = r^*$); moreover, it is higher than at the laissez-faire (where $F_K(1 - \tau_{RD}) = r^*$ and, consequently, $F_K > r^*$).

The economic rationale for the result is as follows. At the point where $F_K = r^*$, the marginal product of capital at home is equal to the world rate of interest. At this point the domestic economy loses nothing in terms of GNP by marginally shifting capital of home residents abroad to home (through the reduction of the quota L on capital exports). In other words, starting at the production efficient point, a marginal change in the allocation of capital must have a negligible effect on output. On the other hand, such reallocation of capital increases the capital-income tax base, thereby allowing reduction of the tax rate for a given public consumption (and, consequently, given tax revenue needs). Such a reduction in the distortionary tax rate must raise welfare. Put differently, a forced reduction in capital exports, at the point where $r = r^*$, essentially amounts to a lump-sum transfer of income from the representative consumer to the government, brought on by the expansion in the tax base. Such a transfer must improve welfare because the social value of a marginal dollar in the hands of the government exceeds the social value of this dollar in the hands of private consumers.[9]

How severe should the restrictions on capital exports be? Should capital exports be altogether banned?

If, under autarky, r is close to r^*, then there is little gain for the society as a whole from investing abroad, because this gain is equal only to the difference between r and r^*. However, the private sector can still gain considerably from investing abroad if $r(1 - \tau_{RD})$ is considerably below r^*. Therefore, a massive quantity of capital may fly abroad, and the government loses a significant amount of tax revenues from such an outflow of capital. Therefore, in this case, it may be efficient to ban exports of capital.

10.3 Conclusion

This chapter examined the efficiency implications of restrictions on capital exports. We showed that when governments can tax the income from this capital, no quantity restrictions should apply. This implies that before-tax rate of return on domestic capital (i.e., the marginal productivity of domestic capital, denoted by r) should be equal to the world rate of interest (denoted by r^*). This equality ensures an efficient allocation of the country's savings between investment at home and investment abroad (see figure 10.1).

When governments cannot effectively tax foreign-source income and apply no restrictions to capital exports (laissez-faire), then the rate-of-return arbitrage condition equates the after-tax rate on domestic capital (i.e., $(1 - \tau_{RD})r$) to the world rate of interest (i.e., r^*). This equality implies that the before-tax rate of return on domestic capital exceeds the world rate of interest (i.e., $r > r^*$). Consequently, the stock of domestic capital induced by the laissez-faire policy exceeds the level of capital that would have been optimal under circumstances where the government is able to fully tax foreign-source income.

Obviously, if governments can effectively tax foreign-source income and choose to impose no restrictions on capital exports, consumers' welfare exceeds the level that prevails in the case where foreign-source income is

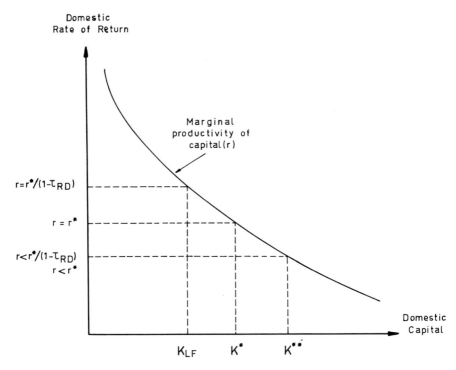

Figure 10.1
Efficient stock of domestic capital with and without taxation of foreign-source income
Note: K_{LF} = Laissez-faire stock of capital with no taxation of foreign-source income
    K^* = Efficient stock of capital with taxation of foreign-source income
    K^{**} = Efficient stock of capital with no taxation of foreign-source income

not effectively taxed and the governments resort to quantity restrictions on capital exports. This consideration may explain why the EC, which is moving toward a single capital market in 1992, searches for ways to enforce taxation of foreign-source income as to eliminate incentives to locate capital abroad [see Giovannini and Hines (1989)].

The issue of whether the government can tax foreign-source income arises in the context of income taxation. With a destination-based consumption tax, all domestic consumption is taxed regardless of the location of production; at least an excise tax can be fully enforced on imports. One may ask whether a destination-based consumption tax eliminates the need for capital-income taxation and the accompanying restrictions on international capital mobility. The answer is no. First, it is not at all clear that an excise tax on imported goods and services can be more easily enforced than a tax on foreign-source capital income. Second, as the literature on direct versus indirect tax controversy suggests [see, for example, Atkinson (1977)], the consumption tax does not drive out the income tax in an optimal tax design. Thus, as long as the income tax coexists with the consumption tax, the problem of enforcement of taxes on foreign-source income brings out the efficiency associated with controls on international capital flows.

10.4 Appendix

In this appendix we derive equations (10.16)–(10.18). The first-order conditions for a solution to the program in equation (10.15) are

$$v_\alpha + v_N L(1 + r^*) - \beta F_K[c_{0\alpha} + c_{0N}L(1 + r^*)]$$
$$- \beta[c_{0\alpha} + c_{0N}L(1 + r^*)] - \beta[c_{1\alpha} + c_{1N}L(1 + r^*)] = 0, \qquad (10.20)$$

and

$$v_N[(1 + r^*)\alpha_1 - 1] - \beta F_K\{c_{0N}[(1 + r^*)\alpha_1 - 1] + 1\}$$
$$- \beta c_{0N}[(1 + r^*)\alpha_1 - 1] + \beta r^*$$
$$- \beta c_{1N}[(1 + r^*)\alpha_1 - 1] = 0, \qquad (10.21)$$

where c_{ij} denotes the partial derivative of c_i with respect to argument j ($i = 0, 1; j = \alpha, N$), and $\beta > 0$ is the Lagrange multiplier.

Recalling that $F_K = r$ and rearranging terms, we can rewrite (10.20) and (10.21), respectively, to yield

$$v_\alpha + v_N L(1 + r^*) - \beta(1 + r)[c_{0\alpha} + c_{0N}L(1 + r^*)]$$
$$- \beta[c_{1\alpha} + c_{1N}L(1 + r^*)] = 0, \qquad (10.22)$$

and

$$[v_N - \beta(1 + r)c_{0N} - \beta c_{1N}][(1 + r^*)\alpha_1 - 1] + \beta(r^* - r) = 0. \qquad (10.23)$$

Recalling Roy's identity ($v_\alpha = -v_N c_1$) and the second-period budget constraint ($c_1 - (1 + r^*)L = K/\alpha_1$), we can rewrite (10.22) as

$$-v_N\left(\frac{K}{\alpha_1}\right) - \beta(1 + r)[c_{0\alpha} + c_{0N}L(1 + r^*)]$$
$$- \beta[c_{1\alpha} + c_{1N}L(1 + r^*)] = 0. \qquad (10.24)$$

The Hicks-Slutsky equations for this case are

$$c_{0\alpha} = \bar{c}_{0\alpha} - c_1 c_{0N} \qquad (10.25)$$

and

$$c_{1\alpha} = \bar{c}_{1\alpha} - c_1 c_{1N},\tag{10.26}$$

where $\bar{c}_{i\alpha}$ denotes the Hicks-Slutsky compensated derivative of consumption in period i with respect to α_1. The Euler's equation states that

$$\bar{c}_{0\alpha} + \alpha_1 \bar{c}_{1\alpha} = 0,\tag{10.27}$$

where use is made of the adding-up properties of the Slutsky matrix. Putting differently, (10.27) follows from the envelope theorem: the compensated demand changes from any price change cannot alter expenditures to a first-order approximation, since these expenditures are initially minimized. Substituting $\alpha_1 = [1 + (1 - \tau_{RD})r]^{-1}$ into equation (10.27) yields

$$(1 + r)\bar{c}_{0\alpha} + \bar{c}_{1\alpha} = r\tau_{RD}\bar{c}_{0\alpha}.\tag{10.28}$$

Also, upon differentiating the individual consolidated budget constraint, equation (10.5), with respect to income (namely, $E + L[(1 + r^*)\alpha_1 - 1]$), we obtain

$$(1 + r)c_{0N} + c_{1N} = \frac{1}{\alpha_1} + r\tau_{RD}c_{0N}.\tag{10.29}$$

Substituting (10.25), (10.26), (10.28), and (10.29) into (10.24) and (10.23) yields the following first-order conditions for the optimal policy:

$$\beta - \lambda = \frac{\alpha_1 \beta r \bar{c}_{0\alpha}}{(K/\alpha_1)}\tag{10.30}$$

and

$$\beta(r^* - r) = \frac{(\beta - \lambda)[(1 + r^*)\alpha_1 - 1]}{\alpha_1},\tag{10.31}$$

where

$$\lambda = v_N \alpha_1 + r\tau_{RD}(-c_{0N})\alpha_1.\tag{10.32}$$

11

International Tax Competition and Gains from Harmonization

The creation of a single capital market in the European Community raises the possibility of tax competition among the member countries, in the absence of a full-fledged harmonization of the income tax systems. The possibility of capital flight from the EC to low-tax countries elsewhere also has strong implications for the national tax structures in the EC. These developments have renewed the interest among public finance and international finance economists in the issues of tax harmonization, tax coordination, tax competition, and the structure of international taxation. This chapter focuses on the structure of taxation for countries that are engaged in tax competition and on the potential gains from tax harmonization among them.

In this chapter we are interested in highlighting the distortions and inefficiencies of the international allocations of world savings and investments that are caused by capital-income taxation. We thus abstract from market power considerations. It is well known that tax competition introduces the possibility of terms-of-trade manipulation among countries. If, however, the economic community for which the tax competition or the tax harmonization applies consists of many relatively small member countries, each member must also have relatively small market power. Consequently, the terms-of-trade manipulation through tax competition becomes insignificant.

We focus here on the issues of tax design and resource allocation that are generated by tax competition for given terms of trade (including interest rates). We have already demonstrated (see chapter 5) that it is efficient to employ residence-based taxation in a small open economy. Therefore, it is still efficient for each of the competing countries to employ such a tax system if it cannot manipulate the international terms of trade to its own advantage. Because residence-based taxation leads to complete equalization of marginal productivities of capital across countries, it follows that tax competition generates an efficient allocation of the *world's* stock of capital. If the previously competing governments were to harmonize their fiscal policies, the most they would achieve is an efficient allocation of the world's capital, as implied by the analysis of chapter 5. Such an efficient allocation is achieved, anyway however, through tax competition. Hence, there are no gains from international harmonization of tax systems, if the individual governments are unable to manipulate the terms of trade.[1]

11.1   Analytical Framework

International tax competition, or fiscal policy competition in general, has major effects on the resource allocation across countries as well as within each country. For example, the aggregate (worldwide) level of savings as well as its cross-country composition may be distorted by such competition. Similarly, the volume of world investment and its international allocation among countries may become inefficient. In general, these effects on the allocation of the world resources can be decomposed into two elements. One concerns the indirect manipulation of the international terms of trade by various fiscal measures (other than explicit trade barriers such as tariffs and quotas) that is akin to the familiar "trade wars." The second element concerns the international and domestic misallocation of resources that is generated by tax competition for given terms of trade (see also chapter 2). As mentioned in the opening paragraph, we ignore the first element (which plays a role in chapter 8) to highlight the saving-investment distortions that result from the tax competition.

To simplify the exposition we assume that the competing group consists of two small countries, denoted by superscripts H (for home) and F (for foreign); superscript R denotes the rest of the world. We suppose that the world capital market is fully integrated (as in Europe of 1992)—that is, there exist totally free international movements of capital. We assume other factors of production (such as labor) to be immobile internationally.

To focus on the issues of tax competition and tax harmonization, we employ a simplified version of the stylized workhorse model of chapter 5. This simplified model has the following features. In the first period the economy possesses an initial endowment of the composite good. Individuals can decide how much of their initial endowments to consume in the first period and how much to save. Saving is allocated to either domestic or foreign investments. In the second period, output (produced by capital and labor) and income from foreign investment are allocated between private and public consumption. To simplify we assume that government spending takes place in the second period, and investment cost adjustments are insignificant. As in the tax model of chapter 5, the government employs taxes on labor, taxes on income from domestic investments, and possibly taxes on income from investments abroad to finance optimally public consumption.

For simplicity we assume that government spending on public goods does not affect individual demand patterns for private goods or the supply of labor. That is, only the taxes that are needed to finance these expenditures affect individual demands and supplies, but not the expenditures themselves. Formally, we assume that the individual (direct) utility function is weakly separable between private goods and services on the one hand and public goods and services on the other hand. That is, the representative individual in the home country (country H) has a utility function of the form

$$U^H(C_0^H, C_1^H, \ell^H, G^H) = u^H(C_0^H, C_1^H, \ell^H) + m^H(G^H), \tag{11.1}$$

where u^H and m^H are the private and public components of the utility function, respectively; C_0^H, C_1^H, and ℓ^H are first-period (present) consumption, second-period (future) consumption, and second-period labor supply, respectively; and G^H is second-period public consumption.

We denote savings in the form of domestic capital by S^{HH}, savings exported to country F by S^{HF}, and savings exported to the rest of the world by S^{HR}. The budget constraint of the representative individual (the private sector) in the first period is

$$C_0^H + S^{HH} + S^{HF} + S^{HR} = E^H, \tag{11.2}$$

where E^H is the fixed endowment.

In the second period the private sector finances its consumption from labor income, which is taxed at the rate τ_ℓ^H, and its capital income, which stems from one domestic source and two foreign sources, from country F and from the rest of the world. Gross returns on capital income from these sources are r^H, r^F and r^R, respectively.[2] These capital-income sources may be taxed by the home country and by the foreign countries. We denote by τ_{rD}^i, τ_{rA}^i, and τ_{rN}^i the tax rates imposed by country i ($=H, F$) on capital income of a resident from a domestic source, of a resident from a foreign source, and of a nonresident from a domestic source.

Thus, the private sector faces the following budget constraint in the second period:

$$C_1^H = (1 - \tau_\ell^H)w^H \ell^H + S^{HH}[1 + (1 - \tau_{rD}^H)r^H]$$

$$+ S^{HF}[1 + (1 - \tau_{rA}^H)(1 - \tau_{rN}^F)r^F]$$

$$+ S^{HR}[1 + (1 - \tau_{rA}^H)r^R], \tag{11.3}$$

where w^H is the real wage rate (in terms of second-period consumption).

Since a resident in country H is free to invest either in his own country, H, or in the foreign country, F, or in the rest of the world, R, it follows that if his or her portfolio is diversified, he or she must earn the same net (after-tax) return everywhere. That is,[3]

$$(1 - \tau_{rD}^H)r^H = (1 - \tau_{rA}^H)r^R \tag{11.4}$$

and

$$(1 - \tau_{rA}^H)(1 - \tau_{rN}^F)r^F = (1 - \tau_{rA}^H)r^R.$$

Upon cancellation of the common term $1 - \tau_{rA}^H$, the second of these two conditions becomes

$$(1 - \tau_{rN}^F)r^F = r^R. \tag{11.5}$$

Hence, the second-period budget constraint may be rewritten as

$$C_1^H = (1 - \tau_\ell^H)w^H \ell^H + S^H[1 + (1 - \tau_{rD}^H)r^H], \tag{11.6}$$

where

$$S^H = S^{HH} + S^{HF} + S^{HR} \tag{11.7}$$

denotes the aggregate saving of the private sector in country H. As usual, the budget constraints for the first and second periods, (11.2) and (11.3), may be consolidated into a single lifetime budget constraint:

$$C_0^H + q_C^H C_1^H = E^H + q_\ell^H \ell^H, \tag{11.8}$$

where

$$q_C^H = [1 + (1 - \tau_{rD}^H)r^H]^{-1} \tag{11.9}$$

and

$$q_\ell^H = (1 - \tau_\ell^H)w^H[1 + (1 - \tau_{rD}^H)r^H]^{-1} \tag{11.10}$$

are the present-value (posttax) consumer prices of second-period consumption and labor, respectively.[4]

Maximization of the utility function (11.1), subject to the budget constraint (11.8), yields the demand for private consumption in the first period, the supply of saving in the second period, and the supply of labor by the private sector in the second period, respectively:

$$c_0^H(q_C^H, q_\ell^H, E^H), \quad c_1^H(q_C^H, q_\ell^H, E^H), \quad S^H(q_C^H, q_\ell^H, E^H), \quad \text{and} \quad \ell^H(q_C^H, q_\ell^H, E^H).$$

As usual, the indirect utility function is defined by

$$v^H(q_C^H, q_\ell^H, E^H, G^H)$$
$$= u^H[c_0^H(q_C^H, q_\ell^H, E^H), c_1^H(q_C^H, q_\ell^H, E^H), \ell^H(q_C^H, q_\ell^H, E^H)] + m^H(G^H).$$
(11.11)

This comprises the consumption-labor supply side of the economy. We turn now to the production-labor demand side.

Production-Labor Demand Side

Domestic output, Y^H, of the composite consumption good in the second-period is produced by capital, K^H, and labor, ℓ^H, according to a neoclassical, constant-returns-to-scale production function:

$$Y^H = F^H(K^H, \ell^H).$$
(11.12)

The stock of domestic capital is composed of savings by domestic residents channeled to domestic uses, S^{HH}; savings by the residents of country F channeled to country H, S^{FH} and savings by the rest of the world channeled to country H, S^{RH}. That is,

$$K^H = S^{HH} + S^{FH} + S^{RH}$$
$$= S^H - [(S^{HF} + S^{HR}) - (S^{FH} + S^{RH})],$$
(11.13)

where use is made of equation (11.7). In other words, the domestic capital stock is equal to aggregate domestic saving, S^H, less net capital exports, $S^{HF} + S^{HR} - (S^{FH} + S^{RH})$.

The marginal productivity conditions determine the (pretax) interest rate and the wage rate:

$$r^H = F_K^H(K^H, \ell^H)$$
(11.14)

and

$$w^H = F_\ell^H(K^H, \ell^H),$$
(11.15)

where the subscript denotes the partial derivative with respect to variables K and ℓ.

As usual, the equilibrium conditions (reflecting the resource constraints) for country H require that the supply be equal to the demand for first- and second-period consumption. Accordingly, the conditions are[5]

$$C_0^H = E^H - S^H \tag{11.16}$$

and

$$G^H + C_1^H = F^H(K^H, \ell^H) + K^H + (S^{HF} + S^{HR})(1 + r^R)$$
$$- (S^{FH} + S^{RH})[1 + (1 - \tau_{rN}^H)r^H]. \tag{11.17}$$

Note that $S^{HF} + S^{HR}$, the savings of the residents of country H that are invested abroad, earn the social (i.e., before tax) return at the rate of r^R, no matter whether invested in the rest of the world or in country F [see also the arbitrage condition (11.5)]. The sum $S^{FH} + S^{RH}$, denoting the foreign savings invested in country H, earn the domestic rate of return, r^H. But the foreign residents can extract from country H only a net-of-tax return $(1 - \tau_{rN}^H)r^H$, because a tax of τ_{rN} (per unit) remains in country H. The equations describing country F are similar, except that the superscripts F and H are interchanged.

If we assume an interior solution, the rate-of-return arbitrage conditions (11.4) and (11.5) become

$$(1 - \tau_{rD}^F)r^F = (1 - \tau_{rA}^F)r^R, \tag{11.18}$$

and

$$r^R = (1 - \tau_{rN}^H)r^H. \tag{11.19}$$

When we consolidate the first- and second-period equilibrium conditions for country H, described in equations (11.16) and (11.17), it follows that country H faces the following (future-value) lifetime equilibrium condition:

$$G^H + c_1^H(q_C^H, q_\ell^H, E^H) = F^H\{E^H - c_0^H(q_C^H, q_\ell^H, E^H)$$
$$- [(S^{HF} + S^{HR}) - (S^{FH} + S^{RH})], \ell^H(q_C^H, q_\ell^H, E^H)\}$$
$$+ E^H - c_0^H(q_C^H, q_\ell^H, E^H)$$
$$+ [(S^{HF} + S^{HR}) - (S^{FH} + S^{RH})]r^R, \tag{11.20}$$

where use is made also of equations (11.13) and (11.19). This condition merely states that total private and public consumption in the second period (i.e., $G^H + c_1^H$) must be equal to the sum of (1) output generated by domestic capital, which is financed by domestic saving (i.e., $E^H - c_0^H$), less net capital exports (i.e., gross capital exports, $S^{HF} + S^{HR}$, less gross capital imports, $S^{FH} + S^{RH}$), and labor; (2) domestic capital; and (3) the return on net capital exports. Notice that by Walras's law the government budget constraint in each country is automatically satisfied at equilibrium.

11.2   International Tax Competition

International tax competition works as follows. Each of the two competing governments designs its fiscal policy so as to maximize the welfare of the representative resident. In so doing, it takes into account the equilibrium and arbitrage conditions set forth by the adherence to a market economy and also takes as given the fiscal instruments employed by the government in the other country. This leads to a Nash equilibrium between the two countries.

Enforcement of Taxes on Income Originating in the Rest of the World

Let us suppose that fiscal policies are not harmonized internationally. Consequently,the two countries engage in tax competition. We assume, however, that some minimal degree of coordination among the two countries and the rest of the world prevails, so that they can effectively tax, should they wish, their residents on foreign-source (including the rest of the world) income.

In this case the government in country H chooses G^H, q_C^H, q_ℓ^H, $(S^{HF} + S^{HR}) - (S^{FH} + S^{RH})$, r^H, w^H, τ_ℓ^H, τ_{rD}^H, τ_{rN}^H, and τ_{rA}^H so as to maximize the (indirect) utility function (11.11) subject to the equilibrium condition (11.20), the definition of q_C^H and q_ℓ^H in (11.19) and (11.10), respectively, and the relevant arbitrage conditions, (11.4) and (11.19). Notice that the other two arbitrage conditions, (11.5) and (11.18), are irrelevant for country H because they have no effect on the economy of country H. That is, the endogenous variables in (11.5) and (11.18) appear nowhere else in the equations describing the economy of country H. In addition, r^H and w^H are derived from the marginal productivity conditions (11.14) and (11.15).

This optimization can be simplified a great deal by a two-stage solution. First, the government chooses public consumption, G^H, consumer prices of second-period consumption and labor, q_C^H and q_ℓ^H, respectively, and net capital exports so as to maximize the indirect utility function (11.11), subject to only one constraint—the resource constraint (11.20), Then, in the second stage, the government sets r^H and w^H from (11.14) and (11.15), respectively;

τ_{rD}^H from (11.9); τ_{ℓ}^H from (11.10); τ_{rN}^H from (11.19), and τ_{rA}^H from (11.14). In the first stage of the optimization process it follows from the first-order condition for net capital exports that the marginal product of capital, F_K^H, should be equal to the world rate of interest, r^R. Since $F_K^H = r^H$, by (11.14), we thus have

$$F_K^H = r^H = r^R. \tag{11.21}$$

This gross rate-of-return equalization (which, for the same reasons, must hold also in country F) implies that physical capital must be efficiently allocated among country H, country F, and the rest of the world. Thus, even though we are in a second-best situation where many distortions exist both within and across countries (e.g., the saving-consumption tradeoffs and consumption-leisure tradeoffs are distorted), the world production is efficient.

Because $r^H = r^R$, it follows from (11.19) that $\tau_{rN}^H = 0$. Equation (11.4) also implies that $\tau_{rD}^H = \tau_{rA}^H$. Thus, country H does not tax foreigners on income originating in country H.[6] Also, it taxes its residents uniformly on their capital income from all sources, domestic as well as foreign. Evidently, a similar result holds for country F as well. Thus, each country employs the residence (or worldwide) principle for the taxation of income from capital in the Nash equilibrium of the tax competition.

Can there be gains from tax harmonization? Notice that in the optimization problem carried out by the government of country H, the only variables that pertain to country F are S^{HF} and S^{FH}. However, country H is indifferent between the various forms of savings, S^{HF} and S^{HR}, and between S^{FH} and S^{RH}, as long as net capital exports, $S^{HF} + S^{HR} - (S^{FH} + S^{RH})$, stay constant. That is, because net capital exports from country H to the rest of the world can offset any fiscal policy that country F may implement, it follows that country F has no meaningful effect on country H, and vice versa. We can thus conclude that nothing is gained from tax harmonization, and the international tax competition leads to a *second-best optimum*.

Taxes on Income Originating in the Rest of the World are Not Enforceable

To tax effectively worldwide income, a considerable degree of coordination among countries is required. Such coordination takes the form of information exchange among the tax authorities, withholding arrangements, breachments to bank secrecy laws, and the like. We assume now that even though they continue to engage in tax competition (that is, the countries do not jointly determine the tax rates), countries F and H can reach such coordination between them. This coordination enables each country to effectively tax its residents on capital income that is invested in the other country. However, due to the lack of coordination with the rest of the world, they cannot tax the income from capital that is invested in the rest of the world. This specification captures the essence of a problem hindering European integration: that of European capital moving to low-tax countries in the rest of the world.

The arbitrage conditions (11.4)–(11.5) and (11.8)–(11.19) now become:

$$(1 - \tau_{rD}^H)r^H = r^R, \tag{11.22}$$

$$(1 - \tau_{rA}^H)(1 - \tau_{rN}^F)r^F = r^R, \tag{11.23}$$

$$(1 - \tau_{rD}^F)r^F = r^R, \tag{11.24}$$

and

$$(1 - \tau_{rA}^F)(1 - \tau_{rN}^H)r^H = r^R, \tag{11.25}$$

If there is an interior solution for the allocation of capital invested by the rest of the world in countries H and F, it must also be the case that the rest of the world earns a net return of r^R on such investments. That is,

$$(1 - \tau_{rN}^H)r^H = r^R = (1 - \tau_{rN}^F)r^F. \tag{11.26}$$

Then (11.26), (11.23), and (11.25) imply that

$$\tau_{rA}^H = \tau_{rA}^F = 0. \tag{11.27}$$

That is, when countries F and H cannot tax their residents on the income from capital that is invested in the rest of the world, then the rate-of-return arbitrage prevents each of them from taxing its residents on their income from capital invested in the other country, even though their tax authorities can cooperate on such things as tax withholding. This may explain why the EC dropped the idea of imposing a withholding tax on capital income.

We now turn to the Nash equilibrium resulting from tax competition in this case. Consider one of the two competing countries, say country H. As in the preceding section, the government in country H faces the same optimization problem, except that constraints (11.22) and (11.25) replace (11.4) and (11.19), respectively. Here too, it follows from the first-order condition for net capital exports that $F_K^H = r^R$. Because $F_K^H = r^H$, by (11.17), we have

$$F_K^H = r^H = r^R = r^F = F_K^F. \tag{11.28}$$

The equalization of the domestic marginal productivity of capital in country H (and in country F) with the world rate of interest generates a worldwide efficient allocation of physical capital. From (11.22) and (11.24) we can therefore conclude that

$$\tau_{rD}^H = \tau_{rD}^F = 0. \tag{11.29}$$

It follows from (11.27), (11.23), and (11.25) that

$$\tau_{rN}^H = \tau_{rN}^F = 0. \tag{11.30}$$

We can conclude therefore that no capital-income tax whatsoever is imposed by either country if capital flight to the rest of the world cannot be effectively stopped. Consequently, all the tax burden falls on the internationally immobile factor, labor. As in the preceding section, it is straightforward to show that countries F and H cannot gain anything from tax harmonization between them. That is, tax competition leads to a constrained optimum, relative to the set of tax instruments that is available. Since the set of tax instruments in this case is more restricted than if taxes on income from sources in the rest of the world were enforceable, it follows that the constrained optimum in the capital-flight case is inferior to the second-best optimum that is reached if worldwide income taxation is implementable.[7]

We conclude that if the two countries are not coordinated with the rest of the world and cannot effectively tax their residents on their income from capital invested in the rest of the world, then competition among the tax authorities leads to a full exemption from tax for the mobile factor (such as capital, or skilled labor). Accordingly, the entire tax burden is placed on the immobile factors (such as unskilled labor or land). However, even with this asymmetric treatment of capital and labor income there are no gains from tax harmonization.

11.3   Income Distribution Considerations

So far we have dealt with a representative individual in each country, thereby abstracting from intracountry income distribution considerations. Nevertheless, although in general the size of government and the structure of taxation depends on income distribution considerations, the international taxation propositions of the preceding sections do not depend on such considerations. Specifically, (1) the optimality of the residence principle in case each country can tax its residents on their capital income originating in the rest of the world, (2) the optimality of not taxing capital income in the case where it cannot, and (3) the redundancy of tax harmonization in both cases all hold with consumer heterogeneity, as well. To see this, notice that with many consumers the indirect utility function $v(q_c, q_\ell, E)$ is replaced by an indirect *social welfare function*, $v(q_c, q_\ell, E_1, \ldots, E_n)$, that depends, in addition to prices, also on the distribution of initial endowments $E_1, \ldots, E_n$, among the n consumers.[8]

Similarly, each individual demand or supply function is replaced by an aggregate demand or supply function. Thus, for example, the demand function for first-period consumption of the representative individual, namely, $c_0(q_c, q_\ell, E)$, is replaced by an aggregate demand function, $c_0(q_c, q_\ell, E_1, \ldots, E_n) = \sum_{i=1}^{n} c_{0i}(q_c, q_\ell, E_i)$, where $c_{0i}(q_c, q_\ell, E_i)$ is the demand function of individual i for first-period consumption, and so on. By carrying out this extension, it can be verified that none of the qualitative results of the preceding sections are altered.

V

Epilogue

12

Conclusions and Extensions

This book, dealing with international taxation in the integrated world economy, reflects the continuous process of increased economic integration of national economies. This process has stimulated a new international perspective to economic policy making. The growing integration of the world economy and the globalization of policy making, since the end of World War II, is evidenced in eight rounds of world wide General Agreements on Tariffs and Trade (GATT) in which tariff barriers were gradually slashed and nontariff barriers (NTB) were eased. The process of economic integration is most pronounced in the European Community and its move toward a single market for goods, services, and factors of production (particularly capital) in 1992. Bilateral Free Trade Agreements have been signed by the United States and Canada and by the United States and Israel, and another Free Trade Agreement is being negotiated by Canada, the United States, and Mexico. Recently the United States and Japan have reached a comprehensive agreement on economic policy coordination (the Structural Impediments Initiative), which aims at dismantling structural impediments to trade such as those affecting aggregate savings and investment. Similarly, the European Community has entered into trade agreements with several countries or blocks of countries, such as the European Free Trade Association (EFTA) countries. In another part of the globe, Australia and New Zealand operate under a free trade agreement (the Closer Economic Relations Agreement, CER). Several Latin American countries (such as Chile) have unilaterally slashed their tariff and nontariff barriers, and currently the Eastern European countries are intensively strengthening their commercial and financial ties with the rest of the world.

Underlying many of these developments have been the ongoing efforts by the International Monetary Fund, the World Bank, and the Organization for Economic Cooperation and Development (OECD) that have worked with notable success to dismantle exchange controls and international capital barriers. Between 1950 and 1980, the average tariff rate in the industrial countries fell from about 40 percent to less than 5 percent. At the same time, the ratio of exports to gross national product in industrial countries rose from about 7 percent to about 17 percent.[1]

Nevertheless, individual countries still maintain separate monetary and fiscal systems. A key issue addressed in this book is the interaction among fiscal policies of sovereign countries (each with its own national agenda) and the magnitude and direction of capital and goods flows in the integrated world economy. Particular emphasis is placed on the relations among direct and indirect taxes on the one hand, and savings, investment, consumption, and production on the other. In this context, we have analyzed the implications of alternative national tax system for efficiency, equity, and incidence. A distinction has been made between concepts and efficiency viewed from the individual-country perspective and from the perspective of the world economy. The latter focuses on the worldwide allocation of aggregate savings and investment and the geographic location of consumption and production of individual commodities. Our analysis of the incidence of taxes has focused on the *intratemporal* terms of trade (the relative price of goods), the *intertemporal* terms of trade (the interest rate), and the balance of payments. In this context we have studied the implications of capital flight, tax harmonization, and tax competition for the design of efficient national tax systems.

Although the menu of tax instruments seems enormous, we have reduced their number considerably by making use of the numerous equivalence relationships among various tax instruments. These equivalence relationships are important for both analytical and practical reasons. They facilitate the economic analysis of the various tax instruments and, at the same time, they enable the tax authorities to find ways around internatonal agreements on trade taxes by employing equivalent domestic tax instruments.

To examine the implications of alternative tax systems on the international transmission of domestic tax policies, we have paid attention to the global effects of budgetary imbalances. Our analysis has demonstrated how the details of the public finance (such as a destination versus origin-based VAT system) determine the international consequences of budget deficits. In the normative part of the book we have applied the concepts of optimal taxation (familiar from the closed economy literature of public finance) to the design of optimal tax systems for internationally open economies. In this context we have examined the implications of the growing trend toward capital-market liberalization in enforcing tax policies on foreign-source income and their implications for the incidence of taxes on internationally mobile and immobile factors of production. We have also analyzed the desirability of international tax harmonization when governments engage in tax optimization.

This book has developed the analytical infrastructure of international taxation and has applied the analysis to examine several specific issues. It can be applied further to illuminate various other issues, some of which would require an adaptation of the model to the specific circumstances. Among such key issues of international taxation, awaiting future research, are:

(1)   International taxation, growth, and productivity.
In an integrated world, the international flows of physical and human capital (direct foreign investment, brain gain, or brain drain) have profound implications for growth and productivity. International taxation generates strong incentives and disincentives for investments in physical and human capital. Therefore it affects the overall rate of growth of the world economy as well as the differential rates of growth among national economies. The analytical framework developed in this book can be extended to examince both the positive and the normative effects of taxation on factor mobility, growth, and productivity.

(2)   Fiscal requirements for a monetary union.
The move toward a greater harmonization of monetary policy and the developments of the accompanying institutional framework [as illustrated for example by the Delors report (1989) and by the plans for the creation of a European Central Bank] pose new challenges for the design of fiscal policies. A useful application and extension of the approach developed in this book would be the examination of the fiscal conditions necessary for the viability of such trends. In this context a central issue to be examined is the nature of the constraints that need to be imposed on fiscal deficits (including the guarantees that deficits would not be monetized and debt bail-out would not be granted), international fiscal transfers, the distribution of seigniorage, and the like.[2] Such analysis should provide the information necessary to assess the need for tax reforms.

(3)   The future of the welfare state.
In a world economy with free movements of capital and labor (especially highly skilled labor), the ability of governments to impose a high tax burden on such internationally mobile factors of production is severely restricted unless a high degree of international coordination and tax enforcement is

reached among national tax authorities. Consequently, the tax burden is likely to shift to some extent toward the internationally immoble factors of production (such as land or low-skilled labor). This tax shift limits the ability of national governments to pursue independent policies of distribution and subsidized public services, which are at the center of the welfare state. A useful area of research could apply the analysis in this book to address the issue of international coordination of national income-distribution policies and their burden sharing.

(4)   Vanishing tax on capital income.
Optimal taxation of capital income is subject to two conflicting forces. On the one hand, the income from existing capital is a pure rent. Taxing it away is therefore efficient. On the other hand, taxation of the returns on current and future investment may lead to inefficient stagnation.

Following Lucas (1990), consider a small open economy with an infinitely lived representative agent, endowed with one unit of leisure and K_0 units of capital. The representative agent's problem is specified by

$$\sum_{t=0}^{\infty} \beta^t [u(c_t, \chi_t) + \lambda P_t(w_t(1 - \chi_t) - c_t)], \tag{12.1}$$

where β denotes the subjective discount factor, c and χ denote consumption of goods and leisure, respectively, P denotes the consumer (tax-adjusted, present-value) price of consumption, w denotes the post-tax wage rate, and λ is the Lagrange multiplier. The first-order conditions are given by

(a) $u_c(c_t, \chi_t) - \lambda P_t = 0,$

(b) $u_\chi(c_t, \chi_t) - \lambda P_t w_t = 0.$
$$\tag{12.2}$$

Underlying the specification in (12.1) is the idea that the household sells its endowment of capital to the firm at $t = 0$ and the government confiscates the household income from this transaction since it is a lump-sum income. Consequently, the lifetime budget constraint implies that the discounted flow of consumption should be equal to the discounted flow of labor income and capital income appears nowhere in the household problem. Substituting the first-order conditions into the budget constraint yields the implementability constraint for the optimum tax problem as follows:

$$\sum_{t=0}^{\infty} \beta^t [u_c(c_t, \chi_t)c_t - u_\chi(c_t, \chi_t)(1 - \chi_t)] = 0. \tag{12.3}$$

The optimal tax problem is then given by

$$\text{Max} \sum_{t=0}^{\infty} \beta^t u(c_t, \chi_t)$$
$${}_{\{c_t, k_t\}}$$

$$+ \phi \sum_{t=0}^{\infty} \beta^t [u_c(c_t, \chi_t)c_t - u_x(c_t, \chi_t)(1 - \chi_t)]$$

$$+ \mu \sum_{t=0}^{\infty} R^{-t}[F(K_t, 1 - \chi_t) + (1 - \delta)K_t - K_{t+1} - c_t - g_t], \qquad (12.4)$$

where ϕ denotes the Lagrange multiplier associated with the implementability constraint, μ denotes the Lagrange multiplier associated with the resource constraint, and δ is the rate of depreciation. The resource constraint for the small open economy is equal to the discounted sum (where the world rate of interest, $R - 1$, used for discounting) of the gap between the flow of output, $F(\ ) + (1 - \delta)K_t$, and the sum of investment, K_{t+1}, private consumption, c_t, and public consumption, g_t.

Setting the derivative of the Lagrangean expression in (12.4) with respect to K_t equal to zero yields

$$- R^{-t+1} + R^{-t}[F_k(K_t, 1 - \chi_t) + 1 - \delta] = 0. \qquad (12.5)$$

Equation (12.5) implies that the marginal product of capital must be equal to the sum of the world rate of interest and the depreciation rate. This production efficiency condition implies that the tax rates on domestic capital income and foreign source capital income should be equalized—the residence principle. The other first-order conditions are given by

$$\beta^t [u_c(c_t, \chi_t) + \phi(u_{cc}(c_t, \chi_t)c_t + u_c(c_t, \chi_t) - u_{cx}(c_t, \chi_t)(1 - \chi_t)]$$
$$- \mu R^{-t} = 0, \qquad (12.6)$$

and

$$\beta^t [u_\chi(c_t, \chi_t) + \phi(u_{cx}(c_t, \chi_t)c_t - u_{xx}(c_t, \chi_t)(1 - \chi_t) + u_\chi(c_t, \chi_t)]$$
$$- \mu R^{-t} F_L(K_t, 1 - \chi_t) = 0. \qquad (12.7)$$

Suppose that the system has a steady state. As usual for a small open economy, this requires a specific relationship between the discount factor and the world rate of interest:

$$\beta R = 1. \qquad (12.8)$$

In this case equation (12.5) implies that

$$F_k(K_t, 1 - \chi_t) + 1 - \delta = \beta^{-1}. \qquad (12.9)$$

Matching up equation (12.9) with the firm's equilibrium condition

$$(1 - \tau)(F_k(K_t, 1 - \chi_t) - \delta) = (1 - \beta)\beta^{-1}, \tag{12.10}$$

where τ is the tax rate on capital income, we conclude that in the steady state the tax on capital income vanishes. For some specific functional forms, the result is even stronger. Consider the log utility function

$$u(c_t, \chi_t) = \alpha \log c_t + (1 - \alpha) \log \chi_t \tag{12.11}$$

In this case (since $u_{c\chi} = 0$ and $u_{cc}c = u_c$) the first-order condition in (12.6) reduces to

$$u_c(c_t, \chi_t) = \mu(\beta R)^{-t}. \tag{12.6'}$$

Substituting (12.6') into (12.5) yields

$$F_k(K_t, 1 - \chi_t) + (1 - \delta) = \frac{u_c(c_{t-1}, \chi_{t-1})}{\beta u_c(c_t, \chi_t)}. \tag{12.12}$$

Equation (12.12) implies that there is no tax wedge between the consumption marginal rate of substitution and the marginal productivity of capital. Hence, the tax on capital income is zero in every period. This, however, holds only in the case of zero transfers. In general, the Ramsey tax rules [equations (12.4)–(12.7)] do not imply zero taxes on capital income.

The work in this book attempts to break what seems to have been a traditional monopoly of international law experts and explain to the economics profession the conceptual issues underlying international taxation. In developing the analysis in this book, we have combined key elements and concepts from fields of international economics and public economics. A selected reference list from this body of literature is provided in the next chapter.

Notes

Chapter 1

1. For a comprehensive analysis of tax systems, see Pechman (1987), and for a thorough analysis of effective marginal tax rates on income from capital, see King and Fullerton (1984).

2. In calculating tax rates, we divide the general government tax-revenue data from OECD (1987a) by a corresponding computed tax base from OECD (1987b). We thus generate series of average tax rates for the major industrial countries. For the definitions of various tax rates, see the note to table 1.2.

3. See also Dooley (1990).

4. See, for example, Bernard and Weiner (1990), Hines and Hubbard (1990), Jun (1990), and Slemrod (1990).

5. See, for example, Ault and Bradford (1990).

Chapter 2

1. The residence principle and the source principle are also referred to as the worldwide and territorial principles, respectively.

2. Notice that the last set of equalities in equation (2.5) (namely, $\tau_{rN} = \tau_{rN}^* = 0$) is not necessary for the joint constraint (2.2) to hold. This means that for a viable equilibrium to hold, it suffices that each country taxes its residents according to the residence principle and, at the same time, levies taxes on nonresident incomes, provided that each country offers appropriate foreign tax credits with refunds for excess credits.

3. With no loss of generality, it is assumed that the product of the government sector is also taxed.

4. The source principle is also called the origin principle in the case of indirect taxation.

5. More precisely, exports are zero-rated rather than exempted. When a good is merely exempted from VAT, then no refund is offered to the producer for the VAT on the intermediate goods used in the production of the good. When exports are zero-rated, then not only the value-added of the exporting firm is exempted, but rather also the value-added of the firms producing the intermediate goods embodied in the exported good. Thus, the total value of exports is excluded from the VAT base in this way.

6. This is accomplished, as explained in the preceding note, by imposing a zero-rate VAT on exports.

7. The choice of a *common* numeraire for both countries implicitly assumes that the numeraire good is internationally mobile.

8. If, however, factors of production are not internationally mobile, the two polar tax principles are equivalent. See Berglas (1974). Hamilton and Whalley (1986) explored the issue of the nonuniformity of tax rates across goods that generates a difference between destination and origin systems. See also Feldstein and Krugman (1990) and Sinn (1990a,b).

Chapter 3

1. Examples of the large body of literature bearing on this subject are Aschauer and Greenwood (1985), Barro (1974), Buiter (1981), Brock and Turnovsky (1981), Frenkel and Razin (1985a, b), (1986b), (1987), Sachs (1981), Sachs and Roubini (1987), and Svensson and Razin (1983).

2. For the literature on investment costs of adjustment see Hayashi (1982, 1985), Lucas (1967), and Treadway (1969).

3. Depreciation is dealt with in later chapters.

4. For the early literature on the transfer problem see Johnson (1956), Keynes (1929), Meade (1951), Metzler (1942), Mundell (1960), Ohlin (1929), Rueff (1929), and Samuelson (1952).

Chapter 4

1. It is based on Alan Auerbach, Jacob Frenkel, and Assaf Razin, "Notes on International Taxation," February 1989. We are indebted to Alan Auerbach for agreeing to include this chapter in the book.

2. See Lerner (1936) and the dynamic extension in Razin and Svensson (1983b). Another useful equivalence is the relationship between taxes on international borrowing and dual exchange rates (see Frenkel and Razin (1987), and Mendoza (1990)).

3. Gordon and Levinsohn (1990) analyze emprically to what extent governments use domestic tax instruments in an attempt to offset the reduction in border distortions (tariffs, export subsidies, and import quotas).

4. See Kotlikoff (1989), who argues that for these reasons measured government budget deficits may not be an economically meaningful concept.

Chapter 5

1. Examples of the large body of literature bearing on this subject are Atkinson and Stern (1974), Atkinson and Stiglitz (1976), Balcer and Sadka (1982), Diamond (1970, 1975), Diamond and Mirrlees (1971), Dixit (1985), Dutton, Feldstein, and Hartman (1979), Gordon (1986), Mirrlees (1972), and Sadka (1977).

2. It should be noted at the outset that the working capital (cash) yields no real return, except possibly some tax advantage.

3. Up to now we have assumed that $r_0 \leqslant r_0^*$, so that the firm borrows domestically only. If $r_0 > r_0^*$, then the firm borrows only from abroad. In this case, r_0 plays no role in the economy, and the relevant interest rate becomes r_0^*. The alternative investment rules (5.22)–(5.25) are still valid, with r_0^* replacing r_0 everywhere.

4. To verify, subtract the household's and the firm's budget constraints, (5.1) and (5.20), respectively, from the goods-market equilibrium condition in period zero, (5.33), to obtain the government's budget constraint, (5.28). A similar procedure applies to period one by using equations (5.2) and (5.21), (5.34) and the arbitrage condition, (5.3), to yield (5.29).

5. In deriving this frontier we use the production-investment technology [equations (5.14)–(5.16)] and the resource constraints [equations (5.33)–(5.34)]. Some substitutions and rearrangements of terms yield equation (5.35).

6. In principle the constraint in (5.19) may be binding if the optimal policy is constrained with respect to the choice of the tax instruments.

7. It is noteworthy that even though direct taxes on business are absent, the firm's profits are still taxed indirectly through dividend taxes.

Chapter 6

1. The ideas underlying the model were developed by Barro (1974, 1979), Diamond (1965), Samuelson (1958), Stiglitz (1983), and Yaari (1965). See also Dornbusch (1985), Persson (1985), and Weil (1985). For a discussion of the measurement of public-sector deficits, see Blejer Cheasty (1991) and Kotlikoff (1989).

2. For an alternative interpretation of this overlapping-generations model, in which this coefficient indicates population growth rate, see Weil (1989).

3. For an analysis of similar tradable-nontradable models see Frenkel and Razin (1988b) and Van Wijnbergen (1986).

Chapter 7

1. Examples of the literature of the tax effects on savings, investment, and growth are Auerbach and Kotlikoff (1983, 1987), Boskin (1978), Bovenberg (1986, 1989), Buiter (1987), Feldstein (1974a,b), Fisher (1939) Goulder and Eichengreen (1988), Judd (1987a,b), King (1983), Kotlikoff (1989).

2. The income tax is a cash-flow tax as investment is fully deductible at the time it is made. See chapter 4.

3. No distinction is drawn here between the individual and the firm; capital income is subject to a single tax rate of τ_{yt}, which is also the tax rate on labor income.

Chapter 8

1. Based on Jacob Frenkel, Assaf Razin, and Steven Symansky, "Simulations of Global Effects of VAT Harmonization," in Horst Siebert (ed.), *Reforming Capital Income Taxation*, Tübingen, Mohr: Institute für Weltwirtschaft on der Universität Kiel, 1990. We are indebted to Steven Symansky for agreeing to include this chapter in the book. Examples of the literature bearing on this subject are Bourguignon and Chiappori (1989), Bradford (1984), Bryant et al. (1988), Cnossen (1988), Cnossen and Shoup (1987), Emerson, et al. (1988), Frenkel, Razin, and Symansky (1991), Musgrave (1987), Pechman (1987), Perraudin and Pujol (1990), and Sinn (1990b).

2. Zero-rated products involve the reimbursement of taxes levied on inputs with the result that the final good is completely untaxed; see also chapter 2.

3. For a recent broad survey of the international practice and problems in the area of VAT see Tait (1988).

4. For examples of such an analysis see Frenkel and Razin (1987, 1989) and Frenkel, Razin, and Symansky (1990).

5. As was already explained in chapter 2, a cash-flow income tax is equivalent to a VAT system imposed according to the *source* (rather than *destination*) principle.

6. Intuitively, the rise in the home-country VAT accompanied by an equiproportionate fall in the income tax broadens the tax base and raises tax revenue in the current period if the home country runs a current-account deficit. To restore tax revenue the income tax rate must be lowered. The opposite changes occur in the future period in which the current-account position is in surplus, reflecting the intertemporal budget constraint. Similar considerations imply that the path of income tax abroad also steepens. As a result, the tax incentives to investment decline, yielding a fall in the world rate of interest. See Frenkel and Razin (1987, ch. 8).

7. As an example of induced changes in the functional distribution of income consider the left-hand column of table 8.2. There, the VAT harmonization raises

the share of labor and lowers the share of capital income in the home economy for both the short and medium runs while inducing opposite redistributions in the foreign economy.

8. The intratemporal labor-supply elasticity, indicated by σ, is 0.3; the cost-of-adjustment coefficient investment, indicated by g, is 40; and the intertemporal elasticity of substitution for consumption is unitary (see the Appendix). To examine the sensitivity of the results with respect to the values of the elasticities we also simulated the model with a lower cost-of-adjustment coefficient and a higher labor-supply elasticity. Under these circumstances the welfare cost of VAT diminished relatively, whereas the welfare cost of income taxes increased relatively. In fact, in searching for the Ramsey's second-best tax structure (alternatively, the Diamond-Mirrlees optimal tax structure) we find for this set of parameter values that the income tax dominates the VAT.

9. Our formulation reflects the assumption that, except for the final period, bolted capital cannot be consumed. However, in the final period the capital stock, K_t, can be transformed into consumption at the rate aK_T, where $0 \leqslant a \leqslant 1$. This assumption serves to mitigate abrupt changes in the behavior of the economy arising in the final period of the finite-horizon model. Accordingly, the budget constraint applicable to the final period (period T) is analogous to the one shown in equation (8.1) with an added term on the right-hand side equal to ak_T. For a formulation of a model highlighting the interaction between investment, government spending policies, and international interdependence within an infinite-horizon model see Buiter (1987) and Frenkel and Razin (1987).

Chapter 9

1. Note that in earlier chapters q_c was denoted by α_1^H, the individual discount factor. The notation is modified here as we try to denote consumer prices by q.

2. A few special cases are of interest. Suppose that individual h' is the poorest member of society, while individual h'' is the richest. The social welfare function (9.14) reduces to the Rawlsian max-min criterion when $\gamma_{h'} = 1$ and $\gamma_h = 0$ for all $h \neq h'$. When $\gamma_n = \gamma_j$ for all n and j, the social welfare function (9.14) is Bentham's sum-of-utilities. When $\gamma_{h''} = 1$ and $\gamma_h = 0$ for all $h \neq h''$, (9.14) reduces to the max-max criterion.

Chapter 10

1. Examples of the literature bearing on this subject are Giovannini and Hines (1990b), Greenwood and Kimbrough (1985), McLure (1988), and Slemrod (1988).

2. Nevertheless, the results about the efficient investment incentives are valid also in the case of a two-way capital flow.

3. This assumption is inessential and completely separate from the issue of the inability of governments to tax foreign source income. We maintain this assumption purely for analytical convenience.

4. This specification assumes that all the capital stock is available for consumption at the end of period one. In the terminology of chapters 3, 6, and 7, it is assumed that $a = 1$.

5. The government budget constraint is $r\tau_{RD}K + F(K) - rK = G$. Note that the term $F(K) - rK$ represents the revenue from taxes on pure profits. Notice also, that by Walras's law this constraint is satisfied in equilibrium and henceforth deleted.

6. See the appendix.

7. This is strictly correct in the case where U is weakly separable between (C_0, C_1) and G.

8. In a many-good economy (including leisure) the determination of the sign of $\beta - \lambda$ is more complicated; the sign is positive under the assumption of certain substitutability in consumption. See Atkinson and Stern (1974).

9. An interesting question in this context is whether an increase in the domestic stock of capital is necessarily brought about by a reduction in the quota on capital exports. Under certain stability conditions, the answer is yes; see Razin and Sadka (1989a).

Chapter 11

1. Examples from the literature bearing on this subject are Bird and McLure (1989), Giovannini (1990a,b), McLure (1986, 1989), Siebert (1989), Tanzi (1988), and Tanzi and Bovenberg (1990).

2. The gross return, r^R, on capital income from the rest of the world is net of taxes paid in the rest of the world.

3. Note that the specification of the second condition in (11.4) is (inessentially) different than the specification in chapter 2 [equations (2.1)–(2.2)].

4. Notice that q_C^H is also the discount factor that was denoted earlier by α_1.

5. As before, we assume that the entire stock of physical capital is available for consumption at the end of period one.

6. The economic intuition behind this result is that since the supply of capital faced by the country is infinitely elastic, there is no benefit in taxing foreigners on income originating in the host country.

7. Note, however, that there exist incentives to limit capital exports to the rest of the world, as shown in chapter 10. Thus, if internationally feasible, the fiscal

harmonization between countries H and F can take the form of quantitative restrictions on exports of capital to country R.

8. To simplify the notation, the superscripts H and F were dropped.

Chapter 12

1. See Twentieth Century Fund (1989).

2. Issues of time inconsistency and rules vs. discretion arise in this context [see, for example, Calvo (1978), Calvo and Obstfeld (1988), Fischer (1980), Lucas and Stokey (1983), and Persson and Svensson (1984)].

Selected References

Aschauer, David A., and Jeremy Greenwood (1985). "Macroeconomic Effects of Fiscal Policy," in Karl Brunner and Alan H. Meltzer (eds.), *The New Monetary Economics, Fiscal Issues and Unemployment, Carnegie-Rochester Conference Series on Public Policy*, Vol. 23 (Amsterdam: North-Holland), pp. 91–138.

Atkinson, Anthony B. (1977). "Optimal Taxation and the Direct versus Indirect Tax Controversy," *Canadian Journal of Economics* 10, 590–606.

Atkinson, Anthony B., and Nicholas H. Stern (1974). "Pigou, Taxation and Public Goods," *Review of Economic Studies* 41, 119–128.

Atkinson, Anthony B., and Joseph E. Stiglitz (1976). "The Design of Tax Structure: Direct versus Indirect Taxation," *Journal of Public Economics* 6, 55–75.

Auerbach, Alan J., Jacob A. Frenkel, and Assaf Razin (1989). "Notes on International Aspects of Taxation," International Monetary Fund.

Auerbach, Alan J., and Lawrence J. Kotlikoff (1983). "National Savings, Economic Welfare, and the Structure of Taxation," in Martin Feldstein (ed.), *Behavioral Simulation Methods In Tax Policy Analysis* (Chicago: University of Chicago Press).

Auerbach, Alan J., and Lawrence J. Kotlikoff (1987). *Dynamic Fiscal Policy* (New York: Cambridge University Press).

Ault, Hugh J., and David F. Bradford (1990). "Taxing International Income: An Analysis of the U.S. System and its Economic Premises," in Assaf Razin and Joel Slemrod (eds.), *Taxation in the Global Economy* (Chicago: University of Chicago Press).

Balcer, Yves, and Efraim Sadka (1982). "Horizontal Equity, Income Taxation and Self-Selection with an Application to Income Tax Credits," *Journal of Public Economics* 19, 291–309.

Barro, Robert J. (1974). "Are Government Bonds Net Wealth?", *Journal of Political Economy* 82 (November/December), 1095–1117.

Barro, Robert J. (1979). "On the Determination of the Public Debt," *Journal of Political Economy* 87, no. 5, pt. 1 (October), 940–971.

Bernard, Jean-Thomas, and Robert J. Weiner (1990). "Multinational Corporations, Transfer Prices, and Taxes: Evidence from the U.S. Petroleum Industry," in Assaf Razin and Joel Slemrod (eds.), *Taxation in the Global Economy* (Chicago: University of Chicago Press.

Berglas, Eitan (1974). "Devaluation, Monetary Policy, and Border Tax Adjustment," *The Canadian Journal of Economics* 7, no. 1, 1–11.

Bird, Richard M., and Charles E. McLure Jr. (1989). "The Personal Income Tax in an Interdependent World," Paper presented at International Seminar in Public Economics (ISPE), Erasmus University, Rotterdam (January).

Blanchard, Olivier J. (1985). "Debt, Deficits, and Finite Horizons," *Journal of Political Economy* 93 (April), 223–247.

Blejer, Mario, and Adrienne Cheasty (1991). "Analytical and Methodological Issues in the Measurement of Fiscal Deficits," *Journal of Economic Literature*, forthcoming.

Boskin, Michael J. (1978). *Federal Tax Reform: Myths and Realities*, Institute for Contemporary Studies.

Bourguignon, F., and P. A. Chiappori (1989). "Exploring the Distribution and Incentive Effects of Tax Harmonization," mimeo, Delta, Paris, November.

Bovenberg, A. Lans (1986). "Capital Income Taxation in Growing Open Economies," *Journal of Public Economics* 31, no. 3, 347–376.

Bovenberg, A. Lans (1989). "The Effects of Capital Income Taxation on International Competitiveness and Trade Flows," *American Economic Review* 79, (Sep.) no. 5, 1045–1064.

Bovenberg, A. Lans, Krister Andersson, Kenji Aramaki, and Sheetland K. Chand (1990). "Tax Incentives and International Capital Flows: The Case of the United States and Japan," in Assaf Razin and Joel Slemrod (eds.), *Taxation in the Global Economy* (Chicago: University of Chicago Press).

Bradford, David F. (1984). *Blueprints for Basic Tax Reform*, 2d ed., rev. (Arlington, Va.: Tax Analysts).

Bradford, David F. (1986). *Untangling the Income Tax* (Cambridge: Harvard University Press).

Brock, William A., and Stephen J. Turnovsky (1981). "The Analysis of Macroeconomic Policies in Perfect Foresight Equilibrium," *International Economic Review* 22, 177–209.

Bryant Richard C., Dale W. Henderson, George Holtham, Peter Hooper, and Steve A. Symansky (1988). *Empirical Macroeconomics for Interdependent Economies* (Washington, D.C.: The Brookings Institution).

Buiter, Willem H. (1981). "Time Preference and International Lending and Borrowing in an Overlapping Generations Model," *Journal of Political Economy* 89, no. 4, 769–797.

Buiter, Willem H. (1986). "Structural and Stabilization Aspects of Fiscal and Financial Policies in the Dependent Economy," P. I, Washington, World Bank, Macroeconomics Division, DRD (August), unpublished manuscript.

Buiter, Willem H. (1987). "Fiscal Policy in Open, Interdependent Economies," in Assaf Razin and Efraim Sadka (eds.), *Economic Policy in Theory and Practice* (London: Macmillan), pp. 101–144.

Buiter, Willem H., and Ken M. Kletzer (1990). "The Welfare Economics of Cooperative and Noncooperative Fiscal Policy," *Journal of Economic Dynamics and Control* 14 (Aug.), no. 4, 632–645.

Calvo, Guillermo (1978). "On the Time Consistency of Optimal Policy in a Monetary Economy," *Econometrica* 46, 6 (Nov.), 1411–1428.

Calvo, Guillermo A., and Maurice Obstfeld (1988). "Optimal Time-Consistent Fiscal Policy with Finite Lifetimes," *Econometrica* 56, 411–432.

Cnossen, Sijbren (1988). "More Tax Competition in the European Community," paper presented at 44th Congress of the International Institute of Public Finance, Istanbul (August).

Cnossen, Sijbren, and Carl S. Shoup (1987). "Coordination of Value-Added Taxes" in Cnossen Sijbren (ed.), *Coordination in the European Community* (Antwerp: Kluwer Law and Taxation Publishers).

Cumby, Robert, and Richard Levich (1987). "On the Definition and Magnitude of Recent Capital Flight," in Donald R. Lassard and John Williamson (eds.), *Capital Flight and Third World Debt* (Washington, D.C.: Institute for International Economic).

Deveraux, M., and M. Pearson (1990). "Harmonizing Corporate Taxes in Europe," *Fiscal Studies* 11, 21–35.

Diamond, Peter A. (1965). "National Debt in a Neo-Classical Growth Model," *American Economic Review* 55, 1126–1150.

Diamond, Peter A. (1970). "Incidence of an Interest Income Tax," *Journal of Economic Theory* 2, 211–224.

Diamond, Peter A. (1975). "A Many-Person Ramsey Tax Rule," *Journal of Public Economics* 4, 335–342.

Diamond, Peter A., and James Mirrlees (1971). "Optimal Taxation and Public Production," *American Economic Review* (March and June), 8–17 and 261–278.

Delors Report (1989). "Report on Economic and Monetary Union in the European Community," Committee for the Study of Economic and Monetary Union (April).

Dixit, Avinash (1985). "Tax Policy in Open Economies," in Alan Auerbach and Martin Feldstein (eds.), *Handbook on Public Economies*, Chap. 6, 314–374, (Amsterdam: North-Holland).

Dooley, Michael P. (1987). "Comment on the Definition and Magnitude of Recent Capital Flight, by Cumby, Robert, and Richard Levich," in Donald R. Lassard and John Williamson (eds.), *Capital Flight and the Third World Debt* (Washington, D.C.: Institute for International Economics).

Dooley, Michael P. (1988). "Capital Flight, a Response to Differences in Financial Risks," *International Monetary Fund Staff Papers* 35, no. 3 (September), 422–436.

Dooley, Michael P. (1990). "Comment," in Assaf Razin and Joel Slemrod (eds.), *Taxation in the Global Economy* (Chicago: University of Chicago Press).

Dornbusch, Rudiger (1985). "Intergenerational and International Trade," *Journal of International Economy* 18 (February), 123–139.

Dutton, John (1982). "The Optimal Taxation of International Investment Income: A Comment," *Quarterly Journal of Economics* 46, 373–380.

Emerson, Michael, Michel Aujean, Michel Catinat, Philippe Goybet, and Alexis Jacquemin (1988). "Fiscal Barrier," *European Economy* (March), 45–107.

Fair, Ray C. (1979). "On Modelling the Economic Linkages among Countries," in Rudiger Dornbusch and Jacob A. Frenkel (eds.), *International Economic Policy: Theory and Evidence* (Baltimore: Johns Hopkins University Press).

Feldstein, Martin S. (1974a). "Tax Incidence in a Growing Economy with Variable Factor Supply," *Quarterly Journal of Economics* 88 (November), 551–573.

Feldstein, Martin S. (1974b). "Incidence of a Capital Income Tax In a Growing Economy with Variable Savings Rates," *Review of Economic Studies* 41 (October), 16–33.

Feldstein, Martin S., and David Hartman (1979). "The Optimal Taxation of Foreign-Source Investment Income," *Quarterly Journal of Economics* 93 (August), 613–624.

Fischer, Stanley (1980). "Dynamic Inconsistency, Cooperation and the Benevolent Dissembling Government," *Journal of Economic Dynamics and Control* 2, 1 (Feb.), 93–107.

Fisher, Irving (1939). "The Double Taxation of Savings," *American Economic Review* 29 (March), 16–33.

Frenkel, Jacob A., and Assaf Razin (1985a). "Fiscal Expenditures and International Economic Interdependence," in Willem H. Buiter and Richard C. Marston (eds.), *International Economic Policy Coordination* (Cambridge: Cambridge University Press).

Frenkel, Jacob A., and Assaf Razin (1985b). "Government Spending, Debt, and International Economic Interdependence," *Economic Journal* 94 (September), 619–636.

Frenkel, Jacob A., and Assaf Razin (1986a). "The International Transmission and Effects of Fiscal Policies," *American Economic Review* 76 (May), 330–335.

Frenkel, Jacob A., and Assaf Razin (1986b). "Fiscal Policies in the World Economy," *Journal of Political Economy* 94, pt. I (June), 564–594.

Frenkel, Jacob A., and Assaf Razin (1986c). "Real Exchange Rates, Interest Rates and Fiscal Policies, "*The Economic Studies Quarterly* 37 (June), 99–113.

Frenkel, Jacob A., and Assaf Razin (1987). *Fiscal Policies and the World Economy; An Intertemporal Approach* (Cambridge, Mass.: MIT Press).

Frenkel, Jacob A., and Assaf Razin (1988a). "International Effects of Budget Deficits," *International Monetary Fund Staff Papers* 35 (June), 297–315.

Frenkel, Jacob A., and Assaf Razin (1988b). *Spending, Taxes and Deficits: International-Intertemporal Approach*, Princeton Studies in International Finance, no. 63 (Princeton, N.J.: International Finance Section).

Frenkel, Jacob A., and Assaf Razin (1989). "International Effects of Tax Reforms," *Economic Journal* 98 (March), 38–58.

Frenkel, Jacob A., Assaf Razin, and Steve Symansky (1990a). "International Spillovers of Taxation," in Assaf Razin and Joel Slemrod (eds.), *Taxation in the Global Economy* (Chicago: University of Chicago Press), pp. 211–254.

Frenkel, Jacob A., Assaf Razin, and Steve Symansky (1990b). "Simulations of International VAT Harmonization," in Horst Siebert (ed.), *Reforming Capital Income Taxation* (Tübingen: J. Mohr Publishing).

Frenkel, Jacob A., Assaf Razin, and Steve Symansky (1991). "The International Effects of VAT Harmonization," International Monetary Fund, *Staff Papers*, forthcoming.

Giovannini, Alberto (1989). "National Tax Systems vs. The European Capital Market," *Economic Policy* 9 (October), 345–386.

Giovannini, Alberto (1990a). "Reforming Capital Income Taxation in the Open Economy: Theoretical Issues," in Horst Siebert (ed.), *Reforming Capital Income Taxation* (Tübingen: J. Mohr Publishing).

Giovannini, Alberto, and James R. Hines (1990b). "Capital Flight and Tax Competition: Are There Viable Solutions to Both Problems?" in Alberto Giovannini and Colin Mayer (eds.), *European Financial Integration* (Cambridge: Cambridge University Press).

Gordon, Roger H. (1986). "Taxation of Investment and Savings in a World Economy," *American Economic Review* 76, 1087–1102.

Gordon, Roger H., and James Levinsohn (1990). "The Linkage Between Domestic Taxes and Border Taxes," in Assaf Razin and Joel Slemrod (eds.), *Taxation in the Global Economy* (Chicago: University of Chicago Press).

Goulder, Larry H., and Barry Eichengreen (1988). "Savings Promotion, Investment Promotion and International Competitiveness," in Robert Feenstra (ed.), *Trade Policies for International Competitiveness* (Chicago: University of Chicago Press).

Greenwood, Jeremy, and Kent P. Kimbrough (1985). "Capital Controls and Fiscal Policy in the World Economy," *Canadian Journal of Economics* 18 (November), 743–765.

Grubert, Harry, and John Mutti (1987a). "Taxes, International Capital Flows and Trade: The International Implications of the Tax Reform Act of 1986," *National Tax Journal* 15, no. 3 (September), 315–330.

Grubert, Harry, and John Mutti (1987b). "The Impact of the Tax Reform Act of 1986 on Trade and Capital Flows," in *Compendium of Tax Research 1987*, Office of Tax Analysis, Department of the Treasury, Washington, D.C.

Hall, Robert E. (1978). "Stochastic Implications of the Life Cycle–Permanent Income Hypothesis: Theory and Evidence," *Journal of Political Economy* 86 (December), 971–987.

Hall, Robert E., and Alvin Rabushka (1983). *Low Tax, Simple Tax, Flat Tax* (New York: McGraw-Hill).

Hamada, Koichi (1984). "Strategic Aspects of International Fiscal Interdependence" (Tokyo: Tokyo University) Unpublished manuscript.

Hamilton, Robert, and John Whalley (1986). Border Tax Adjustment in U.S. Trade," *Journal of International Economics* 20 (Aug.) 377–383.

Hayashi, Fumio (1982). "Tobin's Marginal q and Average q: A Neo-Classical Interpretation," *Econometrica* 50, 213–224.

Hayashi, Fumio (1985). "Corporate Finance Side of the Q Theory of Investment," *Journal of Public Economics* 27 (August), 261–280.

Hines, James R., Jr., and R. Glenn Hubbard (1990). "Coming Home to America: Dividend Repatriations by U.S. Multinationals," in Assaf Razin and Joel Slemrod (eds.), *Taxation in the Global Economy* (Chicago: University of Chicago Press).

Horst, Thomas (1980). "A Note on the Optimal Taxation of International Investment Income," *Quarterly Journal of Economics* 44, 793–798.

Johnson, Harry G. (1956). "The Transfer Problem and Exchange Stability," *Journal of Political Economy* 59 (June), 212–225.

Judd, Kenneth L. (1987a). "A Dynamic Theory of Factor Taxation," *American Economic Review, Papers and Proceedings* 77, no. 2 (May), 42–48.

Judd, Kenneth L. (1987b). "The Welfare Cost of Factor Taxation in a Perfect-Foresight Model," *Journal of Political Economy* 95, no. 4, 675–709.

Jun, Soosung (1990). "U.S. Tax Policy and Direct Investment Abroad," in Assaf Razin and Joel Selmrod (eds.), *Taxation in the Global Economy* (Chicago: University of Chicago Press).

Keynes, John M. (1929). "The German Transfer Problem," *Economic Journal* 39 (March), 1–7.

King, Mervyn A. (1983). "The Economics of Saving," NBER Working Paper 1247 (December), Cambridge, Mass.

King, Mervyn A. (1987). "Prospects for Tax Reform in 1988," Discussion Paper No. 0010, LSE Financial Markets Group Discussion Paper Series, London.

King, Mervyn A., and Don Fullerton (1984). *The Taxation of Income From Capital* (Chicago: University of Chicago Press).

Kotlikoff, Lawrence J. (1989). *What Determines Savings?* (Cambridge, Mass.: MIT Press).

Paul Krugman and Feldstein Martin (1990). "International Trade Effects of Value Added Taxation," in Assaf Razin and Joel Slemrod (eds.), *Taxation in the Global Economy* (Chicago: The University of Chicago Press), pp. 270–282.

Lerner, Abba, P. (1936). "The Symmetry Between Import and Export Taxes," *Economica* 3 (August), 306–313.

Lucas, Robert E., Jr. (1967). "Adjustment Costs and the Theory of Supply," *Journal of Political Economy* 75 (August), 321–334.

Lucas, Robert E., Jr., (1990). "Supply Side Economics: An Analytical Review," *Oxford Economics Papers* 42, 293–316.

Lucas, Robert E., Jr., and Nancy L. Stokey (1983). "Optimal Fiscal and Monetary Policy in an Economy without Capital," *Journal of Monetary Economics* 12 (July), 55–93.

Meade, James E. (1951). *The Theory of International Economic Policy: The Balance of Payments*, Vol. 1 (London: Oxford University Press).

Mendoza, Enrique (1990). "Capital Controls and the Dynamic Gains from Trade in a Business Cycle Model of a Small Open Economy," IMF Working Paper WP/90/109.

Metzler, Lloyd A. (1942). "The Transfer Problem Reconsidered," *Journal of Political Economy* 50 (June), 397–414.

Micossi, Stefano (1988). "The Single European Market: Finance," *Banca Nazionale del Lavoro Quarterly Review*, no. 165 (June), 217–235.

Mirrlees, James A. (1972). "On Producer Taxation," *Review of Economic Studies* 39, no. 117, 105–112.

Mundell, Robert A. (1960). "The Pure Theory of International Trade," *American Economic Review* 50, 67–110.

Musgrave, Peggy (1987). "International Tax Competition and Gains From Tax Harmonization," NBER Working Paper No. 3152 (October), Cambridge, Mass.

McLure, Charles E. (1986). "Tax Competition: Is What's Good for the Private Goose also Good for the Public Gander?" *National Tax Journal* 39 (September), 341–348.

McLure, Charles E. (1988). "U.S. Tax Laws and Capital Flight from Latin America," NBER Working Paper No. 2687 (August), Cambridge, Mass.

McLure, Charles E. (1989). "Economic Integration and European Taxation of Corporate Income at Source: Some Lessons from the U.S. Experience," *European Taxation* 29, 243–250.

Office for Economic Cooperation and Development (1987a). *Quarterly National Accounts*, no. 2 (diskettes).

Office for Economic Cooperation and Development (1987b). *Revenue Statistics*: 1965–1968 (tapes).

Ohlin, Bertil (1929). "The Reparation Problem: A Discussion," *Economic Journal* 39 (June), 172–178.

Pechman, Joseph A. (ed.) (1987). *Comparative Tax Systems: Europe, Canada and Japan* (Arlington, Va.: Tax Analysts).

Perraudin, William R. M., and Thierry A. Pujol (1990). "European Fiscal Harmonization and the French Economy" (April), International Monetary Fund.

Persson, Torsten (1985). "Deficits and Intergenerational Welfare in Open Economies," *Journal of International Economics* 19 (August), 67–84.

Persson, Torsten, and Lars E. O. Svensson (1984). "International Borrowing and Time-Consistent Fiscal Policy," Seminar Paper No. 283 (Stockholm: University of Stockholm, Institute of International Economic Studies).

Razin, Assaf, and Efraim Sadka (1990). "Integration of the International Capital Markets: The Size of Government and Tax Coordination," in Assaf Razin, and Joel Slemrod (eds.), *Taxation in the Global Economy* (Chicago: University of Chicago Press), pp. 331–348.

Razin, Assaf, and Efraim Sadka (1989a). "Optimal Incentives to Domestic Investment in the Presence of Capital Flight," IMF Working Paper WP/89/79.

Razin, Assaf, and Efraim Sadka (1989b). "International Tax Competition and Gains from Tax Harmonization, Foerder Institute, Working Paper No. 37–89 (Tel Aviv: Tel Aviv University), *Economics Letters* 1990–91.

Razin, Assaf, and Efraim Sadka. "Efficient Investment Incentives in the Presence of Capital Flight," *Journal of International Economics* (forthcoming in 1991).

Razin, Assaf, and Lars E. O. Svensson (1983a). "The Current Account and the Optimal Government Debt," *Journal of International Money and Finance* 2 (August), 215–224.

Razin, Assaf, and Lars E. O. Svensson (1983b). "Trade Taxes and the Current Account," *Economic Letters* 13, no. 1, 55–58.

Rueff, Jacques (1929). "Mr. Keynes' Views on the Transfer Problem: A Criticism," *Economic Journal* 39 (September), 388–399.

Sachs, Jeffrey D. (1981). "The Current Account and Macroeconomic Adjustment in the 1970s," *Brookings Papers on Economic Activity* 1, 201–268.

Sachs, Jeffrey D., and Nuriel Roubini (1987). "Sources of Macroeconomic Imbalances in the World Economy: A Simulation Approach," NBER Working Paper No. 2339 (August), Cambridge, Mass.

Sadka, Efraim (1977). "A Note on Producer Taxation and Public Production," *Review of Economic Studies* 44, no. 2 (June), 385–387.

Samuelson, Paul A. (1952). "The Transfer Problem and Transport Cost: The Terms of Trade When Impediments are Absent," *Economic Journal* 62 (June), 278–304.

Samuelson, Paul A. (1958). "An Exact Consumption-Loan Model of Interest with or without the Social Contrivance of Money," *Journal of Political Economy* 66 (December), 467–482.

Siebert, Horst (1989). "The Harmonization Issue in Europe: Prior Agreement or a Competitive Process?", Kiel Institute of World Economics Working Paper No. 377, June.

Seidman, Lawrence S. (1984). "Conversion to a Consumption Tax: The Transition in a Life-Cycle Growth Model," *Journal of Political Economy* 92, no. 2, 247–267.

Sinn, Hans-Werner (1990a). "Tax Harmonization and Tax Competition in Europe," NBER Working Paper No. 3248 (January), Cambridge, Mass.

Sinn, Hans-Werner (1990b). "Can Direct and Indirect Taxes be Added for International Comparisons of Competitiveness?", NBER Working Paper No. 3263 (Feb.), Cambridge, Mass.

Slemrod, Joel (1988). "Effects of Taxation with International Capital Mobility," in Henry Aaron, H. Galper, and Joseph A. Pechman (eds.), *Uneasy Compromise: Problems of a Hybrid Income-Consumption Tax* (Washington, D.C.: The Brookings Institution), pp. 115–148.

Slemrod, Joel (1990). "Tax Effects on Foreign Direct Investment in the United States: Evidence from a Cross-Country Comparison," in Assaf Razin and Joel Slemrod (eds.), *Taxation in the Global Economy* (Chicago: University of Chicago Press).

Stiglitz, Joseph E. (1982). "Utilitarianism and Horizontal Equity: The Case for Random Taxation," *Journal of Public Economics* 18, 1–33.

Stiglitz, Joseph E. (1983). "On the Relevance or Irrelevance of Public Financial Policy: Indexation, Price Rigidities, and Optimal Monetary Policy," in Rudiger Dornbusch and Mario H. Simonsen (eds.), *Inflation, Debt, and Indexation* (Cambridge, Mass.: MIT Press).

Summers, Lawrence H. (1981a). "Taxation and Corporate Investment: A Q-Theory Approach,' *Brookings Papers on Economic Activity* 1, 67–127.

Summers, Lawrence H. (1981b). "Capital Taxation and Accumulation in a Life-Cycle Growth Model," *American Economic Review* 71 (September), 533–544.

Summers, Lawrence H., and Chris Carroll (1987). "Why is U.S. National Saving so Low?", *Brookings Papers on Economic Activity* 2, 607–642.

Svensson, Lars, E., and Assaf Razin (1983). "The Terms of Trade and the Current Account: The Harberger Laursen-Metzler Effect," *Journal of Political Economy* 91, no. 1 (February), 97–125.

Tanzi, Vito (1987a). "Income Taxes, Interest Rate Parity, and the Allocation of International Savings in Industrial Countries," Working Paper 87/53, International Monetary Fund (August).

Tanzi, Vito (1987b). "Tax Reform in Industrial Countries and the Impact of the U.S. Tax Reform Act of 1986," IMF Working Paper Series No. 87/61 (September).

Tait, Alan A. (1988). *Value Added Tax: International Practice and Problems* (Washington, D.C.: International Monetary Fund).

Tait, Alan A. (1987). "The Response of Other Industrial Countries to the U.S. Tax Reform Act," *National Tax Journal* 4, no. 3 (September), 339–355.

Tait, Alan A. (1988). "Capital Mobility and the Need for Tax Coordination Among Industrial Countries," mimeo, International Monetary Fund, unpublished.

Tait, Alan A., and Lans A. Bovenberg (1990). "Is There a Need for Harmonizing Capital Income Taxes Within EC Countries?", International Monetary Fund, Fiscal Affairs Department, mimeo (January).

Tobin, James (1969). "A General Equilibrium Approach to Monetary Theory," *Journal of Money, Credit and Banking* 1, 15–29.

Treadway, Arthur B. (1969). "On Rational Entrepreneurial Behavior and the Demand for Investment," *Review of Economic Studies* 36, 227–239.

Twentieth Century Fund (1989). *The Free Trade Debate*, Reports of the Task Force on the Future of American Trade Policy (New York: Priority Press Publication).

Van Wijnbergen, Sweder (1986). "On Fiscal Deficits, the Real Exchange Rate and the World Rate of Interest," *European Economic Review* 30 (October), 1013–1023.

Weil, Philippe (1985). "Overlapping Families of Infinitely Lived Agents," (Cambridge, Mass.: Harvard Univ.), unpublished manuscript, May.

Yaari, Menahem E. (1965). "Uncertain Lifetime, Life Insurance, and the Theory of the Consumer," *Review of Economic Studies* 32 (April), 137–150.

Index